PRAISE FOR
MY OLD MAN AND THE MOUNTAIN

"Here's an entertaining coming-of-age yarn from a likable, talented diarist."

—*The Seattle Times*

"*My Old Man and the Mountain* is Leif Whittaker's engaging and humorous story of what it was like to "grow up Whittaker"—the youngest son of Jim Whittaker, the first American to summit Mt. Everest, and Dianne Roberts, in an extended family of accomplished climbers."

—*Rock & Ice*

"Leif's book, *My Old Man and the Mountain* is a beautiful piece of writing, funny and sad, insightful and engaging. It chronicles both his father's experiences on Mt. Everest as well as his own."

—American Alpine Institute

"Leif Whittaker, son of the first American to summit Everest, has given us a deliciously irreverent perspective on growing up in the shadow of a famous father, and how that journey helped shape a unique perspective on one young man's own relationship with a mountain . . . and a dad."

—Tom Hornbein, author of *Everest: The West Ridge*

"It might be easy to feel lost in the shadow of a father who was the first American to stand on top of Mount Everest. Leif Whittaker tells the unique story of finding his own identity—as a son, and as a climber—with humility, candor, and a wonderful sense of humor."

—Brendan Leonard, author of *Sixty Meters to Anywhere*

"The trials and tribulations of sharing the Whittaker family name and his journey up Everest is what Leif Whittaker shares with a dash of sarcasm and humour in the book, *My Old Man and the Mountain*."

—*The Himalayan Journal*

A MEMOIR

MY OLD MAN AND THE MOUNTAIN

LEIF WHITTAKER

**MOUNTAINEERS
BOOKS**

MOUNTAINEERS BOOKS is dedicated to the exploration, preservation, and enjoyment of outdoor and wilderness areas.

1001 SW Klickitat Way, Suite 201, Seattle, WA 98134
800.553.4453, www.mountaineersbooks.org

Printed in the United States of America
Distributed in the United Kingdom by Cordee, www.cordee.co.uk
22 21 20 19   1 2 3 4 5

Copyeditor: Kirsten Colton
Design and layout: Heidi Smets Graphic Design
Cover illustration: Jen Grable
All photographs © Whittaker family unless credited otherwise

Photo insert, all clockwise from top: Page i: *Joss and Leif Whittaker; Dianne Roberts, Leif, Joss, and Jim Whittaker; Jim, Leif, and Dianne; Joss, Jim, and Leif; Leif, Joss, and Jim.* Page ii: *Ama Dablam; Dave Hahn, Lam Babu, and Buddhist Lama; David Morton and Melissa Arnot; Kaji, Lam Babu, Yubaraj, Chhering; Lama Geshe.* Page iii: *Climbing team at Base Camp; South Col.* Page iv: *Base Camp; Melissa and Kent Harvey; Camp 3; Hillary Step.* Page v: *Dave at Geneva Spur; Dave; Melissa; Melissa and Kent at South Col.* Page vi: *Leif and Jim; Namche Bazaar.* Page vii: *Lhotse; Porters near Lobuche; Leif; Jake Norton and Dave at Everest Base Camp.* Page viii: *Leif, Dave, Melissa, Kurt, Kaji, Pasang (back row); Leif Whittaker on summit of Everest, May 26, 2012; Jim Whittaker on summit of Everest, May 1, 1963.* Text page 13: *Leif at Base Camp in 2003;* page 46: *Leif slacklining on the Washington coast (©Freya Fennwood);* page 65: *Buddhist stupa on the trail to Everest Base Camp; Nuptse, Everest, and Lhotse in the background;* page 153: *Kent Harvey crosses a ladder in the Khumbu Icefall while Dave Hahn watches.*

Library of Congress Cataloging-in-Publication Data is on file

Mountaineers Books titles may be purchased for corporate, educational, or other promotional sales, and our authors are available for a wide range of events. For information on special discounts or booking an author, contact our customer service at 800-553-4453 or mbooks@mountaineersbooks.org.

♻ Printed on recycled paper

ISBN (paperback): 978-1-68051-069-0
ISBN (ebook): 978-1-68051-070-6

An independent nonprofit publisher since 1960

For Dad, Mom, and Joss

CONTENTS

PART FOUR: CLIMB ON

AUTHOR'S NOTE

All descriptions, events, and dialogue described herein are based on my personal memories, journals, and discussions with other participants. Any errors or misinterpretations are mine alone. In a few instances names have been changed to protect privacy. I have also taken certain liberties with chronology and structure by drawing from my two expeditions to the summit of Mount Everest in 2010 and 2012. In combining details from these two expeditions into a single, more cohesive narrative, I hope the reader will gain a more authentic perspective on the Everest experience and how these events have shaped my life.

The descriptions of the 1963 American Mount Everest Expedition are based in part on the many stories I heard while growing up; on review of family photo archives; and on my readings of *Americans on Everest* by James Ramsey Ullman, *Everest: The West Ridge* by Tom Hornbein, and *A Life on the Edge* by Jim Whittaker. Please see the resources in the back of this book for additional references.

PRELUDE

Three more steps and another loud breath, and finally I crest the South Summit and I look past Dave, across a dip in the snowy ridgeline, and feel my heart swan dive out of my chest and plummet down the Kangshung Face eight thousand feet into Tibet. There's a queue of about a hundred climbers coming down as we're trying to go up. I don't see any way to get over, around, or past them without taking the same ride as my heart. All I can think about is the disappointment in Dad's eyes when he hears we bailed three hundred feet from the summit and says, "What a shame. I'm sure you would've made it if it weren't for the damn crowds." I've been training for years and I've done everything right and I'm *so* close, but it's like the mountain won't *let* me climb it. Dave sighs into the clunky valve of his oxygen mask and says, "Just like usual on Everest. Hurry up and wait."

But waiting can kill you at 28,700 feet. The rhythm—step, breathe, step, breathe—is what keeps you alert and alive. The moment you stop moving is the moment you start to die. I've seen what happens. I saw it a few hours ago when we shuffled past the corpses of people who died just a week ago. Your body closes in on itself, cutting off extremities in an effort to sustain the vital core, and before you know it you're unable to walk or even lift your arms. Your oxygen-starved mind plays tricks on your body. The pain in your lungs and toes disappears and the cold no longer feels so cold. You lose consciousness not long after that and drift off into a dreamless slumber from which you never wake. I think about all the frozen corpses I've seen, their leathery skin bleached white as fresh snow and their limbs contorted unnaturally. How long can we wait?

Dave trudges into the dip in the ridgeline, clips his tether to a ten-foot ribbon of fixed rope, and waves for me to join him. There's a rocky cleft here and I guess he's thinking it'll protect us from the wind. I plant my crampons on a convex patch of snow and crouch, wrapping my arms around my knees. Maybe I'll stay warmer if I squeeze myself into a ball. Melissa, Kent, Chhering, Kaji, and Pasang clip in next to us. Kent twists the regulator on my oxygen bottle, reducing the flow, and I return the favor because we have to ration our breaths. Then I curl my hands into fists inside my gloves and settle in to watch the crowd pass.

Where the hell did all these people come from? We've been climbing through empty wilderness for the past six hours, but now the mountain looks like a Best Buy on Black Friday when the credit-card reader at the checkout suddenly craps out. The crowd is backed up at the Hillary Step, a forty-foot tower of gray stone jutting from the ridgeline into the cobalt sky. It's a notorious bottleneck with a sheer drop on both sides. From where I'm crouched I count fifty-seven people. Three more come into view on the corniced skyline. I keep adding.

Seventy.

Eighty.

I'm at ninety-three and I can't keep track of who I've counted and who I haven't.

A man wearing an oxygen mask rests his elbow on his front knee like he's about to puke. I hear a raspy sound in his lungs and then he continues his unsteady descent. A woman in a yellow down suit trudges past, breathing twenty times per step, unaware of the traffic jam behind her. Higher up, a rappeling climber in a blue suit tilts forward and bangs his chest and face into the rock. He lowers himself ever so slowly until his feet touch the ground. He takes a step and almost falls, but his tether catches him, jerking against his waist. Then he walks forward again with painstaking care like a drunk driver attempting a field sobriety test.

What a shame. I can't believe my story ends here, trapped in a queue three hundred feet from the summit. This was my one chance and I'm going to fail. I'll never be able to tell people I climbed Mount

Everest. I'll never be able to give Dad a straight look in the eye without thinking about today.

I doubt he ever thought Mount Everest would look like this. The crowd makes it hard to imagine the Hillary Step when Dad and Gombu were here forty-nine years ago, but I try anyway.

The crowd vanishes. A ten-inch layer of snow plasters the rock. A seventy-mile-per-hour wind rips across the ridgeline, tossing the snow into a blizzard. The clouds are bruises blocking out the sun. The fixed ropes disappear and in their place I see a single thread of nylon connecting two hunched figures. The man in front leans his tall frame into the wind. He breaks a chunk of frozen saliva off the front of his oxygen mask and slides the ice under the mask between his lips to drink his own spit. He's wearing gold overboots, navy-blue pants, and a crimson parka with a wolverine fur–lined hood. His external-frame backpack has the initials "JW" written on the yellow fabric in permanent black ink. His ice axe has a steel head and a wooden shaft with a small American flag lashed to it. The second man is not much taller than five feet, but he matches the other man's pace so there's no slack in the rope between them. The red double-pennant flag of Nepal is tied to his ice axe. The two men climb in unison along the sloping gray rock toward the base of the Hillary Step. They're completely alone in the middle of a storm, yet they press onward without a hint of hesitation. Their rhythm is a ticking clock.

The crowd reappears and the storm disintegrates. One man has a hole in the leg of his down suit, and each time he bends his knee, a cloud of feathers shoots into the air around him and flies away in the breeze. Another man removes an oxygen bottle from his backpack and launches it off the ridgeline to the east. It falls without a sound. He attaches his regulator to a new bottle and slides his backpack over his shoulders and trudges onward.

I rip my eyes away from the crowd and gaze off into the blue distance. I make out Cho Oyu, the sixth-highest mountain in the world, its summit ridge as flat as a Utah mesa. There's the Tibetan Plateau, a rolling expanse of umber hills stretching to the horizon. Today's the type of day that happens only once or twice a year at 28,700 feet—pacific, balmy, and cloudless. On a day like today, footsteps and deep breaths are the only sounds that break the vast silence.

There's a pair of boots sticking out from behind a crag about thirty feet beneath me. I can see the boots, but not the legs and torso and arms and head connected to them. I'm crouched right where Rob Hall died eighteen years ago, but I don't think that's him. The boots are the same model I'm wearing, with built-in yellow gaiters and black piping. The deep-lugged soles have almost no dents or nicks. They look brand new. One boot's twisted sideways, toe pointing uphill, contorted in an unnatural position. If I were to fall from this convex patch of snow, I might end up in the same configuration.

Pasang waves his hand at Dave and points to a gap in the crowd. The Hillary Step is unoccupied for a moment, but there are still about fifty people above it and another twenty below. "We go now. We can make it through," says Pasang. His voice is Darth Vader's beneath his oxygen mask.

Dave looks at the Hillary Step and the crowd, and then turns back to Pasang and shakes his head no.

Pasang points to his oxygen mask. "Almost empty."

"I know. We're all low on O's and we're all getting cold, but going up there right now is suicide."

"How long can we sit here?" I ask.

"If it weren't for this weather, we would've turned around already," says Dave.

The sky is a type of dark blue I've never seen before. The wind is a feather brushing my cheeks, the sun as warm as a freshly laundered sheet. But we're slowly dying. The rhythm—step, breathe, step, breathe—is the only antidote and I'm already beginning to forget what it sounds like. It's growing fainter with every second we wait.

PART ONE
SCOUTING

1.
NO PARENTS

Four hours from the trailhead I hike around a bend in the trail and there's Joss, standing dead still, watching something ahead. The meadow is full of knee-high grass and gnarly trees and this moss called "old-man's beard" because it hangs down from branches in hairy strips. Rays of sunlight shoot through the canopy into the meadow and I glimpse an entire herd of elk hiding in there. It's not like I haven't seen elk before but it's always been on the side of the highway. This is different. We're ten miles from the nearest road. There aren't any parents or guides or chaperones. It's just Joss and me. We're in *their* territory and they don't mind that we're close enough to hear them breathe. They're way bigger than they look from the seat of a speeding car, but they're graceful and quiet too. I'd watch them for the rest of the afternoon if I could, but we've got five more miles to hike before camp tonight and another five to the summit of Mount Olympus, so we can't waste time smelling elk if we want to be able to tell everyone that we climbed the highest peak in the Olympic Mountains.

The trail has been flat for the first twelve and a half miles, thank heavens. As it is, I can barely keep Joss in sight on the long straightaways next to the sudsy Hoh River. He's the one who knows where we're going. He has the map and the plan and this whole adventure was his idea. He says he'll get us to the summit alive. I know a couple of knots and stuff, but I don't have the first clue how to climb a mountain.

My backpack weighs a thousand pounds. It's full of gear I found in the garage and don't really know how to use: a ratty harness that's too big for me, a bunch of carabiners that look like they're from the seventies, crampons with leather straps, and an ice axe with all sorts of dents and nicks in the shaft. I'm wearing stiff-as-a-board leather boots that must've been Dad's back in the day and they're killing me already, but I can't stop to adjust my laces because Joss'll give me a look that says, *Stop being a pussy.* I don't want him to think I'm a pussy, so I keep hiking.

The river is the color of pavement. We hike past rhododendrons and hemlocks and chartreuse moss as thick as a down comforter. A black slug paints a trail of slime along a nurse log. An ivory flower on the edge of the trail shudders as Joss hikes by. A pool of dew drips from a salal leaf. A bird sends looping melodies through the forest. A swarm of mosquitoes spins and dives above a muddy pit. The wilderness is happening constantly and we're just passing through.

The sun is still out and I'm drenched with sweat when we finally reach Elk Lake. There's a ten-foot log as wide as a diving board sticking out into the water. I drop my backpack and strip to my underwear and walk out on the log with bare feet. The lake is a reddish-brown color like rusty iron. Feeding trout rise to the surface amongst lily pads. Ripples collide with the shore. I feel the water with my toe and it shocks my skin, but I tell myself, *It's not going to kill you,* and then I dive in. The cold takes my breath away.

Joss jumps in too. We swim until we're shivering. We swim until the sun dips below the treetops. There's nobody around to tell us it's time to get out.

Early the next morning a man in a tan-and-green uniform comes into our camp and threatens to give us a ticket. He's a wilderness ranger and he says we have to camp in designated campsites only. We're camped right next to the lake and the log. The ranger is in the middle of explaining the rules when he notices the ice axes on our packs.

"Are you planning to climb Olympus?" he asks incredulously.

"Yes. Heading up tomorrow morning," says Joss.

"Are you sure about that? Have you boys climbed before?" the ranger asks.

"Of course," says Joss a little defensively, but in the back of my head I'm thinking, *I haven't climbed a thing.*

The ranger frowns. "Do you have a backcountry permit?" he asks.

Joss unties the permit from his backpack and passes it to the ranger. His eyes soften as he reads our names.

"Are you related to *the* Whittakers?" he asks.

"Which Whittakers do you mean?" says Joss.

"*The* Whittakers. The famous ones. The climbers," says the ranger.

"Jim is our dad," says Joss.

The ranger smiles and folds up the permit and hands it back to Joss. "Okay, I'm going to let you off with a warning this time, but in the future make sure you camp in designated campsites only."

"Thank you. We will."

"Oh and, uh, how's your dad doing?" asks the ranger.

"He's doing well."

"Is he still climbing?"

"He likes to say he climbs onto barstools and into bed," says Joss.

The ranger chuckles from his belly. "That's great. You boys be safe now," he says, and walks off up the trail.

It's early afternoon when we get to Glacier Meadows, which means we still have time for Joss to teach me how to mountaineer before morning, so we hike up to the moraine and find a patch of snow where we can practice.

Joss shows me how to attach my crampons to my boots with the confusing web of worn leather straps and then he demonstrates how to walk on the snow. He splays out his feet like a duck so all the points of his crampons are digging in. He says this technique's called "floppy bunny ears." Then he shows me how to tie the climbing rope through my harness. The harness feels like a pair of saggy jeans, but Joss says, "It'll be fine," and he shows me how to tie in with a figure eight. Finally, he explains how to hold my ice axe and how to self-arrest. He says I'm supposed to self-arrest if I fall, or if he falls, or if anyone falls. He says if I fall, I'm supposed to scream *Falling!* "But don't worry," he says, "we're not going to fall."

Then why is he showing me how to self-arrest? And how to scream?

"Where did you learn all this stuff?" I ask. "Did Dad teach you?"

"No. Of course not. Did he ever teach you a thing about mountaineering?" he replies.

"Not really. Except for pressure breathing and the rest step when we climbed Pinnacle Peak that one time."

"I guess he showed me a few basics with the ice axe. And some knots," says Joss.

"The knots we learned, that's mostly from sailing. Why do you think they didn't teach us more?" I ask.

"I don't really know," says Joss. He pauses for a few moments and then says, "It's like they want to shield us from climbing for some reason."

"Maybe because it's dangerous?"

"Maybe. But they're always talking about how it's important to take risks and live life on the edge and that whole spiel. Besides, it's only dangerous if you're stupid."

"So then where did you learn all this stuff?"

"Books. I remember I asked Dad to teach me how to rappel once and he told me to go read *The Freedom of the Hills*. It's like a textbook about climbing. So I went and read the whole thing and then started doing rappels off the walls at Fort Worden," he says.

I look at my brother. He's seventeen, older than I am by a year and eight months. He has a 'fro of curly dark hair and this sharpness in his golden eyes that gives him the appearance of a mad scientist trapped in a climber's body. Six feet three inches tall with Dad's kingly nose, Joss inherited many of the same features I did. He has a ravenous mind and a pinpoint memory, and he was a college-level reader by age six. He read Michael Crichton's *Jurassic Park* in the first grade and proceeded to terrify his classmates with stories about bringing dinosaurs back from extinction. We were enemies from birth. I hated his braininess and he probably despised my goofiness. We used to trade blows all the time, but when I was eleven Dad and Mom sold our house and moved us onto a fifty-three-foot sailboat, where there simply wasn't enough room to fight. Instead, we learned to scuba dive together. That's where our friendship really began, underwater. Now he's holding a shiny ice axe and all this badass equipment is dangling from his harness and, without a doubt, Joss looks like he's ready to lead me through a throng of bloodthirsty velociraptors.

"So you're saying you learned all this stuff from reading a book?" I ask.

"Well, yeah. Pretty much."

Does Joss really know what he's doing? Probably not, but what are my options? I can either chicken out or I can trust him, and chickening out really isn't an option. I shrug and say, "Cool. What time are we getting up in the morning?"

The Blue Glacier is the color of a Tahitian lagoon. It's a jungle gym of shallow crevasses and bottomless moulins and ribs of night-hardened corn. Sunrise is a purple explosion. Up ahead, Joss wends through a narrow slot and clambers over a wall of ice. We're angling toward an outcrop of red rock beneath a feature called the Snow Dome and I'm pretty sure we're lost.

The Snow Dome is a rolling mound of pure-white snow like the skull of a bald man. Somehow, we're supposed to get on top of the Snow Dome, so we might as well climb directly up the outcrop of red rock. There's probably an easier way, but does it really matter? The red rock has this beautiful iridescent sheen and we're making good time. Joss scrambles up a ramp. I follow him and, man, this is fun. We're just playing around in the mountains.

We crest the Snow Dome and meander around a crevasse. Joss walks to the edge and peers over. His feet are inches from the hole, the rope stretching between us. What would I do if he fell? I'd do the self-arrest thingy. I know that much. But how would I get him out? No clue.

Joss keeps moving and I follow his tracks to the edge of the crevasse. It's only about three feet wide, but it darkens to an abyssal black; I can't see the bottom. My legs go all tingly when I look down. The rope pulls against my harness and Joss looks back to check on me. I wave at him and grin big to show him I'm not scared even though my legs are still tingling like crazy.

We climb through Crystal Pass and a ridge of peaks appears on our right. One of them has to be the summit. Joss gets out the map and we confer.

"It's got to be that one," I say, pointing at a clump of rock at the top of a gradual snowfield. It's really the only thing that makes sense based on the map and it's the only peak around that looks climbable. All the other peaks are dead vertical. Joss agrees, so we trudge off for the summit.

"Hey, you two!" A shrill voice flies across the snow. I look to my left and there's a man standing and waving from a knobby ridge of stone about a hundred yards away. I wave back to him and he yells, "That's the false summit. You don't want to go that way. Come over here."

As we approach I notice he has an ice axe logo on his jacket and a casual posture that exudes confidence. He must be a guide. There are two other people with him. Joss asks them how it's going and the man gushes, "Spectacular! We're on our honeymoon and we couldn't have asked for a better day."

"Trudging twenty miles through a rainforest sounds like a cruel way to elope," says the guide. His smirk hints at sarcasm. "But at least we'll have a decent view when we get to the top." He points over his shoulder at what's got to be the true summit.

My eyes travel from the end of his finger to a spire of rock shaped like a missile and, oh fuck, that's not what I was expecting. It falls away vertically for thousands of feet on all sides. The tingling's instantly back and my throat closes up. We're not actually going to climb that thing, are we?

If Joss is scared, he sure is hiding it well. He sticks out his lower lip and tilts his head and nods like he's pondering a mediocre piece of art.

"The easy route traverses along those ledges and then wraps around the corner. There's just one airy move," says the guide, motioning toward some crumbly looking blocks. "We're going up the north side, but it's 5.4, so you'll want to place some gear if you go that way."

Do we have the necessary gear to protect fifth-class climbing? Do we have the necessary gear to protect any sort of climbing? Nope.

"We were planning on doing the traverse," says Joss.

"Good idea." The guide sends me a you're-in-way-over-your-head glance.

"See you on top," says Joss.

My brother leads while I belay like he taught me. Belaying's essentially useless in this situation because Joss has nothing except a few pieces of webbing to secure to the rock. In fact, the only thing the belay does is ensure that if Joss falls, he'll pull me off the rock with him. He's looking pretty smooth, though, as he traverses the summit missile. He disappears behind the corner and then there's a loud "Woot!" It's the sound of utter exhilaration. Joss tells me to take him off belay. "It's not too bad," he yells. "Only one scary part."

The rope draws tight, beckoning me upward.

The climbing's easy at first, but then I reach the corner and, shit shit shit shit, there's a sheer million-foot drop to an unforgiving glacier. I freeze. The tingling runs up my spine and around my neck and all the way to the top of my head. I can't move. I'm frozen.

Above me, a shoulder-width chimney leads to what appears to be an easier ridgeline. The chimney is adorned with all sorts of knobs and flakes and horns, but they look like nothing more than brittle wrinkles to me. Joss tugs impatiently on the rope. The nylon strand is a cobweb floating in a thousand feet of air. Now it matters that I don't have the first clue how to climb a mountain.

I'd prefer not to move. I could just stay in this position forever and I'd be completely happy here if it weren't for one thing: Joss is already on the summit. He was in this exact same position and he hardly hesitated, and now he's at the highest point in the Olympic Mountains and I'm not. I *have* to get to the summit too.

It's not going to kill you, I tell myself, even though I know it could. Then I take one enormous breath and go for it.

2.
QUESTION

It's like it always is when Joss and I get dragged along to one of Dad's lectures. We're slouching with Mom at the very back of a packed banquet room and Dad's onstage, towering over a podium to the left of a twenty-foot-tall screen. The crowd is two hundred strong in glistening suits and strappy high heels, sitting at round dining tables with linen tablecloths and polished salad forks and crystal champagne flutes that reflect the blue glow of the screen. Dad's baritone booms, drowning out the clings and clangs of dishware. The servers are taking painstaking precautions not to block a single person from seeing the six-foot-five-inch bald man at the podium. Dad is talking about Everest, of course, and the crowd's gobbling it up like each word's a scoop of mint chip, but I've heard these stories for sixteen years and Dad's voice is lulling me to sleep.

The screen flashes. It's *the* photograph, the one that people have in the back of their minds when they think of Jim Whittaker, first American on the summit of the highest peak on planet Earth. He's in his crimson jacket and navy pants and gold overboots. His back leg's locked straight and his uphill knee's bent, and he looks like a big game hunter who has just bagged the prize. The clouds swirl around him and he thrusts his ice axe into the storm. There's a small American flag tied to it and a much larger one tied to an aluminum stake planted in the snow behind him. He looks invincible, like Ali standing over Sonny Liston or George Washington crossing the Delaware River.

The crowd goes wild—whistles and cheers and clapping hands. Dad says, "Thank you," into the microphone and bounces his hand in the air, ordering people to sit down, but it just makes it worse. Now everyone's standing and, gimme a break, we're supposed to stand too. Mom yanks me up by the back of my nicest shirt. I put my hands together so it looks like I'm paying attention, like I care, but I'm really thinking about what Spencer and Chris and Danny are doing right about now. They'll be out on a sunset sail, Spencer strumming that cheap guitar and Chris cracking a Black Butte Porter bought with Spencer's fake international student ID. Danny, at the helm, will be trying to heel our little Islander over as much as he can. I'd much rather be there, or practicing my reverse layups, or sniping with Oddjob on *GoldenEye 007*, or driving back and forth on Water Street with Led Zeppelin's "Whole Lotta Love" cranked to the max. Dad sidesteps away from the podium and bows, which means we're supposed to clap louder. Look at all the gold cuff links and diamond earrings and ultrawhite teeth. A server slips my plate away and our eyes connect and her face says, *Hang in there, kid.*

Dad is bald except for a close-cut ring of peppery hair. When he's around the right friends, he jokes that his hairless noggin is the catchment system for a solar-powered sex machine. His nose is a wedge and his hazel eyes are creased deeply around the edges because he squints and smiles too much. He's built like an NFL tight end. No wonder his Mount Everest teammates called him "Big Jim." He's seventy-two this year, but I often forget how old he is because most of my friends' parents are in worse shape than he is. He whips ski turns like his knees are brand new, and I can't stop his post moves one on one even though I'm almost as tall as he is now. He's still Big Jim, more or less.

Dad says, "People often ask me what my first thought was when I made it to the summit. In fact, after our climb, a reporter asked that very same question of Gombu. He replied for both of us when he said, 'How . . . to . . . get . . . down.'" The crowd rumbles as if on cue, but they don't stand up again, thank God.

I lay my head on the linen tablecloth and stick my tongue out at Joss. What will we climb next? Baker? Rainier? He said we should try Chimacum Rock again. It's a dirty crag out in the county behind a trailer park. There's graffiti in places and most of the holds are growing moss, but it's only a fifteen-minute drive from town and nobody's ever there. He made me follow him up this one route with knobby holds sticking out at odd angles. We went all the way to the summit, two pitches. I wanted it to be over the moment I left the ground, but it felt good to tell people I'd done it and the view of the trailer park was top notch. I guess I wouldn't mind a second go.

Dad's still talking about a past life—the REI years and his friendship with the Kennedys. Back when he was the first employee and first CEO of REI, he grew the business from a one-room store to a $46 million company. The eyes in the crowd are gleaming attentively. After President John F. Kennedy's assassination in 1963, the Canadian government named their highest unclimbed peak in honor of the fallen president. In 1965, Dad led Senator Robert F. Kennedy on the first ascent of the 13,944-foot peak in the Yukon. Climbing together in that frozen wilderness, Dad and Bobby Kennedy became lifelong friends. The screen flashes and there are Dad and Bobby skiing in Sun Valley. Another flash and there's Dad—skinny black tie, starched white shirt, and tailored suit—stepping off a plane behind Bobby. Another flash and there's Dad carrying a flag-draped coffin with seven other pallbearers through a throng of dark suits at Saint Patrick's Cathedral. The crowd's silent and contemplative now. What Dad doesn't say is that all he's got to show for those experiences is a low membership number at REI, a lifetime 30 percent discount, and a shitload of grief. At least that's *my* sense of it, but it all happened way before I was born, so what do I know.

Flash.

Gasp.

This one's from K2. Two tents balance on a steep-as-hell knife-edge ridge. Dad's like, "This was a beautiful camp and it had one interesting attribute, as we discovered the first time our teammate John Roskelley crawled out of the tent to relieve himself. He walked onto the ridge, squatted down, and did his business. Right in the middle of it, he started laughing. We asked him what was so funny and he said, 'This is probably the only place in the world where a person, without moving their feet, can take a poop in China and a pee in Pakistan.'" Dad's timing is perfect, like usual, and the crowd erupts in laughter.

Dad and Mom would probably appreciate it if I were paying attention and laughing at Dad's jokes and chatting amiably with the other people at the table like Joss is, but I just can't take it tonight. I tuck a napkin under my ear and drift off thinking about the balsa bridge I'm supposed to be building in physics, and the basketball game against Bainbridge Island next week, and eating Swiss Orange Chocolate Chip from Elevated Ice Cream or a slice of Waterfront pizza, and the sophomore girl with the strawberry hair and . . .

. . . Mom jiggles my shoulder and I jolt awake. She pulls me up by the arm this time and drags me over to a group of suits and high heels. They're surrounding Dad, each waiting their turn to shake his hand. The slideshow's over and I guess it's time to schmooze, which I hate because I'm supposed to act like the perfect son—well mannered and obedient with a dab of holier-than-thou and a pinch of ambition. In truth I made it into the police blotter twice this year: "A seventy-one-year-old woman reported seeing a group of young men jumping into hedges and shrubbery on Cherry Street, causing damage to the plants" and "Due to a number of incidents in which hundreds of plastic forks have been stabbed into lawns during the night, Safeway will now be asking for iden-tification from anyone purchasing more than one box of plastic forks." Port Townsend can get dull. Imagine how the crowd would react if *those* exploits were flashing on the twenty-foot screen.

Dad sees us approach and introduces us to everyone in sight—"This is my wife, Dianne, my son, Joss, and my other son, Leif." I try not to flinch when Dad calls me his "other" son, but I'm sure my face is a steamed beet now and there's nowhere to hide. I try to look each person directly in the eye when I shake hands, just like Dad taught me. I shake hands with a gray-haired man in a shimmering tuxedo. He sizes me up while our hands are clasped. He glances approvingly at my tidy little button-down shirt and my striped tie and my pleated slacks, but his eyes turn to slivers when he sees my ratty sneakers.

"I thought movie stars were the only people who could wear sneakers with a suit," says Shimmering Tuxedo.

I try a lighthearted laugh, but it comes out as an embarrassed squeal and, son of a bitch, Shimmering Tuxedo is keeping my hand firmly clenched. I glance at Dad for help. He's got to see me squirming out of the corner of his eye, but I guess the person he's talking to is a senator or governor or CEO because they're obviously more important than I am. Joss is telling a guy in a black cap about how he was recently accepted to Brown University. Mom's fending off some creep who must have no idea how much Dad can bench press. I'm on my own. Shimmering Tuxedo leans down toward me until his face is only a few inches away. White curls protrude from his nostrils and ears.

"Just tell me one thing," he says, his salmony breath wafting over me. "Do *you* want to climb Mount Everest someday? Do you want to follow in your daddy's footsteps?"

If I had a dime for every time someone's asked me that question, I could probably fund an expedition to Olympus Mons, the highest peak on the planet of Mars, and then I could really outdo Dad. I imagine Mom and Dad's friends used to coo that question in my ear as they cradled my newborn body in their arms. They probably asked me when I learned to crawl up the stairs at nine months, exclaiming, "He's already *such* a good climber." When I learned to talk and walk, they asked me and expected an answer. How am *I* supposed to know if I want to follow in Dad's footsteps? I mean, it's kind of a loaded question.

I try another lighthearted laugh, but it comes out as croak. "Maybe someday," I say. "You never know."

3.
NOW TENSE

It's Thanksgiving and our living room in Port Townsend reeks of armpits and roast turkey and candied yams and booze. My cousins Liz and Sarah are arguing about whether grapes or apples are the proper ingredient for Waldorf salad. Another cousin, Brad, is chasing his eight-year-old sister across the bamboo floors, slipping around corners in his socks and crashing into an ornate Pakistani bookshelf and shrieking the whole time. I'd say about two-thirds of the twenty-person party consists of brothers and sons. Most of them are over six feet tall, many of them are mountaineers, and all of them have these booming voices. I'm normally pretty boisterous myself, at least when I'm around Spencer and Chris and Danny and any girls I'm trying to impress, but whenever the Whittaker clan gets together, I prefer to observe. I'm still shorter than most of them and it's pretty easy to sneak around without attracting attention, so I go to the cabinet where Mom keeps the liquor and spike my orange juice with a dash of rum, just enough to feel like I fit in. Joss notices and shoots me a shame-on-you look, but I'm sure that's not a glass of grape juice he's holding and he's still six months from twenty. I know he's not going to rat on me because I'd rat on him and then he'd have to suffer through this evening without any sort of buzz.

Dad is next to the fireplace talking to his identical twin brother, Uncle Lou. Along with Uncle Barney, Dad and Lou are the patriarchs of the family and they gaze over their offspring with a kingly aura. Dad's holding a glass of his signature drink: Myer's dark rum, Coca-Cola, and a squeeze of lime juice. Dad and Lou are both wearing black turtleneck sweaters with vertical ribs that make them look ripped. According to family legend, they could each bench press three hundred pounds back in their army days.

Mom is hunched over a roasting pan whisking viscous gravy that's the color of brown sugar. She simultaneously checks the contents of three pots with her free hand, lifting lids and peeking inside. She's almost twenty years younger than Dad and she's the most active person I know. Most people assume Dad's the big adventurer, but Mom is the one who sailed all over the world—after spending her early years on the parched Canadian prairies, hundreds of klicks from the ocean. She came to tae kwon do class with me, stuck with it after I quit, and earned her black belt even though the brick she tried to chop in half during the final test just wouldn't break. Boards were like toothpicks to her, but the brick bruised her arm from elbow to pinkie. She keeps it in her office as a reminder. Of what, I'm not quite sure. This month her hair is dyed a kind of reddish brown, and it's always cut short so it won't interfere with her favorite tools, which are cameras, oars, sewing machines, coping saws, paintbrushes, notebooks, spatulas, winches, and skis. The tank top she's wearing shows off the shoulders and arms of a rower who rises every morning—including this morning—at five to pull a blade through the forty-eight-degree waters of Port Townsend Bay. Her dangly earrings are, in fact, miniature sculling oars.

She sets the whisk on the counter next to her and swallows a sip of red wine. She surveys the scene with a look that says, *I hope the brothers and their sons don't kill each other tonight.*

Welcome to Thanksgiving.

I take another sip of OJ.

Dad sidles up to my forty-something cousin, Peter, and asks, "Was it a busy year on the mountain?"

Peter is a guide on Mount Rainier. He's taken over Lou's business, Rainier Mountaineering Inc. (RMI). "Busier than ever. We had the entire summer booked out by January," he says.

"Jeez! Incredible. How many people are climbing it these days?" asks Dad.

"The park service says more than ten thousand attempts every year."

"And still about half of them make it to the top?"

"Yep. About that. We keep *our* success rate much higher but it all depends on the conditions," says Peter.

"I guess I should've stayed in the business," says Dad. "It wasn't so popular when Louie and I started up there."

Peter nods knowingly and says, "It's growing every summer."

"So how many times have you been to the summit now?" asks Dad, squeezing Peter's shoulder.

"I got my two hundredth this year."

"You passed me long ago," says Dad. "I think I've got about eighty."

"I imagine you might get one or two more before you're done."

"You never know," says Dad, winking. He sticks his chest out and holds his breath and flexes his arms and beats his fists against his sternum like King Kong. "Ten thousand stainless-steel bands," he says.

"All right, Jim, come and carve the turkey." Mom's voice floats into the living room.

The table in the dining room is the preferred table because it's oak and it has these hand-carved lion's heads for feet and it's set to accommodate fourteen people. The other table in the living room is a folding Costco variety with space for ten. Mom's covered it with a colorful tablecloth, which she sewed together herself. Uncle Lou quickly claims a seat opposite Dad at a head of the oak table. Uncle Barney, not to be outdone by his younger brothers, claims a seat at the head of the Costco table. Now that each of the patriarchs has claimed his respective domain, the rest of the family members rush to occupy a desirable space in the hierarchy.

Chairs scratch hardwood. Wine glasses tinkle. Pant legs swish and the younger Whittakers squeal. We're all finally seated, but more than a few cousins are dissatisfied—squished between an unruly child and a table leg, or pinned in a corner next to a broad-shouldered, left-handed mountaineer. The latter is exactly where I am, at a corner of the Costco table, sitting next to Peter.

Dad carves the turkey like it's a mastodon and he's a caveman—giant slabs of meat and bone. He pauses to say it's nice to have the family together, and with that we attack. There's plenty of food for everyone, but you'd never guess. It's a competition. Swallow your share and ask for more before there's nothing left.

The mashed potatoes and gravy are to die for. I'm digging into my second helping when Peter asks, "Have you gotten up Rainier yet?"

"Yeah, Mom and Dad've taken me up there a few times," I reply.

"To the *summit*?"

"The summit? Oh. No. Just up to Camp Muir," I say. Camp Muir's at the top of the Muir Snowfield, and it's where a lot of the guides and climbers spend the night on their way to the summit.

"So you haven't actually *climbed* it before?" he says.

"No."

"What're you waiting for? I climbed it for the first time when I was twelve."

I'd like to say, *Good for fucking you*, but I'll never hear the end of it if I say something like that. I could tell him about climbing Mount Olympus with Joss, but he'd probably just pooh-pooh it because Mount Rainier's about five thousand feet taller. Rainier's the tallest in Washington State and one of the tallest in the Lower 48, and I guess that means it's more important than other mountains.

Stay calm and nod politely. Dammit, I'm almost out of juice.

I could tell anyone who'd listen how we won a basketball tournament in Oregon on a last-second layup, beating a team that was ranked in the top ten, and now we're ranked too, but Richard starts talking about a construction deal that's sure to make him a boatload of money. Richard finishes and I'm ready to boast about my 4.0 GPA and how my balsa bridge held fifty-three pounds, which was third-best in the class. Then Ingrid starts talking about her brand-new Jeep. That conversation dwindles and I'm thinking I should joke about how the mountain of mashed potatoes I just ate was taller than anyone else's mountain of mashed potatoes, but now Win's into a story about climbing Mount McKinley, the tallest mountain in North America. My mountain of mashed potatoes doesn't seem very big anymore, so I ask for a third helping.

Dessert's on the way and I'm ready for all these people to get out of our house. They're milling about the living room, waiting for the pie. Mom's in the kitchen, pouring cream into two steaming mugs. I ask her if she needs help because it's an easy way to earn brownie points.

"Thanks, but I just have to pop the pies in the oven for a few minutes. Could you please take these to your dad and Uncle Lou?" she says, handing me the mugs of coffee.

Dad and Uncle Lou are standing in front of the fireplace again, chatting.

"Thank you, young man," says Lou. He takes a sip and exhales audibly and says, "A little better than the coffee in the army, eh, Jim?"

Dad's eyes crinkle at the edges. "You know about the coffee in the army, right, Leif?"

"I think I remember," I say. Do I really have to hear it again?

"The coffee in the army, they say is mighty fine. Good for cuts and bruises, and tastes like iodine," says Lou in a singsong voice.

"And what about the biscuits in the army?" I say, because now it can't be avoided.

"You know about the biscuits too," says Dad. "The biscuits in the army, they say are mighty fine. One rolled off the table—"

"And killed a friend of mine," I blurt. Dad and Lou chuckle.

"You've gotten a lot bigger since the last time I saw you," says Lou.

"You think so?" I ask.

"Definitely. Roll up that sleeve and let me see your muscles."

I raise my arms over my shoulders into a double biceps pose like I'm "Macho Man" Randy Savage. The various conversations in the living room, dining room, and kitchen come to a stop. It's suddenly dead silent and the entire family's looking at me. Lou wraps his hand around my right arm and squeezes. His fingers dig into my doughy muscle all the way to the bone. I flex as hard as I can and hold my breath, but Lou's fingers don't move. His face changes like he thinks I'm a massive disappointment and he says, "Now tense."

Son of a bitch. I fell into Lou's trap and everyone's laughing at me. I should run to the garage and hide where Dad keeps the weights and fire out some bicep curls while the family eats pumpkin pie. I'll be bigger and stronger and louder and taller than Lou one of these days and then I'll be the one laughing.

Lou releases me. "Feel this," he says, curling his left arm toward me. It's made of oak. My fingers can't even make an impression. I bug out my eyes because that's what he wants me to do. He draws in an enormous breath and sticks out his chest. He flexes each boob one at a time—first the left, then the right—like a pirate showing off tattoos. Lou bounces his fist on his chest and says, "Ten thousand stainless-steel bands!"

4.
OLD FRIEND

If I had to guess, I'd say it's 7:00 a.m., but I can't be sure because I left my Timex at home, seven thousand miles and a fifteen-hour plane ride away, along with my phone and keys and the twelfth-grade English assignments I'm supposed to be doing. It's chilly here at twelve thousand feet. The sun would probably be shedding warmth by now if it weren't for the giant peak that's blocking it. Which peak is that? Thamserku? Kangtega? I know it's not Everest. The Big E's directly in front of us, way off in the hazy distance, to the left of Ama Dablam and Lhotse, and partially hidden behind Nuptse. Morning in Solukhumbu reeks of juniper and mud and cakes of dried yak dung burning in nearby stoves. There's a ramshackle army base fifty yards behind us, complete with rusty barbed wire and armed guards in woodland camo, but we're not on their property and they're not paying attention to us. Mom's snapping photos with her two-foot-long lens. Dad's chatting with a trekker. Gombu's tracing his thick finger along the glowing horizon, naming each peak for Joss.

"Thamserku," he says when he gets to the silhouetted spire. I thought so.

"And, of course, *Chomolungma*," says Gombu. Chomolungma is the Tibetan name for Everest. Dad always says it means "Goddess Mother of the Earth," which is better than being named for a dead white guy, I guess. Still, Everest has a fittingly grandiose ring to it.

According to family legend, when Dad saw Mount Everest for the first time from the window of a Royal Nepalese Airlines DC-3, he stared at it for a long time with the odd thought that he wanted to become its friend. At thirty-four, he was one of the preeminent mountaineers in the United States and he hadn't been very surprised when Norman Dyhrenfurth, the leader of the expedition, asked him to join the team. He left behind his family and a promising job at REI for a chance to test himself in the Himalaya. I imagine a mild odor of sweat floated through the stuffy passenger cabin as Dad and his teammates strained their necks for a glimpse out the window. They were en route to Kathmandu to embark on a three-month expedition to the summit. A Nepali flight attendant served juice and soda, but the men were preoccupied with the image in the window. The mountain was a triangle of licorice-black rock cutting into a pale sky. A plume of windblown snow trailed from the massif like the train of a gossamer gown. To Dad, it wasn't an enemy to be fought and destroyed. It was a friend to be respected.

Dad was crazy. Mount Everest looks about as friendly as a hurricane. Golden light is now dripping from the top. Mom gasps, a shutter goes *click, click, click*, and Dad says, "There she blows." Everest capturing dawn, that's why we awoke at this ridiculous hour and trudged up the hillside behind the guesthouse, our breath like steam. That's why we came all this way in the first place.

The idea was to trek to Base Camp for the fortieth anniversary of Dad's climb. Mom had said, "Here's a note to give your teachers. Tell them you'll be gone a month."

I wasn't that surprised. When I was in sixth grade, they sold everything we owned—house, cars, TV, trampoline, basketball hoop—and bought a sailboat. Then they yanked Joss and me out of school so we could sail around the world with them. We cruised for four years, and when we got home they put me right back into school as if I never left. Still, getting As was easy after that, which could mean one of two things: either it's crazy what you can learn from scuba diving on World War II–era shipwrecks, taking night watches and navigating the open ocean ten days from land in every direction, fixing waterlogged diesel engines, playing dodgeball with Fijian kids, and spearfishing amongst marauding grey reef sharks; or the American public school system just sucks. Maybe it's a little of both. Anyway, they're kind of weird, my parents, so when Mom told me we'd be hiking in the Himalaya, my first question was whether I'd be home in time for prom.

I don't mind missing physics and American history and Current World Problems as long as I get to graduate with Spencer and Chris and Danny and everyone else. I'm planning to walk down the aisle wearing flippers and a dive mask, and I can't wait to see the expression on Principal Ehrhardt's face. Besides, this trek's more important than reading a textbook version of the Lewis and Clark Expedition, or debating if the Patriot Act is a breach of the Fourth Amendment. I've been hearing about Mount Everest my whole life, so it's about time I see it for myself.

Seeing it in real life *is* different from grainy documentaries and coffee-table books and slideshows and my imagination. The other peaks are still shivering in the shadows, but Everest is sunbathing now. A plume boils. A puff of fog hovers in the valley. The summit's *so* far away. I might as well be looking at the moon.

Joss says Buddhist monks call Solukhumbu the "world above the world," and I can see why. At the top, corniced pinnacles thrust from turquoise glaciers. Below the horizon are flutes of snow and sheer faces of inky stone and crooked Dracula teeth. Lower down, livestock trails crisscross pastures of tan grass. Lower still, the faint churning of a river plays from the heart of an emerald V-shaped valley. It's majestic as hell. I climb onto a boulder and raise my arms like Jack from *Titanic* and Joss scoffs in the background while Mom's shutter clacks like a typewriter. Mount Everest doesn't flinch. It's way, way, way back there and it doesn't care about us. I drop my arms and take a seat on a boulder next to Dad. He's gazing at the mountain like he sees something nobody else can see.

Does it look different than it used to?

I peer at the triangle. Sure, it's beautiful and powerful and mysterious and all that, but it's not friendly. No fucking way.

Shrill birdsong emerges from waist-high bushes. A soldier rides a roan horse back and forth along the barbed wire. Dust curls up from its hooves and hangs in still air. *Do* I want to climb Mount Everest someday? I wouldn't even know where to begin.

Dad catches my eye and tilts his head toward Everest. "What do you think, son?" he asks.

"I can't believe you actually climbed that thing," I reply.

Dad's face changes like he's been reminded of an amusing memory he hasn't thought about in a long time. "Sometimes," he says, "neither can I."

5.
GO-RACK

To the left of Tengboche Monastery, between two papery trunks and beneath a string of faded prayer flags, Gombu leads us along a secret trail. There's no sign, just a faint imprint of footsteps hugging the crest of a sepia hill. A gust brushes the prayer flags. They're so thin and tattered it looks like they're about to turn to dust. Joss says the colors symbolize elements. He says blue's for sky and space, white for air and wind, red for fire, green for water, and yellow for earth. Joss knows these sorts of things so I believe him. I ask what the writing on the prayer flags means. He gives me an are-you-really-that-stupid look and says, "They're *prayers,* dude." I can think of some comebacks—at least I don't look like Gene Wilder from *Young Frankenstein,* at least I can dunk a basketball—but he'll just get angry and when he's angry he's unpredictable. Now's not the time for a fight.

The trail's empty except for the five of us. If it weren't for the swish of pant legs and the distant static of the river, it would be silent here. Off to my left there's a ramshackle home with a sooty hole in its slate roof. The door's open and I glance inside as I'm stepping past and there's a young girl—she can't be more than ten—sitting on a white plastic lawn chair, her feet swinging back and forth over the dirt floor. She must sense movement out of the corner of her eye because she spins my way and hops out of the chair and leans her shoulder against the door frame, watching us with her enormous eyes like she wishes she could come with us. Around a bend and she's gone. The monastery's gone too. I inhale dust and yak and a hint of Himalayan glacier. Dad sways back and forth as he walks, his head down and his hands clasped behind his back like he's a monk doing a walking meditation.

A bird floats high overhead. It's completely black and if I had to guess, I'd say it's a raven only even bigger than the ones you see pestering bald eagles back home. Gombu tells me it's a *gorak*. I watch it swoop and dive, bouncing between invisible layers in the air. It croaks—*go-rack, go-rack*.

Farther along the ridge, a copse of rhododendrons blooms. We duck wrist-thick branches and crawl into a cave of petals just large enough for us to stand. The roof is a tangle of branches and the floor is a sponge of moss. It smells like the perfume section in the Bon Marché, only purer and softer and far more inviting. *It's really pretty in here* is what I'm about to say when I notice the hurt on Dad's face, so I swallow my words and follow Dad's gaze. Right in front of us but kind of hidden in the branches are four shrines made of stone, with mortar crumbling and falling out in places. Names and epitaphs are carved on the front of each shrine: Lute Jerstad, Barry Bishop, Gil Roberts, Jake Breitenbach. No wonder everyone's so quiet. This is where Dad and Gombu's teammates are remembered.

As far as I know, three of the men—Lute, Barry, and Gil—died long after the 1963 American Mount Everest Expedition (AMEE), but the fourth, Jake Breitenbach, a twenty-seven-year-old guide from Jackson, Wyoming, was the first person to die in the Khumbu Icefall. It happened on the team's second day of real climbing. On the first day, a rope team that included Dad and Gombu had forged a route into the unstable center of the Khumbu Icefall, then returned to Base Camp in darkness, exhausted. Jake was part of a second team that intended to push the route farther the following morning. However, before the second team had made any progress on the previous day's work, a serac the size of two shipping containers collapsed. Jake was crushed beneath twenty feet of frozen debris. There was no saving him.

In the days following Jake's death, the American Mount Everest Expedition analyzed the circumstances of the accident. The climbers unanimously agreed that it was an "act of God." Mount Everest didn't judge. They knew it didn't care who they were or what they'd done. It shifted and collapsed without consideration for age, skill, or experience. There was nothing else to it.

But even though reasonable minds said otherwise, it must have been difficult not to think the mountain had, for some reason, *chosen* Jake. After all, there had been no deaths or serious injuries in the Khumbu Icefall during eight prior expeditions, which had sent dozens of men back and forth through the hazard. Why now? Why Jake? Why not Dad?

"1936–1963. Long Live the Crow." Dad touches Jake's shrine with his open palm like he's testing it for warmth. "Jake, we miss you. We wish you could be here with us. You should see it now," he says.

Mom clears her throat. Mine's getting clenched up too, so I put my arm around her because it just feels right. Joss, on the other side of her, does the same. Dad touches the other three shrines. "Barry, we miss you . . . Gil, we wish you were still here . . . Lute, old buddy, we miss your music and your voice . . ."

Do Dad and Gombu want shrines built here when they're gone?

Dad goes into a recitation of Robert Service's "The Cremation of Sam McGee." "There are strange things done in the midnight sun/ by the men who moil for gold . . ." Dad knows the whole poem by heart. He used to memorize poetry to stay occupied when tentbound in a storm. "Lute knew them all. He was the best," says Dad.

He turns toward us and his eyes are leaking, and it reminds me of the day he came into social studies and asked Mrs. Nielsen if he could have me for a minute, and I followed him to the parking lot and he told me Grammy had passed away in the night. That's the only other time I've seen him cry. Mom fishes her arm out from around my back and waves Dad and Gombu into the hug. Then we're all wrapped together, our shoulders and armpits interwoven. Dad says, "Such a good family."

Back on the secret trail, towering gray clouds spread apart and reveal Mount Everest. A churning plume of spindrift spills off the summit. We walk beneath faded prayer flags. Two goraks circle. They catch currents and carve playful patterns in the sky. Then they dive, rocketing down the hillside, until they disappear. The young girl is still in the doorway. I walk past and she waves a little shyly, so I wave back. Her smile's made for the cover of *National Geographic*, but my camera won't capture that as well as my memory. The secret trail weaves through birch trunks and behind the monastery and now I can see the beaten path. Trekkers hike across a bald plateau like their life depends on how fast they can get from one destination to the next.

Go-rack. Look at that. The birds are sailing the updraft, letting it carry them toward the sun. I stop and watch them and wonder what it feels like to fly.

Go-rack. It echoes through the valleys of Solukhumbu.

I wouldn't mind pausing for a minute, but Mom's already zooming away and Dad's right on her heels. I yank the shoulder straps on my backpack so they're nice and tight. We have miles of trail ahead.

6.
TOTTERING CHAOS

Ten days after the secret trail and two weeks until prom, we get to the city of tents called Base Camp. There's a puke-green tent as big as a one-car garage and a yellow tent the size of an SUV and a bunch of orangey, two-person pods anchored to the moraine. I thought Base Camp would be resort-like, with coffee shops and internet cafés and pizza parlors and hot tubs, but instead I see heaps of prayer flags and blue tarps and rusty folding chairs and stainless-steel pots and pans laid out to dry. The sunlight glints and ricochets off them. Beneath my boots is gravel and beneath the gravel there's ice, a whole bunch of ice, the kind that forms gnarly towers and fins that would make Dr. Seuss proud. A voice crackles in Nepali from a radio in a nearby tent. A yak bell goes *clang clang.* Here at 17,500 feet the air is so dry that breathing feels like eating sand. Pumori is off to my left, a T. rex fang tearing at the sky. Lingtren and Khumbutse are up ahead with broad talus flanks and shelves of hanging ice. Then there's Nuptse and the West Shoulder of Everest, covered in blocky glaciers and flutes and aprons that shield the true summit of Everest from view. Base Camp's in a cul-de-sac. The only easy way out is the way we came, back toward warmth and villages and green and life. There are none of those things here. The color and faces and cozy shelters are all temporary.

I've never been this high, not even close. My head is one big throb and my lungs are about three thousand feet underwater, but Joss isn't complaining and Mom's barely breaking a sweat and Dad looks younger than he has in years, so I'm not going to tell them how I feel. Dad always says climbing mountains is just putting one foot in front of the other. That's what I focus on. I keep my head down as we hike past more tents and handmade granite altars.

There aren't many people about. Gombu says most of the climbers are up on the mountain right now. Those left at Base Camp are mostly support staff—cooks, doctors, coordinators. I guess we're nearing the middle of camp because the tents are closer together here. They're pitched in even rows with guylines crisscrossing and stone stairways built into the moraine and efficient, manicured paths leading from kitchen to dining room to toilet and back. A few folks are here to greet us. Dad's already shaking hands. A young Nepali man bows to Dad and Dad bows back, and then the young man puts a silk scarf over Dad's neck. Gombu is already wearing one. This must be the end of the trail.

I shed my backpack and Joss gives me a smile that says *nice job, brother*. I go for a high-five even though Joss doesn't really like to high-five. He slaps my hand without hesitation and actually holds on for an extra second. It's not quite as euphoric as when we hugged it out on the summit of Olympus, but this is like a summit too. Maybe it's okay to show some love when you're in the mountains.

I take in the view. All the peaks are so massive that they almost feel close. Pumori is right there, only a few hours of climbing away. The bone-white face of Lingtren winks at me. There's Khumbutse and the Lho La pass and the West Shoulder of Everest and, gulp, what on earth is that? My stomach's suddenly empty and I can't breathe. It's like my lids are glued open and my head's strapped in place and all I can do is stare and stare and stare into the twisted, shattered, crushed rubble of the Khumbu Icefall.

I've seen terrible, incomprehensible landscapes before. I've peered into a midnight forest and felt something dangerous staring back at me. I've walked to the edge of a cliff and felt my legs wobble. I've felt the vibrations in my bones as thirty-foot curlers slammed against a bluff in a shower of explosive foam. I've gawked at an endless desert horizon from the top of an empty dune and peeked down at a sprawling city from the window of an airplane and wondered how I fit in. I've gazed at the stars for hours and hours. But I've never seen anything like the Khumbu Icefall. It's a shifting and crumbling maze of glacier, a frozen waterfall about fifteen times taller than the tallest waterfall at Niagara

Falls. It's breaking and falling and reorganizing every hour of every day. It's just like Sir Edmund Hillary famously described it: "tottering chaos."

My eyes play over the towering seracs and black crevasses, and I imagine Dad and Gombu and Jake Breitenbach chopping steps with their long axes and spanning holes with tree trunks from a nearby forest and plugging screws into seventy-foot walls of brittle ice. Dad's crampons go *scritch* as he dances across a frozen boulder. Gombu's breaths echo through a white canyon. They're moving as fast as they can, their rhythm unbroken, but it's not fast enough. The Icefall is enormous and they're just specks of black. It could change, it *will* change at any moment, without warning or reason. They're just praying they won't be around when it does.

People have been asking me my whole life if I want to climb Mount Everest, but they've never seen the Khumbu Icefall. Just look at that thing—Space Needle–sized columns and abysmal trenches and mounds of jagged rubble. Would *you* want to go through there?

I was named after a climber who died in the mountains. Leif Patterson was a mathematics instructor who lived in Golden, British Columbia, with his wife, Marijke, his nine-year-old daughter, Marjan, and his twelve-year-old son, Tor. As a mountaineer and rock climber, he was experienced, strong, and devoted. He had climbed extensively in Peru, Alaska, Canada, and the United States, most notably a first ascent of the west face of Yerupajá in the Cordillera Huayhuash, a first ascent of Trollveggen in Norway, and various routes on the big walls of Yosemite. He was invited to join the 1975 American K2 Expedition, of which Dad was the leader.

In addition to Dad and Leif, the team consisted of seasoned mountaineers such as Jim Wickwire, Rob Schaller, Galen Rowell, Steve Marts, and my uncle Lou. Mom joined the expedition as the official photographer, tasked with capturing images for *National Geographic*. It was a star-studded cast and the team had high hopes of making the first American ascent of K2, the second-highest mountain on planet Earth.

However, the 1975 American K2 Expedition was cursed from the outset. Delayed flights, third-world stomach bugs, and porter strikes characterized the first month. It took forty-seven days just to reach Base Camp. Morale was in the gutter even before the weather turned sinister. Heavy snowfall created perilous avalanche conditions on the entire route. The climbers hunkered in their tents and brooded. Supplies dwindled. Time wore on. The snow outlasted them.

Frustrated men ached for someone to blame. Dad, the expedition leader, was the obvious target and it didn't help that every night he cuddled in a tent with Mom, the only woman on the team.

Dad and Lou were at odds for much of the expedition and it must've been something to see them argue. I imagine their collisions produced sparks the size of lightning bolts. Just think about it—two enormous twins with booming voices battling for dominance at nineteen thousand feet like Thor and Loki banging hammers in the clouds.

But through the infighting and bickering and politics, Leif Patterson was a loyal friend and devoted teammate. In his book, Dad wrote, "The consummate diplomat, Leif had an uncanny ability to find just the right words or suggestions to resolve disputes among members of the group, including Louie and me. He retained and communicated a sense of optimism, even when things were at their most difficult."

Patterson's upbeat attitude and selfless spirit failed to transform the weather. The expedition adjourned without a single summit attempt.

The team members went their separate ways, but some experienced a nagging feeling that K2 was unfinished business. Dad and Mom were among those with lingering summit dreams, so not long after, they applied for a climbing permit from the Pakistani government and started to muster another team. Leif Patterson wanted a reprise on K2. Dad and Mom were overjoyed to have him on the team, but their excitement would be short lived.

On a clear December morning in 1976, Leif set off to climb Chancellor Peak, a prominent cone on the western boundary of Yoho National Park in the Canadian Rockies. His son, Tor, and a seventeen-year-old family friend tagged along. It was a nice day and the climbing was easy and the trio was having fun. Then, suddenly, the snow beneath them collapsed and a thundering groan rumbled through the valley. Avalanche. Thousands of pounds of cement-like snow swept over them. A clean white slope transformed into a debris field. Afterward, a magical silence.

That night, when her husband and son and the family friend didn't return, Marijke feared the worst.

The next day a helicopter pilot located Leif Patterson's pack, a flash of color amongst the bleak rubble. Searchers uncovered his body. Tor's remains were close by, buried next to the family friend. A climbing rope connected all three of them.

Nine years later, on a snowy night in January, I was born.

It's been hours since we got to Base Camp, but I still can't stop looking at the Khumbu Icefall. It's captivating and terrifying at the same time. I think about Jake and all the other climbers who've died here. How many people have died in the Icefall? Dozens? Hundreds? How many bodies are still buried under the ice? It's as if I can sense them, their sadness and pain, and it brings tears to my eyes. I don't know how to describe it because I've never felt like this before. If I believed in ghosts, I'd probably say they were swirling around me. It's truly powerful and strange, this energy that's coming from the place. But how do I fit in?

It's easy to imagine Dad and Gombu climbing along, but a knife stabs into my throat when I try to imagine going through there myself. I have absolutely no doubt that if I move one step closer to the Khumbu Icefall, it'll kill me. I'll be crushed or buried or swept away and there will be no way to save me. I'll never climb Mount Everest. Never. I just know it.

A thunderous roar breaks the spell. Avalanche. It's a bone-rattling, earth-shaking bellow of which only Mother Nature can be the creator. It over-powers everything else.

Dad and Mom and Joss and Gombu hurry out of a nearby tent to have a look. It spills down from a hanging glacier onto the Khumbu Icefall. A giant plume, weightless in appearance yet immeasurably heavy, billows outward in every direction like cream poured into coffee.

The roar gradually dissipates and a cloud of frozen dust spreads across the Icefall.

Gombu says the avalanche hasn't hit the climbing route. He says the trail of fixed ropes and aluminum ladders is much farther to the south, toward the center of the glacier. This avalanche filled crevasses, but it didn't bury climbers.

Everyone finds a place to sit. Dad's holding a bottle of rum. Joss hands me a mug and cracks open a plastic bottle of Coke and pours some in the mug. Then Dad pours in a healthy dose of rum. He looks me in the eye.

"Are you all right, son?" he asks.

"Yeah. I think so," I say.

"It's a pretty incredible place, huh?"

"I never imagined."

I stir the rum and Coke together with my pinkie. We face the Icefall. Dad raises his mug in the air and points it in the direction of the summit.

"Hello, old friend," says Dad. And with that, we tip back our mugs and drink.

PART TWO
SLACK-ING

7.
NO SERVICE

I unzip my backpack and start shoving in books next to my water bottle and puffy jacket and tuna sandwich. In goes *Addicted to Danger* and of course *The Freedom of the Hills* and a dog-eared copy of some old tome called *Conquistadors of the Useless*. I lift the backpack and it's not nearly heavy enough yet, so I add Dad's memoir, *A Life on the Edge*, and Uncle Lou's *Memoirs of a Mountain Guide*. Since my back's feeling better lately and it's sunny outside, I might as well include *Americans on Everest* by James Ramsey Ullman and *Everest: The West Ridge* by Tom Hornbein, and now I think I've got enough weight to get a workout, especially if I go fast and nobody gets in my way. Dad yells at me from his recliner in the living room, "Good-bye. Have fun! Don't forget . . ." but I'm already out the door. I'm sure he was just reminding me to bring sunscreen or something anyway.

My car rattles like a tin can when I go over sixty, but it would cost more to repair than it's worth and I'd rather save my money for important things, like another climbing trip to South America, or a new rack of cams, or a new rope. Besides, if I turn the music up I hardly notice the vibrations, and it's only an hour to the trailhead. I turn on the radio. Who is that? Rihanna? It's catchy, whatever it is, and the bass is better than a new muffler.

At the trailhead I check my phone, but it says NO SERVICE in the upper-left corner, so I stash it under the driver's seat. I won't need it where I'm going.

The parking lot is full of Subarus and I'm not surprised, because it's Saturday. Mount Townsend is a popular day hike this time of year. I set out on a trail that's just slightly damp and the color of milk chocolate. Sword ferns and huckleberries and Oregon grape and salal cling to the edges of switchbacks. The forest is mostly Douglas fir with its thick, rough bark. A creek tumbles somewhere below, a bird sings shrill melodies, and the whole place stinks of spring—things sprouting and blooming and getting warmer quickly. It's the perfect place to spend my day off. I put my head down and hike.

Twenty minutes and I'm sweating through my shoulder straps. I probably haven't carried a pack this heavy since before the surgery.

People say climbing's dangerous, but what about basketball? A few years ago, I dove for a loose ball during a game of pickup at the high school gym and felt a tweak in my back. It wasn't that bad and I didn't want anyone to think I couldn't keep up, so I played two more games. I did all the right things that night—ice, ibuprofen, rest. The next morning I woke up in so much pain I could hardly get out of bed. Just thinking about it makes me cringe. Surgery, resulting nerve damage, rehab, and the whole deal, but my right foot still doesn't flex or twist like it should. I try to tell myself it doesn't slow me down too much. But I don't know if it'll ever come back.

Sometimes I think I move faster when I'm wearing a heavy pack or when the trail's steeper. It sets off an urge in me to almost run, or at least hike as fast as my legs can carry me. Dad taught me the guide pace when I was little and I'd say my strongest attribute as a climber is my ability to maintain a measured rhythm over long periods of time, but sometimes I just feel like attacking the trail. That's how I feel right now.

Sweat drips from the tip of my nose. My boots beat the trail like drumsticks on a snare and I can't get Rihanna out of my head. I find a speed that puts my heart on the verge of explosion and I try to keep it there.

I churn up behind a mother and father and their two adolescent sons and their black lab. They step to the side of the trail and pull their elbows in when they hear me breathing down their necks. The father eyes my backpack and shoots me a look that says, *What's wrong with you?*

He has no idea.

Two more switchbacks and the forest thins and I'm out of the shadows onto heather slopes in brilliant sunshine. I see Mount Baker, a cone of wrinkled snow rising from the gray-blue waters of Puget Sound. There's Mount Rainier, a mound of ice and rock thrusting into a hazy sky, thousands of feet higher than its neighbors. I'd like to stop and admire the view, but I'll have a better view from the top so I might as well keep churning.

A gray-haired woman blocks the trail. She's carrying a wooden walking stick and bending over to peer at flowers the size of a thumbnail. They're such a vivid purple color that they look almost artificial. The trail isn't wide enough for me to step around so I guess I'll have to ask her to move. She turns her head slightly and glances at me as I get closer, and her eyes light up with recognition. Oh no.

"Leif? Leif Whittaker?" she asks.

I can't quite place her. "Yep. That's me," I reply. "Beautiful day up here, isn't it?"

"Spectacular," she says, and she's genuinely amazed. "You probably don't remember me, but I've known your parents forever. I used to come to Christmas parties at the log house every year. I'm Sarah."

We shake. Her hand is surprisingly cold, especially compared to my damp palm. "Nice to run into you," I say.

"Yes. It is. Will you tell your parents hello for me?"

"Sure thing," I reply. I'd like to end this conversation and get back to hiking.

"What have you been up to?" she asks.

"Well, I graduated from Western in March. I moved back to town and I'm working at the Wildernest now."

"Good for you. The little outdoor store? I love that place."

"Yeah. It's a nice shop. And I'm also doing carpentry to help pay the bills," I say.

"That's great. So where're you living?"

What's with all the questions? "At my parents' house . . . for now."

"That's nice. I'm sure they love having you home."

I try to give her a realistic smile.

She assesses my large backpack. "Are you spending the night up here?"

"No. Just training."

"Training for what?"

I could tell her about how Dr. Bennardo's eyes blew up when he looked at my MRI and found a "Whittaker-sized" ruptured disc, and how the nurse told me to count down from ten and how I only got to seven before the world went black, and how they asked me to wiggle my toes when I woke up and my right leg wouldn't budge, even though it'd wiggled fine before they put me under. But that's a whole story, so I just say, "I'm not really sure, to be honest. But I want to be ready for the next big trip, whatever it is."

"Are you a climber like your dad?" she asks.

"I don't know if I'm like my dad, but yeah, I love to climb." I can guess what she's going to ask next.

"Are you going to climb Mount Everest someday too?"

I laugh like I'm mildly amused, but it comes out with more than a twinge of annoyance and I give my patented response. "Maybe someday. You never know."

The summit of Mount Townsend is a smattering of lichen-covered rocks with views to Canada and the Cascades and the lush valleys of Olympic National Park. It's crawling with hikers. Smoke from the paper mill streams over Port Townsend Bay through the empty sky.

A gust sends a chill through my soaked T-shirt. As I rummage through my backpack for another layer, I glance at Dad's book cover. It's the iconic photo of him wearing his crimson jacket and navy pants and gold overboots. He stares into the camera through black-lensed goggles. Old Glory flaps in the background. *A Life on the Edge.*

I shove it deeper in my pack. The day's fading quickly and I promised I'd meet Sam at the Uptown for beer and Ping-Pong tonight. He's been talking all week about how he's going to kick my ass and I wouldn't want him to think I chickened out.

One last glance at Baker and Rainier and Puget Sound, and I'm off and running down the trail. The books bounce against my scar. I go faster nevertheless.

8.
WHAT ARE YOU DOING WITH YOUR LIFE?

"Seventeen to twenty?" asks Sam, glancing at me over the frame of his glasses. He's holding the ball against his paddle and leaning over the table like he's about to serve.

"I thought it was *sixteen* twenty," I reply.

"I can't remember."

"All I know is I'm winning," I say.

Sam's thin mouth curls at the corners and his eyes soften with amusement. "That's really all that matters to you, isn't it?"

"You know what? I'll give you the point. Seventeen twenty," I say and tap the table with the edge of my paddle—*bang bang.*

"No. I don't need your charity. Sixteen twenty."

"Fine. Sixteen twenty."

Sam serves, and it's a good one to my right and I barely manage to get there. My return is a floaty meatball. He stings it and follows through hard, but it's way too long. The ball flies off and bounces amongst the legs of the barstools, ruined forever in a pool of spilled beer.

"Fuck!" he yells and tosses his paddle on the table.

I grab my beer—darker than molasses—and raise it in his direction. "Cheers, dude. Good game," I say, but I'm really saying *I kicked your ass* and Sam knows it.

"Yeah, yeah," he says, "good game."

We shake hands because that's what gentlemen do and Ping-Pong is a gentleman's game. "I'm ready for another go whenever you are," I say.

"Let's have a smoke first," he says.

The Uptown's pretty dead for a Saturday night, but this is Port Townsend and most of the eight thousand inhabitants are already in bed, or snuggled up to the TV, or at one of the three bars in town where you can pay with a credit card and order things besides beer. It's just the usual suspects tonight—a few hairy Carhartts-wearing guys hunched over the shadowy bar and a handful of noisy out-of-towners cluttered into one of the peeling booths in the corner. The porch is empty.

I take my beer with me and Sam does too. I'm four and a half deep at this point and I hardly feel the chill in the air when we step outside.

Someone has stapled a string of red Christmas lights to the eave and it gives the porch a cozy feel. We sit across from each other at a small circular table. Sam takes a pouch out of his jacket pocket and starts rolling a spliff on his knees. It's heavy on the weed with only a dusting of Bali Shag, which is fine with me because I'd usually do without the tobacco myself.

Sam's pinching the edges of the paper together when he says, "I've been reading your blog. It's good, dude."

Sam's younger than I am by a few years and I picked on him in high school, but I guess he's forgiven me for that. Maybe what's brought us together is the fact that we're both kind of floating aimlessly. He's back from a walkabout in Southeast Asia and trying to decide about college. Grades aren't the problem; figuring out what you love and what you're good at is the hard part. I'm back from college and a climbing trip to Ecuador, where I spent every dime I've ever made, and I'm *still* not sure what's next. Boo hoo. At least I have a job, two of them. If a liberal-arts education has taught me anything, it's how to complain about having too many options.

"Thanks, man. I appreciate you reading it. I guess my English degree's good for something. I'm sure as hell not using it when I'm pounding nails or straightening clothes," I say.

"Wait, you mean building a house doesn't require perfect grammar?" he says, pinching the spliff in his lips.

"Surprisingly not."

Sam inhales deeply and leans back, letting the smoke twirl around him. "But you've got to keep it up because you never know who's going to read it," he adds.

Sam kind of looks like a professor in a boy's body. He's as thin as Gandhi and he's got these sharp glasses and this contemplative expression.

"My mom says the same thing. I just don't really have as much to write about since I got back from Ecuador. I mean, should I write about having back surgery at twenty-three and smoking spliffs on the porch of the Uptown? I'm not really sure I want my mom and her friends reading that stuff," I say.

He winces and laughs in a fatalistic tone. "Yeah. It might be better to leave some stuff out," he says.

We pass the spliff back and forth.

"Didn't you go up Townsend today? You should write about that," Sam says.

"Yeah. I ran into this woman on the trail, some friend of my parents', and she was asking me all these questions and now they're stuck in my head."

"Like what?"

"You know, the usual stuff. Why am I failing at life? Why haven't I lived up to expectations? Why haven't I climbed Mount Everest yet?" I say, rolling my eyes to make it seem like I don't really care too much.

"So you mean nothing important," says Sam.

"Exactly."

He pauses with his contemplative look. "Well, do you *want* to climb Mount Everest?"

"Oh no. Not you too."

Sam smirks for a second, but he's not giving up. "No. Seriously, man. *Do* you?"

The spliff's mostly cashed, but there's enough of a roach for a few more hits. I stick my fingers out in a peace symbol and he passes it over. The smoke drives into my lungs and I try to think about Mount Everest. I close my eyes and I'm sitting on a white granite boulder in front of the Khumbu Icefall.

I exhale a lungful of smoke and it billows across the porch like the powder cloud from an avalanche. "I really don't know, Sam. But sometimes I feel like my life's been tied to that mountain whether I like it or not," I say.

We're silent for a while and the night's all still and empty. I pass the roach back to Sam and chug the final inch of beer. "I guess I'd climb it for no other reason than to get people to stop asking me if I want to climb it or not." It comes out with more than a hint of bitterness.

Sam squishes the crutch in the ashtray and stands up. The red glow from the Christmas lights reflects off the polished lens of his glasses. He's wearing a wry smile. "You ready to get your ass kicked?" he says, tilting his head at the door.

I reach out my hand and Sam grabs it and pulls me up out of my seat. We're standing face to face and I try to look as intimidating as possible. "Bring it on," I say. "Bring . . . it . . . on."

I'm fifteen minutes late, which means I'll have to bust ass if I want to get the store open by ten. I unlock the door and jump inside and flip the circuit breaker. The overhead lights flicker to life.

The next thing to do is get the music playing—something mellow but upbeat that will erase all remnants of last night. The owners, Steve and Kerry, have a pretty good reggae station on Pandora, so I select that and the first tune is "Love the Life You Live" by Midnite, which'll do. I crank the volume.

I stock the register and open the point-of-sale program on the computer. I run around vacuuming every corner, upstairs and down. Then I systematically move through the store from front to back, straightening every piece of clothing on every hanger, making sure each hanger is perfectly spaced two fingers apart, every carabiner is facing the same direction, every cam is sparkling, every pair of shoes has its laces tied, every glass surface is wiped with Windex, the dressing room is clean, and the hangtags are all facing out. Now I'm ready to sell outdoor gear to the masses.

It's 10:03 a.m. and I prop the front door open and dammit, some guy's already here and he wants to take a look at the headlamps, so the first half an hour of my day is spent explaining the various pros and cons of every single headlamp in the store.

The things I do for employee discounts.

Two hours later I grab a slice of pesto, tomato, and olive pizza from the parlor next door. It's all garlicky and drippy on the paper plate and I'm about to take a massive bite when, of course, a family of four walks inside.

It's a couple and their two sons. The husband is wearing a fleece vest, plaid shirt, leather oxfords, and a pair of professional-looking thin-rimmed eyeglasses. He seems like a pretty normal guy, but there's some-thing intense about him and he's looking right at me like he knows who I am, so I set down the pizza and say, "Can I help you find something?" in my most professional tone.

"You must be Leif," he replies. "I'm Neil Fiske."

Neil Fiske? Neil Fiske? Neil Fiske! I completely forgot.

A few weeks ago my parents mentioned the CEO of Eddie Bauer was coming to town for a visit. "He's been reading your blog," said Mom, "and I think he wants to meet you."

I was like, "Why would he want to meet me?" but in the back of my head, I was thinking with disgust, *This is another one of those times when I'm supposed to use my last name to get ahead.*

"I don't know. I guess you'll have to meet him to find out," said Mom, a dead giveaway that she knew more than she was willing to say.

Since then I hadn't given it a second thought. Maybe that's what Dad was telling me not to forget yesterday.

Thank God I used mouthwash and shaved and put on a clean shirt.

"Yes! Mr. Fiske. It's good to meet you," I say and I hope I don't sound too eager.

We shake hands and he introduces me to his family and I show them around the store. Everything's shiny and organized and Neil says, "This is a great store."

My chest swells with pride. Even though it's not my store, I know how to make it look good. I've been selling outdoor gear for years now and I've been in lots of shops. The Wildernest definitely has a special charm. It's small and full and the owners care about having the best stuff. I'm happy Neil appreciates it.

We're making small talk and Neil's picking through a rack of soft-shell pants and everything's dandy until, out of the blue, one of his sons says, "What are you doing with your life?"

He can't be more than fifteen and he's as tall as my elbow, but he's staring at me with this intense look and expecting an answer. Did Neil set this whole thing up? Is this some sort of covert job interview? Neil's acting like he's not paying attention, but I can tell he is.

I could say all sorts of things, like *I'm trying to figure that out* or *The economy's been tough* or *College degrees just don't mean what they used to.* I could also go with the truth, something like, *I dig ditches in the rain four days a week, sell T-shirts to tourists two days a week, and try to drown my doubts with sweat on my one day off. Oh, and the nerves in my right leg are permanently damaged from back surgery and I fall asleep every night without any idea of where life's taking me.* But I'd like to sound a tad more confident than that.

"Well, right now I'm working here and also building houses. I spend all my free time climbing mountains and I'm open to any opportunities that might arise," I say. It sounds a little unnatural, but the son appears satisfied and, thank God, he leaves me alone, wandering off between the shelves.

Neil sets a pair of pants and a jacket next to the register and hands me his credit card.

"Product research?" I ask.

"Something like that," he says.

"I'll give you the friend discount," I say, "10 percent off." I might pay for this later but Steve and Kerry have become my close friends since they hired me and they usually don't mind if it's not more than 10 percent.

I hand him his bag and the receipt with a smile. He hands me his business card. It's printed on weighty paper with this perfect eggshell texture I notice the moment it's in my hand.

"Send me an email and I'll put you in touch with my secretary. Let's set up a meeting," he says.

He's probably just being friendly, but it feels like more than that because he's a CEO, and who knows how much he's worth. "Absolutely. I will."

I say good-bye to his family and they disappear out the door.

I need time to think about all this without the distraction of the store. There's a good place to hide behind the counter next to the register. I sit on the floor where nobody can see me and inspect the business card. The letters are embossed into the thick stock. What could Neil possibly want from me? Maybe testing outdoor gear or designing backpacks or visiting Eddie Bauer stores around the country like a product rep or writing stories for the Eddie Bauer blog. I'll move to Bellevue and rent an apartment on the twentieth floor and commute to the corporate offices in a glitzy Land Rover and, hmm, is that really what I want to do with my life? Besides, whatever the opportunity is, aren't I getting it just because I'm Jim Whittaker's son?

His business card's a work of art and I'm taking it all in when, son of a bitch, some guy peers over the counter and spots me. I jump up. My head brushes against the paper plate I set on the counter and all of a sudden a piece of pizza flies through the air. It lands with a splat upside down on the carpet next to the men's underwear rack. I glare at the guy.

"Whoopsy-daisy. I didn't mean to surprise you," he says.

"Can I help you with something?" I ask, and I try to conceal my annoyance but I think a little seeps through.

Either he doesn't notice or he doesn't care because he's as jolly as ever when he says, "Well, I was just wondering. Do you guys carry headlamps?"

9.
CHOKE

The boardroom is on the fifth story of a sleek skyscraper in Bellevue, Washington. The walls are all polished glass and the floor is dark rock with a glistening sheen. There's an incredible conference table made from two giant pieces of straight-grain fir, and it's probably bigger than my bedroom and definitely worth more than my car. I can see the Bellevue Square mall and the pulsing arteries of the cityscape and Mount Rainier, a watchtower of ice. Neil Fiske should be along at any moment.

It's been one, two, three months since he handed me his card and I still don't know what Neil wants from me. Product testing? Blogging? I spent a week drafting a long email that described my experience in the industry— "I've been working in outdoor stores since I was eighteen and . . ." His terse reply didn't give me any clues. "Call my assistant and we'll set up a meeting." It was rescheduled four or five times and I haven't quit either of my jobs, but today's finally the day Neil is free for lunch. A ferry ride and a two-hour drive in my car-turned-rattle, and I parked between a black BMW and an Escalade with chrome spinners. The nicest outfit I own is a red-and-orange short-sleeve button-down shirt, khaki pants, and a pair of tattered sneakers. It's a decent shirt, I guess, and it fits okay. The sneakers are three years old and I wear them everywhere. I don't wear the pants often because I'm worried I'll stain them. My hands are all twitchy and my stomach's gurgling a little. I'm pretty nervous.

I see him appear through the glass wall and, phew, he isn't wearing a suit, so I don't feel any more out of place than I already do. We say hello and shake hands. An assistant comes in and sets a brown paper bag on the conference table. Neil thanks her and she quietly departs. The two of us sit down and now it's dead silent.

Awkward.

Neil opens the paper bag and extracts two packages of Lays potato chips, two bottles of water, and a sandwich wrapped in parchment paper. He hands me half of the sandwich. It's turkey with cranberry sauce and a fat layer of mayonnaise. Without a word Neil takes a bite. I haven't had lunch yet and the sandwich looks good, so I sink my teeth into the center where the turkey and mayo are thickest. It's both savory and sweet and I guess the CEO probably gets the best sandwich in town.

Just as I'm swallowing, Neil's like, "What would you say if I told you I wanted to send you to Mount Everest?"

Choke!

A clump of turkey and sourdough bread wedges into the wrong tube in my throat and, oh my God, I can't breathe. I cough, trying to dislodge the blockage, and a limp piece of turkey layered in mayo flips out of my mouth and sticks to the front of my plaid shirt. Another cough and a dollop of cranberry sauce lands on my pants. I'm trying to force the rest of the clump down instead of up. Slowly, painfully, the clump descends. My face is probably purple by now and my eyes are watering and my lungs are aching. I've got to swallow before I can inhale and I've got to inhale before I can respond to Neil. Does he know the Heimlich maneuver? Maybe I should regurgitate the clump onto a napkin, but no, it's too far gone. It's lodged into the crevasse that is my throat and there's no rescuing it.

Finally, painfully, it falls past the choke point and I gasp for air.

"If you give me that opportunity . . ." I begin, but the words are all wheezy and hoarse, like they're coming out through a kazoo. ". . . I promise you . . . I will do everything in my power . . . to make it a success." Maybe it's the oxygen deprivation, but I feel lightheaded. Is this really happening? My mind's a flipbook of majestic images—me climbing through the Khumbu Icefall, gazing at distant peaks from the South Col, and standing on the summit. My heart revs with excitement.

Neil Fiske smiles and nods like he's not surprised. "I'm glad to hear that, Leif. Would you like some water?" he says, handing me a bottle.

"Yes. Thank yoohh," I say and my voice is the voice of a seagull.

The Eddie Bauer store in the Bellevue Square mall is, I'm told, one of the nicest in the country, which makes sense because it's just across the street from the black skyscraper and the all-glass boardroom. My head's whirling and I walk past the front of the store and, look, there's a life-size photo of Jim Whittaker in the window display. Same crimson jacket, navy pants, gold overboots, and American flag. Dad is looking past me through dark goggles into the food court of the mall. He appears to be looking directly at a store that offers frozen fruit drinks. It's true: from his heroic place on the summit of the highest peak on planet Earth, Jim Whittaker gazes longingly in the direction of an Orange Julius.

A security guard ambles past, his hands resting on his belt. A woman in a navy pants suit and heels goes *clickety-clackety* down the concourse, ear to an iPhone. A guy at Sunglass Hut looks like he's about to fall asleep.

I walk into the Eddie Bauer store. I zip and unzip zippers and tug on stretchy fabric and shove my hands into pockets. I try things on. I unfold hangtags and read technical information about materials, waterproofing, and insulation. I unfold one tag and there's my cousin's face staring back at me. It's embossed with his looping signature: Peter Whittaker.

When Eddie Bauer launched a new line of technical outdoor clothing and equipment, Peter signed on as a spokesperson. He even has a hand in designing the gear, and he climbed Mount Everest last May on an expedition that coincided with the release of some new products.

I like Peter but we haven't spent much time together. He's quite a bit older than I am and he's got kids and a whole life. I've often thought about asking him for a guiding job but something makes me hesitate. Maybe it's the idea of climbing with people I don't know or going up and down the same mountain over and over, or maybe I just want people to see me as me instead of as Jim Whittaker's son. But I guess I murdered and dismembered and incinerated that idea in the last twenty minutes. Will *my* face and signature be on a hangtag this time next year? Is that what it takes to get to Mount Everest these days? Half of me wants to run back to the boardroom and call the whole thing off. The other half of me wants desperately for Neil's offer to be real.

Peter is on a flat-screen at the back of the store. His face sparkles in 1080 p. He talks for a few seconds and then the video cuts to a clip of him crossing an aluminum ladder. It's laid horizontally over a crevasse and dozens of other ladders and crevasses and seracs cover every inch of the flat-screen. The Khumbu Icefall. My stomach caves in and my tongue goes dry. What the hell am I thinking? Why did I accept Neil's offer so quickly?

"Can I help you?" The question comes from a middle-aged woman who's straightening clothes—zipping up zippers and organizing garments by size.

"No, thanks. I'm just looking," I reply.

She pauses for a moment and then nods in the direction of the flat-screen. "Pretty inspiring, huh?" she says.

"Uh-huh."

"Are you a climber?" she asks.

"Yes."

"Do you want to climb Mount Everest someday?"

I think about the grainy Nat Geo footage of Dad and Gombu kicking steps in fresh snow and a blizzard tearing across the Southeast Ridge, and the picture of Dad with frostbite on his cheeks, looking like he hasn't slept or eaten or taken a sip of water in days, and that phrase he always uses when people ask what he was thinking: "How to get down." I wish they'd make a device that predicts avalanches. I wish there were a checklist to tell you if you're strong enough for twenty-nine thousand feet. Any book will tell you that Everest has lost its magic, but I'm not so sure, because when Neil made his offer I didn't hesitate for a second.

"Yes," I tell the woman. "I suppose I do."

Pulling into the driveway, I can see through the bright windows of our house Dad and Mom sitting on the couch. Spaghetti and marinara rest in a pot on the range. Dad's halfway through a bowl of vanilla and Mom's tapping her BlackBerry, probably setting a new high score on Brick

Breaker. I try to be quiet as I come inside. I'd rather not talk about Everest until I'm saying good-bye, ticket to Nepal in hand, duffel bags packed. Then I bump against a yak bell in the mudroom.

"Hi, Leif!"

There's no avoiding my parents tonight. They know exactly where I've been.

"Hi, Mom." I try to use a nothing-happened voice, but it comes out as more must-stay-calm. I walk casually into the living room and they stand up to greet me.

"How did it go, son?" asks Dad, his eyes brimming with excitement.

I guess there's no reason to lie. I blurt out, "Neil said he wants to send me to Mount Everest."

"Wow!" says Mom. "That's incredible." She hugs me and holds on for a few seconds longer than usual.

"Congratulations!" says Dad with a that's-my-boy look.

Something's weird. They're proud and excited, but they're not surprised.

"Did you guys know this was going to happen?" I ask.

"We didn't know for sure. But we had an idea," says Dad.

Fuck. Neil's offer has nothing to do with my writing or climbing ability or eloquence or anything except that I'm Dad's son and I'm available and cameras get along with my jawline. "You could've *warned* me," I say in disbelief.

"We didn't have a clue what was going to happen and we didn't want to get your hopes up," says Mom. There's a pause and I'm thinking, *I'm just a spoiled brat*, and maybe Mom sees it in my face because she asks, "Is something wrong?"

"You know that I'm a little sensitive about using my family connections to get ahead," I reply.

Dad shuffles his feet and clears his throat but doesn't speak.

Mom's like, "For heaven's sake, Leif. Everyone uses the connections they have. It's all about *who* you know. And you better use the Whittaker name for all it's worth because Lord knows we're not going to be able to give you a *real* inheritance. You and Joss'll be lucky if we leave you guys without a ton of debt."

Now I'm thinking about Jim O'Malley and the words "jointly and severally." A few years before I was born, Dad received a letter from a businessman, Jim O'Malley, who wanted to produce a new line of rugged outdoor products. They met and decided to cofound Whittaker/O'Malley, Inc. With O'Malley acting as president and CEO, and Dad as chairman and spokesman, the business took off, selling gear to specialty outdoor stores as well as large department stores like Nordstrom. The two men became close friends and Dad viewed it as a good investment in an industry he knew well. Then, when I was about six months old, Dad was invited to meet a bank officer at Seattle Trust and Savings Bank. To his horror, he learned that O'Malley had been fabricating and submitting false invoices from customers in order to increase the amount of money the company could borrow. The financial ramifications were catastrophic. According to the fine print on the original business start-up loan, Dad and Mom were liable "jointly and severally" for all the debts Whittaker/O'Malley owed, a total of almost $1 million. Everything was stolen from them—the condo on Maui, the Swan 441 named *Impossible*, the burgeoning outdoor brand in Seattle, and the Port Townsend acreage. In Dad's book, he uses the phrase "financially ruined." They would've been retired decades ago and I would've grown up with every privilege imaginable if it weren't for Jim O'Malley. They've been struggling to recover ever since; that's a big part of the reason Dad's photo is in the window display at the Bellevue Square mall.

"I know. Thanks, Mom. I've just resisted it for some reason. It'd be nice if my last name didn't matter, but I'm learning to come to terms with it . . . slowly," I say, flashing an it-doesn't-really-bother-me smile.

"I'm sure Neil wouldn't have made the offer if it weren't for the climbing and writing you've been doing . . . and if you weren't *you*," says Mom.

How do Moms always know the right thing to say?

Maybe it's all a little too mushy for Dad because he interjects, "So what happened? What did Neil tell you?"

"He asked what I would say if he told me he wanted to send me to Mount Everest. And I told him if he gave me that opportunity I would do everything in my power to make it a success."

"Well put. And how did he respond?" asks Mom.

"He said he would be in touch soon with more details."

"That's it?" asks Dad.

"Pretty much."

"Fantastic!" says Dad. "Good for you."

My family is so weird. What kind of mother and father celebrate the news that their youngest son is about to put himself in grave danger all for the chance to stand on a special patch of snow?

Dad glances at Mom, then back at me, and asks, "What would you say if Mom and I told you we want to come with you?"

Choke!

PART THREE
TENSION

10.
HEIRLOOMS

Dad flips on the light in the garage. I come in behind him, inhaling cedar and mildew and a hint of linseed oil. It's packed tight with metal shelving and cardboard boxes full of children's books and old family photographs and retired cooking utensils, duffel bags of scuba gear and stacks of varnished trim and a pair of nine-foot oars. The surface of Dad's maple workbench is an accidental Jackson Pollock, speckled white and red and blue. It's pushed up against a window that looks out on San Juan Avenue, F Street, Discovery Road, and the Olympic Mountains.

In the far right corner there's a section devoted to tools of the mountains. Dozens of ropes and ice axes and ski poles hang from painted studs along with an external-frame backpack and a pair of rigid leather boots. Three plastic tubs hold Soviet ice screws and deformed snow flukes and rusty chocks, a collection of artifacts from a bygone era of adventure. It's fun to imagine where all this gear has been. Are the boots from the 1978 K2 expedition, when Lou Reichardt, Jim Wickwire, John Roskelley, and Rick Ridgeway became the first Americans to stand on top of the world's second-highest peak? Dad was the leader of the expedition and Mom carried a fifty-pound load of equipment to twenty-six thousand feet, higher than any woman had ever climbed without oxygen before. Are the backpacks from Dad and Uncle Lou's 1960 expedition to Mount McKinley with John Day and Pete Schoening? They reached the summit in three days only to fall five hundred vertical feet during the descent, initiating a legendary rescue effort. Are the ice screws from the 1990 International Peace Climb? Climbers from the world's three super-powers—China, the Soviet Union, and the United States—reached the summit of Mount Everest together in order to demonstrate what could be accomplished through friendship and cooperation. To me, the garage is like a museum. All this stuff's kind of special and sacred, but I guess Dad doesn't really care because he's rummaging through the shelves and messing everything up.

"Where the hell is my sleeping bag?"

"Which one?" I ask.

"That old blue one. You know which one I'm talking about?" he says.

"The rectangular one?"

"Yeah, with the gray lining," he says, digging around some more. "Ah, here it is." He dusts it off. It looks like something you'd find at Walmart, the type your teenage daughter would use to sleep over at a friend's house. "This'll be fine. Don't you think?"

But I'm thinking about how much gear has changed since Dad's heyday. I'm thinking of his wolverine fur–lined hood and Ventile anorak and thick wool pants and reindeer-skin boots and a Maytag oxygen mask squeezing against his frosty cheeks. It's all bulky and heavy and impractical and, jeez, they didn't even know how rough they had it back then.

"I don't think so, Dad," I say. "Remember how cold it was last time we were there?"

"Yeah, but this bag's pretty warm, isn't it?"

"No. I'd go buy a new bag. Down. Get one that's rated to at *least* zero degrees," I say.

"Really? You think so?"

"Definitely. And you better get it soon because we're leaving in two days."

"I know it. Mom and I are starting to pack." He looks at the blue rectangle and his face changes like he's just discovered a hole in his favorite pair of socks. He rolls it up and wedges it beside a box labeled Leif's Kids Books. "We're going to need your help on the trek, son," he says.

Dad's shrunk an inch or two in the past few years and I'm taller than he is now. How old is he again? I always have to do the math. 2012 minus 1929 equals 83. He's getting up there all right, but you'd probably guess early seventies if you saw him bucking firewood at the cabin or pumping iron at his bench here in the garage or skiing black diamonds at Sun Peaks. I'd be worried about an average octogenarian hiking to 17,500 feet, but Dad is Dad. I remember him lying on the sun bench after his double knee replacement six years ago. He was on his back, pillows propping up his legs. Afternoon sun streamed through the windows. The stitch lines were pink and raw. He'd bend the knees little by little and you could see he was burying a ton of pain, but he kept on bending the knees, stitch lines expanding and contracting like gills. A minute later he was carving ski turns between Joss and me. At least that's how fast I remember it happening. One second he couldn't walk without a walker. The next he was complaining about how the knees would sink him when he was swimming laps in the pool. It's weird how time speeds up as you get older, but Dad's always moving faster than the clock. He'll be fine.

"It might to be a little hard on you and Mom. We'll go slow," I say.

"That's right. I think if I just go slow, I can make it. I don't want to hold you guys up, though," he says.

"Don't worry about *that*. We'll have *months* to get to the summit after you and Mom go home."

He nods and opens the door for me. As if it's an afterthought, he says, "It'd be fun to toast a rum and Coke at Base Camp one last time before I check out."

My bedroom's a pigsty of merino boxer briefs and carrot cake Clif Bars and Halls cough drops and Grabber hand warmers and mocha-flavored GU Energy Gel. My long johns are dangling from a lamp shade. My harness and lockers and wire gates and ascender and slings and tethers and cordalettes are spread across my bed. There's a sleeping bag squished against the bookcase and a big fat down suit crumpled on the seat of my threadbare office chair. I've got a three-page list that I printed off from the RMI website. It's supposed to be a list of pretty much everything I need to climb Mount Everest. Pretty much. It doesn't mention lungs or guts or Schwarzenegger-like quadriceps. I grab a red pen from my writing desk and uncap it with my teeth. 2 DUFFEL BAGS. Mine are rubberized canvas, black and blue, and they're so big that I could probably fit inside if I crunched into a cannonball. I lay them out on the floor, wide open. Check. What's next?

BACKPACK

DAY PACK

COMPRESSION STUFF SACK

In goes my Therm-a-Rest and Buff bandana and helmet, which I've tagged with stickers from Eddie Bauer and RMI and one from the Wildernest. I get my ice axe from the closet. The cold metal feels familiar in my hands. I found it melting out from a bank of snow on the trail to Marmot Pass. Joss and I spent a frozen night up there, our shoulders wrecked from hours of self-arrest practice, and as we were hiking out the next day, a flash caught my eye. It was the spike glinting in the sun, a treasure that the changing seasons had revealed. In it goes.

TREKKING POLES

BELAY DEVICE

AVALANCHE TRANSCEIVER

HEAVYWEIGHT MITTENS

The red pen is slicing through letters and, phew, that's the end of page one.

Page two. MOUNTAINEERING BOOTS. Mine are made from three layers of highly insulative polyethylene foam, waterproof Cordura, Kevlar antiperforation fabric, thermo-reflective aluminum facing, and a built-in yellow gaiter that comes almost up to my knee. They look like they're made for landing on the moon, but are they warm enough for Everest? More importantly, am I ready? It's been eight months since the meeting with Neil and I've devoted almost every day to preparing for this expedition.

I remember Antarctica, where the sun surfed the horizon, never setting. Dave Hahn, the RMI guide who I'll be climbing with on Everest, had suggested I go to Mount Vinson, Antarctica's highest peak, to test myself in the cold. Eddie Bauer generously covered my expenses. At first, I cringed at the idea of climbing with a guide. I mean, I'm a Whittaker—I've climbed all over the world and I don't need a guide to show me what to do. But I'm not going to solo Mount Everest either. My climbing team will include veteran RMI guide and sponsored athlete Melissa Arnot, who is aiming to become the first non-Sherpa woman to summit Mount Everest four times. Kent Harvey, a respected cinematographer and experienced mountaineer, will be filming our ascent for Eddie Bauer. An RMI support staff of Americans and Nepalis will also join our team. Except for Dave, with whom I climbed Mount Vinson, I haven't met any of them. Our bond will be formed on the mountain and in the tent. Hopefully nobody snores.

At least I already know that Dave and I can stand each other. Mount Vinson was a good opportunity to test that. I wanted to prove to Dave that I was worthy of his partnership, so I made sure to do more than my fair share of menial tasks without having to be asked. I dug in the snow for hours to set up camp, cooked quesadillas for the team, and carried the heaviest loads I possibly could. Dave noticed. Within a few days he was treating me like an assistant guide rather than a client. I hope we fall in step the same way on Everest.

After Mount Vinson I was already in the southern part of South America, so it made sense to try Aconcagua as well. It's the highest peak outside of Asia and there was no better place to learn how I handled life at almost twenty-three thousand feet. I met Jake Beren, another RMI guide, in the Argentine city of Mendoza, where we enjoyed a few days of steak, Malbec, and ice cream before charging to the summit. It was a little more than a month ago that I was standing next to a metal cross at the top of the Andes Mountains and I guess I'll never be more ready for Everest than I am right now.

But what about my feet—will they cooperate? My right toes, the ones with the nerve damage, went numb during the ascent of Mount Vinson. I kept wiggling them as we climbed, and when we stopped for breaks, I'd balance on a trekking pole and swing my leg like a pendulum, pitching my heartbeat into my toes. I dodged frostbite that way, but won't Everest be colder than Antarctica? I wish they'd make warmer boots, ones that always stayed dry and cozy and comfortable, but they don't, so in go the moon boots. My bags are almost full.

2 WOOL HATS

GLACIER GLASSES

GOGGLES WITH CLEAR LENSES

4–8 PAIRS SOCKS

SUNSCREEN

LIP BALM

2 WATER BOTTLES

My crampons are a bit dull and I'm guessing the Lhotse Face will be bulletproof, so it'd probably be a good idea to sharpen the front points. I grab a file from the garage and take my spikes onto the porch and grind away—*scritch-scratch, scritch-scratch*. I wore these crampons during my climbing trip to Ecuador more than a year ago. They've never failed me, knock on wood. I remember the ribbon of snow above the Cotopaxi *refugio* and that one icy bridge, thinner than a pencil, less than thirty feet from the summit of Cayambe. Lightning flickered in the marble-shaped clouds over the wind-bent grass of the *páramo*. On the porch, I'm filing away the steel, but not the bitter fog that assailed the ankles of Antisana or the gaze of the *vicuna* staring at me through the Chimborazo rain, its fur matted and its eyes bigger than a whale's. Memories survive, even if you can't smell them or taste them or touch them.

THERMOS

TOOTHBRUSH

WET WIPES

HAND SANITIZER

IMODIUM

PEPTO-BISMOL

ACETAZOLAMIDE

AZITHROMYCIN

CIPROFLOXACIN

KNIFE

IPOD

WATCH

CAMERA

READING MATERIAL

In goes *A Life on the Edge*, of course, and *Americans on Everest* because I need to read it a second time, and Tom Hornbein's *Everest: The West Ridge* because I've never read it before, and Tom Robbins's *Jitterbug Perfume* because I'm guessing I'll need to laugh every once in a while, and a pocket-sized version of the Upanishads. Joss gave it to me. He said it's a great book for high camp because you can read it a thousand times or more and you still won't understand it.

I was nervous to tell him about Neil's offer because I thought he'd be jealous. I mean, *I* would be if our roles were reversed. He's been hearing about Everest his whole life just like I have. These days he's not as serious about climbing as I am because he's busy working for the North Olympic Salmon Coalition and applying to PhD programs in the field of archaeology, which is what he's always wanted to do. Still, he makes time to get up one or two major Washington peaks every year. When I called him, we chatted for a while about habitat restoration and then I was like, "Dude, so, uh, I think I'm going to climb Mount Everest." He was silent for a few long seconds and I could almost feel our relationship disintegrating. I remember the day he received a letter of acceptance from Brown University and the pride on my parents' faces when he read it out loud. He held the letter in the air like a trophy and pranced around the kitchen while Dad and Mom cheered. I said, "Congratulations!" and gave him a high five, but I was thinking, *Aren't you* the perfect son. I'm pretty sure Joss wanted to say the same thing to me when I told him about Everest. He didn't, though.

He said, "Really? Holy shit! That's amazing," and he sounded like he meant it.

"So you think I should do it?" I asked.

"Um, duh. Of course you should do it," he said and it reminded me of our climb on Mount Olympus when he yelled, *It's not too bad. Only one scary part.*

"Yeah. I know. I'm just kind of nervous. It's a big mountain."

"If anyone can climb that thing, you can."

I squirmed for a second because I didn't know how to respond. I was thinking, *You have no idea how good it feels to have your support*, but then I just said, "Thanks, brother."

"Check it out and learn the route so next time you can guide me up it," he said with a half-kidding laugh. If they made a device that could send hugs across phone lines, I would've sent one to Joss right then.

BOWL

INSULATED MUG

2 SPORKS

PEE BOTTLE

PERSONAL FIRST-AID KIT

The list is mostly red lines. The last few items will go in my carry-on, which is a good thing because I'm not sure if I can get these duffels closed. I put my legs on either side of one and squeeze my thighs together and pull as hard as I can on the zipper. Nope. It won't budge. I try the other one, but it's just as full. Do I really need all this crap? Isn't climbing mountains about getting away from stuff? I've been climbing mountains for more than a decade, but I've never had this much baggage.

There's a knock on my open bedroom door. "Need some help?" says Dad.

"Yeah. Could you close the zipper while I pull the sides together?" I ask.

"Okay." Dad crouches over the duffel bag. I pull the sides together and he yanks the zipper closed.

"Now the other one?" he asks, glancing at the second duffel bag.

"No. I've still got a few more *small* things to put in that one," I say. "It's a hell of a lot of stuff."

"Yeah, but nothing like '63," he says.

In '63, Dad was equipment coordinator for the team, responsible for acquiring, organizing, and packing twenty-seven tons of food and equipment—all that the twenty members of the American Mount Everest Expedition would need for a four-month journey to the Himalaya. Everything from scientific apparatus to long underwear to oxygen bottles to cases of Rainier Beer was packed into nine hundred waxed cardboard cartons. They were meticulously organized and marked according to the elevation at which they would be opened. Then they were sealed with steel banding and nylon tape, and finally sent to India on a freighter.

I guess my duffel bags aren't really *that* big.

"A lot's changed since then," I say.

"Yeah, but it's still one foot in front of the other," Dad says. "Remember what my old friend Ed Viesturs always says, 'The summit is optional. Getting down is mandatory.'"

"You know me, Dad. I'm not going to do anything stupid," I reply.

"I know. It's not you I worry about. It's everyone else."

Before I can reply, Mom steps into my bedroom. "Did you get everything in?" she asks.

"Yep. I think so. I hope I'm not forgetting anything," I say.

"I have a little something to give you if you want it," says Mom. She brings her hand out from behind her back, revealing a gold chain with a circular gold pendant about the size of a penny.

"What's this?" I ask.

"It's a Saint Christopher medal—the patron saint of travelers. And this one's special. It's been to the summit of K2 with John Roskelley in 1978 and the summit of Everest with Robert Link in 1990 on the Peace Climb. So I want it back," she says, and she's trying to look casual, but I can tell how much it means to her and I hope she can see how much it means to me.

I slide the chain over my neck and feel the weight of the pendant pressing against my chest. My shoulders bunch together and my back stiffens up. What new story will the pendant have when I return it?

"Thank you, Mom. Don't worry, I'll bring it back," I say.

"And bring *yourself* back," she says, so I wrap her in my arms and hold on.

"I have something for you too," interjects Dad. "Do you have room for this?" He hands me a navy-blue leather-bound journal with James Whittaker embossed on the cover in worn gold letters.

"What's this?" I ask, taking the book in my hands.

"It's my journal from '63. Everyone on the team had one. We were supposed to write in them every night and answer all these questions about how we were feeling. I thought you might find something useful in there," says Dad.

I fold it open and there's Dad's distinctive handwriting—a chicken scratch of capital letters, nothing lowercase. There's a series of simple questions on each page that relate to the journal owner's emotional, psychological, and physical state with a scale from one to five for responses. I flip through the pages, scanning Dad's responses. One day he must've been in good spirits because he wrote the number five next to the question "Mood?" One night he must've been feeling sick because he wrote the number one next to the question "General health?" The questionnaire covers everything from sleep patterns to anxiety levels to team dynamics. Beneath each questionnaire there's plenty of space for personal notes and anecdotes. Dad's handwriting from forty-nine years ago fills each page. Few moments are catalogued in such detail. It's a part of family history. Hell, it's a part of national history. It's a priceless artifact and surely too important to take with me. I'm worried I might ruin it.

"Are you sure?" I ask.

"Yeah. Of course. It's just an old book," says Dad, shrugging.

There's no way I'm going to put Dad's journal in a duffel. Instead, I seal it in two ziplocks and slide it into a hidden pouch in my backpack. It holds the journal right against my spine, pressed into my scar, where, perhaps, I won't notice the extra weight.

It's 2:11 a.m. according to the neon-green numbers next to my bed, but I can't fall asleep. People say pressure produces diamonds, but it produces ulcers too. My back and shoulders are throbbing from the stress and my head's a hive of pissed-off bees. My right calf's twitchy and I keep clenching my jaw even though I'm trying to relax. I go through the three-page list again in my mind. Have I forgotten an essential piece of gear? Have I forgotten how to climb a mountain? Am I strong enough and lucky enough to summit Mount Everest?

I open *Americans on Everest* and flip to one of the many pages I've bookmarked and begin to read.

Before the 1963 American Mount Everest Expedition began, Jim Lester, the team psychologist, conducted confidential interviews aimed at studying the personalities of the climbers. James Ramsey Ullman wrote that one of the questions asked of each man was "whether he thought that he individually would reach the top of Everest." All of them except one gave similar answers. They said "perhaps," "it depends," or "I hope to." One man answered differently. When asked if he thought he would reach the summit of the highest peak on planet Earth, Dad replied, "Yes, I will."

I close the book and slide it back into its place. I think about Dad's journal hidden in the sleeve of my backpack and about my own journal—a brand-new spiral-bound notebook without a single word written on a single page. I *need* to fall asleep, but I can't shut down my mind.

First I imagine a young man climbing through a landscape of shattered ice. Sweat drips from his forehead as he climbs beneath a serac that threatens to collapse and crush him at any moment. Next I imagine the young man climbing a snowy ridgeline above an ocean of mountains. His toes are numb and he's very nearly exhausted, but he sticks to a simple rhythm—step, breathe, step, step, breathe. Finally, I imagine him standing, with one leg bent, on a crest of snow. He's holding his ice axe in the air. A white plume of spindrift trails into the sky. I latch onto this final image and repeat a simple mantra in my head: *I will climb Mount Everest.*

I open my eyes. The pain's gone and a simple rhythm has taken its place. I fiddle with the gold pendant, heavy against my chest, and slide into darkness.

11.
LANDING UPHILL

A flight attendant in a green-and-white Yeti Airlines uniform walks down the aisle in the passenger cabin of a Dornier 228, passing out cotton balls and watermelon-flavored hard candy before takeoff. The twenty seats in the aircraft are full. Dad's sitting across the aisle to my left and Mom's in front of me and Dave Hahn's way in the back, as close to the exit door as he can possibly get. I spin my head to glance at him and he gives me a thumbs-up and a look that says, *I'll be the first one out the door when this thing crashes, but I want you to be right behind me.* I twist the cotton balls into my ears and pop the candy in my mouth, and now the engines are revving up so I yank my seat belt tight.

Out the oval window to my right the tarmac of the Kathmandu airport bakes in the sun. Fuel trucks are parked against a chicken-wire fence and palm fronds undulate in the breeze. If I lean my head into the aisle, I can see into the cockpit too, all the controls and levers and gauges and flashing lights, and even out through the front windows to the gray runway that disappears in front of us in a wave of heat. The pilot and copilot are in full view. They're Nepali and they're wearing identical uniforms—starched white shirts unbuttoned at the collar, black leather jackets, aviator glasses with gold rims, black pilot's hats with faded gold Yeti Airlines insignia, and black leather fingerless gloves. It's like they stepped right out of *Top Gun*. I can't hear over the rattling whine of the engines and the muffle of the cotton balls, but they seem to be chatting casually. Shouldn't they be more focused on what they're doing? For Christ's sake, these two movie stars have my life in their hands.

The rattling whine grows louder and louder now and we gain speed and, shit, there's no turning back. I watch the tarmac rush beneath us and wait for the feeling of weightlessness as the wheels leave the ground. There it is. My stomach sinks a little and my back drives into the seat and an errant spring digs in between my shoulder blades. The aircraft shudders, as if its wings are cutting through the thick haze of the city, and then we break into smooth, clean air.

I lean my forehead against the window and let my eyes play over the cityscape. The place unfolds as we pass over. A shoulder-width alleyway winds beneath an unfinished apartment building. A disheveled marketplace overflows with rugs and prayer wheels and tapestries. A pack of marauding dogs searches for edible garbage along the fringe of a dusty field. Piles of litter choke a meandering creek. A white cow turns its head at passing mopeds from its place in the middle of a traffic divider. Thousands of vehicles—motorcycles, mopeds, trucks, sedans, and vans—send up clouds of dust. Kathmandu is its own sort of adventure. It's all getting smaller and smaller and the picture's getting broader and I see temples and hotels and city blocks and entire districts. In Kathmandu, I've heard, there are ten times as many bricks as people. The whole city's the color of brick, except for patches of bright-green trees and rainbows of clothing hanging on wires between buildings and the occasional blue of a rooftop swimming pool. We're leaving behind the brick and litter and mopeds and bent rebar. We're getting away from real problems as fast as we possibly can. Climbing mountains is such a selfish endeavor.

Ten minutes into the flight and Kathmandu's gone. A rural landscape spreads in its place. Every inch of valley and hillside is terraced. It looks like a topographical map and the terraces are the contour lines. They're different colors too—tilled red earth, dry and yellow, then emerald. An empty dirt road parallels a turbid river. We're flying perpendicularly over the ridges and I see a boy in a bright-orange T-shirt running down a road, waving at the aircraft. He sprints around a house to keep the aircraft in sight as long as he can, waving incessantly. Then we punch into dense cloud and the landscape is suddenly invisible.

The last of the candy dissolves in my mouth and I sneak a glance at Dad. He's smiling, but his eyes are red-rimmed with exhaustion and he's got this leave-me-alone look on his face. I can't blame him; we've been on the move for the last three days and his rhythms are probably still catching up with his location. I know mine are. I'd like to ask him about Kathmandu and northeastern Nepal and if it looks different than it did in 1963? How has it changed in forty-nine years? But the compartment's too loud and Dad's too tired and we've got a bit of a hike ahead of us today, so I'll just keep my mouth shut.

We were here in 2003, but I was just along for the ride then and I hardly knew how special it was to listen to Dad's and Gombu's stories, a personal window into history. Joss and I would hike way ahead, scramble on boulders, get a bit lost, and find our way back to the trail like we always had. We'd point out peaks and argue about how to climb them—which rock face or snowy couloir offered the easiest route? Back then, Dad had his original knees, I had my original spine, and my biggest worry was if my tux would match my prom date's gown. There were no real goals or expectations or risks, but that's all changed. About two weeks from now, if everything goes according to plan, I'll be sitting in front of the Khumbu Icefall again, only this time I'll have to go through it.

It's better not to think about it, so instead I think about the American Mount Everest Expedition. Today, it's about a forty-five-minute flight from Kathmandu to the village of Lukla. Dad and his teammates hiked for two weeks to cover the same distance.

They drove Land Rovers and Jeeps fifteen miles east from Kathmandu to the end of the road in the village of Banepa. From there, it was a 185-mile hike to Base Camp. More than nine hundred porters joined the expedition, each carrying a sixty-five-pound load. The men of AMEE described the horde as a giant millipede, a millipede at least five miles long that needed more than two hours to pass a single point. Dad wrote that he felt like he had "stepped into the middle of some wide-screen, epic film."

Fittingly, much of the expedition was being filmed, thanks in large part to Norman Dyhrenfurth, the overall leader. Born in Germany to famed Himalayan adventurers Günter and Hettie Dyhrenfurth, Norman emigrated to the United States as a young man and pursued his passion for mountain climbing and filmmaking. He participated in the 1952 Swiss Mount Everest Expedition, a 1955 international expedition to Lhotse, and the 1960 Swiss expedition to Dhaulagiri, during which he worked as a high-altitude cameraman. In 1961 the Nepalese government granted him a permit for an American expedition to attempt Mount Everest in the spring of 1963, so he began his search for the country's best mountaineers. At forty-four, he was the oldest climber on the team, but he was also a Himalayan veteran whose egalitarian leadership style and intimate knowledge of the region were irreplaceable. Whether behind the lens or at the head of the millipede, Norman kept the expedition running smoothly.

It must've been an incredible sight when the millipede stirred to life in the morning. Porters spat sleep from their lungs, drank tea, smoked cigarettes, hoisted their loads, and set off to the next camp, eight to fifteen miles away. The millipede climbed dry hillsides and descended into green valleys. Merchants, pilgrims, and other travelers passed by in both directions. Many had used the ancient trail for generations to travel between the highlands and the Kathmandu valley. The trail rose and fell, undulating in front of the team as it led toward a wall of distant white mountains.

On hot afternoons the Americans swam in the rivers. Lute Jerstad and Gil Roberts played ukulele in the evenings around the campfire. Everyone laughed and danced and sang in a flickering glow of light. I can imagine Dad evoking bellows of laughter when he stood up one evening and started doing the twist. The Americans drank Rainier Beer and the porters drank *chhaang*, a cloudy alcoholic beverage made from rice and barley. Dad tasted enough chhaang to get drunk one night and the following morning he swore he would never drink it again.

The climbers complained of blisters and aching feet for a week and many of them suffered from cases of the trots. Combine that with exercise, high altitude, and a new diet, and the climbers started to lose weight. But these troubles didn't change their determination or physical drive. They quickly learned to eat the trail and breathe the mountains. Dad did push-ups to complete each day of hiking. He pressed his palms against dust or stone for sixty or more repetitions, enough for thick blood to fill his arms and shoulders. He wanted to be ready.

Days and miles passed. They hiked through the villages of Risingo, Kirantichap, Those, Junbesi, Ghat, and Phakding. The lower altitudes were planted with rice, sugar cane, bananas, and wheat. Higher up, forests of blue pine and rhododendron flourished. Yaks patrolled broad pastures and steep hillsides. The millipede gained a snow-dusted pass, dropped to a river valley, and started to climb again, repeating the same seesaw process day after day.

It was safe walking for the most part, but not always. One morning, when eleven porters shuffled onto an aging bridge at once, sixty-five-pound loads on their backs, there was a wrenching collapse. Three porters crashed into the rushing river and were sucked downstream before they escaped from their loads and swam to shore. Eight landed on the rocks. There were contusions and lacerations and one broken foot. The expedition doctors treated the wounds, relieved that nobody had died. A crisis had been avoided and the millipede slithered along the trail with the same vigor as usual, ever higher and closer to their mountain.

The plane seat's errant spring is digging into my back again. I'd change seats if I could but the flight is completely full, and besides I'm too chicken to unbuckle my seat belt. I wouldn't mind having a glass of orange juice with that tubular ice they always serve on airplanes, but the flight attendant is still strapped tightly into a jump seat next to Dave Hahn. I'm guessing the plane's bouncing too wildly for beverage service.

Dave has probably done this flight more times than the flight attendant, but from the deer-in-the-headlights look on his face, you'd think he was forced on the plane against his will. He's fifty this year, and at first glance he's not what you'd picture when you think badass mountaineer, but I've seen what he's hiding in his quads and lungs. He's a little over six feet tall with ash-brown hair and a tapered smile that's wide open on the left side of his face and tight-lipped on the right. He sports a perpetual goggle tan. He holds his shoulders high and clustered together as if counteracting a heavy backpack. His forearms are bone and sinew and his size-fifteen feet are a little clunky, even compared to my size-twelve shoes. I think Dave's center is where his talent comes from. It's like he's got all this uncluttered space inside him that's there for filling with oxygen.

Dave's followed a similar annual schedule for more than two decades: In winter, he works as a ski patroller at Taos in New Mexico and guides on Mount Vinson. In summer, he guides on Mount Rainier and Denali. In spring, he guides on Mount Everest. Google says he's been to the summit of Mount Everest eleven times, more than any other non-Sherpa. He's also been to the top of Mount Vinson more than thirty times, summited Denali more than twenty, and led over 250 climbs up Mount Rainier. In 2009, *Men's Journal* voted Dave Hahn "Best Mountain Guide." It's a slightly dubious honor and I'm sure his guide buddies give him shit for it, but I bet they're jealous deep down, because how many mountain guides have been profiled in a magazine that's on the shelf of every gas station and Walmart in America?

Dave has spent his life managing risk and maybe he looks so terrified right now because he has absolutely no control.

Looking between the pilots and through the cockpit windows, I see only white clouds, but we've been flying for almost forty minutes now and the landing strip can't be too far ahead. Sure enough, the clouds break apart and we punch into a pocket of clear air and, I kid you not, we're heading straight for a mountainside. The landing strip is just a ribbon of asphalt laid onto the hill. No flat bench or terrace carved out for it or anything like that—it's like a Band-Aid stuck to a forehead. A concrete retaining wall marks the far end and a rusty barbed-wire fence wraps around it. Everyone in the plane leans into the aisle and looks through the cockpit, and if it weren't for the blaring engines, I'm sure I'd hear a collective gasp.

The idea of hiking 185 miles just to get to Base Camp sounded like Chinese water torture a second ago, but we're all envying Dad and his teammates now. Even if we somehow hit the uphill runway at the correct angle, which looks highly unlikely, there's no way we'll have enough space to stop before we smash into the retaining wall and get torn to pieces in the barbed wire.

CNN will have a field day with this one. I imagine the headlines: JIM WHITTAKER AND NINETEEN OTHERS KILLED IN HIMALAYAN PLANE CRASH. And the article: "Jim Whittaker, who became the first American to conquer Mount Everest in 1963, died today in a plane crash in the Himalayan mountains of Nepal. Nineteen others were also killed in the crash, including Whittaker's wife and his youngest son. Pilot negligence is suspected."

The article will fail to identify Mom, me, or anyone else by name, but it will go on for another 1,500 words, mostly describing Jim Whittaker's life and accomplishments.

We're getting super close now and I can see cliffs of gray rock and individual trees jutting from bands of red earth. A yak grazes in a pasture. A string of prayer flags hangs between branches. The plane is shuddering and lurching and I can't help myself, so I look across the aisle again at Dad. Our eyes connect and he bugs his out, as if to say, *Wouldn't it be funny if I died in a plane crash after all the other risks I've taken in my life?*

How the hell does he remain so nonchalant? I try to make my face look calm and composed and a little excited, but I think it's probably paler than chalk. I can't hold his gaze for more than a second anyway because I have to look ahead again to see if it's all going to end like I suspect.

The nose of the aircraft points directly at the ribbon of asphalt. We're heading straight into the hill and, Jesus Christ, we're so close I can see splotches of oil staining the runway.

The view through the cockpit windows rotates upward to a tin-roofed building and the concrete retaining wall in front of it. We hit the pavement. The wheels bounce once and then settle again. Rubber screeches hard. My seat belt mashes my stomach and digs into my guts and the aircraft comes to a nearly immediate halt less than fifty feet from the retaining wall. The pilot turns around and looks into the passenger cabin. He brings his gloved hand to the side of his aviator glasses, tilts his head forward, and slides the gold frame down his nose, revealing his eyes. He fixes his gaze on me and pronounces, "Welcome to the Himalaya!"

12.
MADE WEAK BY TIME AND FATE

Before I step out of the death trap, I tap MODE on my Suunto watch and the screen reads 9,317 feet, which means 17,500 minus 9,317 equals how many vertical feet we have to climb to get to Base Camp. Sort of. It's actually a lot more than that because the trail goes down and up, down and up, rolling like a wave. Besides, I haven't recalibrated since walking North Beach three days ago—rotting kelp, squawking gulls, and a sea lion spying me from the surf. How far have we traveled since then? One thousand miles? One million? People like to break down experiences into bite-sized factoids so they can file them in a folder in their brain. What's 29,035 minus 9,317? It's a hell of a long way to go, that's what it is.

I duck out of the shadowy cabin into yak bells and juniper and prayer flags and broken sunshine. Dave greets me with a handshake and a tapered grin. Dad comes out behind me and he's all smiles too. A local boy puts a *khata*, a ceremonial prayer scarf, around his neck and then looks shyly at me. I bow low with my hands pressed in front of me and the silk slides beneath my collar. It's rougher than I expected. The dangly tails cling to my soft shell. Mom's camera shutter is already clicking, so I adjust my hair and make sure there's nothing on my face and zip all my zippers closed, which will be important from this point on because Kent Harvey's here too and his camera's constantly rolling. Every word and step and breath is recorded. There's no hiding, so I might as well embrace it. I put my arm over Dad's shoulder and grin hard enough to taste shit.

If I had to guess, I'd say Kent Harvey's in his midforties. According to Google, he's been to the summit of Mount Everest once before. He's taller than average, with close-cut brown hair and crow's-feet emanating from his calm eyes. From the moment we met at the Yak and Yeti Hotel, Kent was asking questions about my life—what did I study at Western, what do I love about climbing, how many brothers do I have—and he actually listened, which is rare. Kent joked that his friends call him "Old Man Harvs" because of his mellow nature and grandpa-ish aches and pains. He told me he recently worked on the newest Jason Bourne film, during which he ran around the streets of Manila with a handheld camera and hung from wires above car-chase scenes. He said he's carving out a niche for himself in the film industry as an "extreme, high-risk cameraman." When I told him I don't do anything high risk, he said, "Yeah, you're right. It's only Mount Everest."

Melissa Arnot is the last person out of the plane. I think she's a few years older than I am and she's got this palpable air of confidence and purpose. Google says she's a guide and sponsored climber who's been to the summit of Mount Everest three times. It also says she's been to the top of Mount Rainier more than ninety times and has guided on high peaks in Africa, Ecuador, Argentina, Alaska, and the Himalaya. She's a wilderness Emergency Medical Technician (EMT) and an instructor for Remote Medical International, a company that provides medical training to organizations operating in remote locations worldwide. About five feet four inches tall with copper-blond hair that catches the sunlight and a Natalie Portman smile, Melissa's easily the most photogenic person on our team. Easily. Like Dave Hahn and me, and hopefully even more so, she'll often be the focus of Kent's camera.

Dad is shaking hands with a middle-aged Nepali man with a beatific smile. He squeezes the man's shoulder like they've known each other for years even though they've never met before. Dave says, "Let me introduce you to Lam Babu. He's our *sirdar*, leader of our Sherpa teammates, so he'll be climbing with us. He's here for the walk to Base Camp too. *Great* guy. You'll love him."

Lam Babu is the average height for a Nepali man, which means I tower over him, but as his hand ratchets closed on my palm, I get the feeling I'd have to chew through my wrist if I wanted to escape him. I don't feel the need to escape. Not at all. Beneath his blue-and-white RMI baseball cap, his eyes are gentle and wise. "Good to meet you, Leif-*bai*," he says, so kindly it's like I really am his little brother.

"Good to meet you too. I'm really excited to climb together."

Then he introduces the last two team members. "This is Lhakpa and this is Kami." Lhakpa is lanky with downcast eyes and an oasis of black fuzz on his chin. Kami is kind of stout and square jawed with a close-cut do. They can't be much over twenty and they're so quiet that I can barely hear them say hello. Someone starts unloading the plane, mounding duffels on the tarmac. Lam Babu darts his eyes that way and Lhakpa and Kami jump to life. They heft the bags, guesstimating their weight with outstretched arms, and organize them into stacks of two to be carried up the trail.

I've read it's about forty miles to Base Camp. About. Of course, it depends on which branch of trail you choose and which guesthouses you visit and how many times you walk back and forth over a suspension bridge, admiring the curve of the river. Who knows how fast we'll move and what we'll encounter on the trail. There's no time to waste.

I hike along the cobbled trail between stone walls and almost run into Mom. She's crouched low, aiming her camera at the head of a yak. Or is it a *dzopkyo*? You can see the cow in it—longer neck and thinner coat—so it's probably a dzopkyo. It dips its curved horns and plucks a few blades of grass from a crack in a plastered wall. Dave steps past it without a second glance, strolling on. We're moving now and we can't stop for every shaggy beast if we want to make it to Base Camp by April, but I can't blame Mom for stopping because there's just so much to take in.

Through a gap in the buildings, I glimpse two young men wearing muddy jeans and flip-flops. They're playing a game on a square of plywood that's balanced on an empty fifty-gallon drum, sliding polished stones across it like they're trying to land them in a corner marked with red paint. Maybe it's the Himalayan version of shuffleboard. They're having fun, whatever it is. One man slides a white stone across the plywood and it knocks three blue stones off the board and both men yell *"Swooo!"* Their laughter bounces through the alleyway. I think of Ping-Pong at the Uptown and cribbage at the cabin. I guess people are all the same in certain ways, but it's the differences that make the world beautiful.

Farther down the cobbled trail, a woman and a toddler watch me walk past. The woman scoops handfuls of water from a plastic tub and splashes them onto the toddler's face and head. She washes away streaks and smudges while the toddler shrieks playfully, pushing her face into her mother's hands like a kitten wanting to be petted. The Dudh Koshi river churns in the distance. I remember that Gombu told me it means "milk river." We'll be walking against the downward flow for however long it takes us to get to Base Camp. That distant roar, that churning and tumbling, is guiding us to the glacier.

I take a deep breath and the air's kind of sharp but has this familiar taste of dirt and spring and green. It's different from the Mount Townsend trailhead, but something about it reminds me of the Olympic Mountains. Maybe it's just the fresh complexity of it, the aliveness of it. It helps me settle in. It simplifies things. Forget about the expectations, at least for a minute. Forget about Kent's camera, my face on a hangtag—puke— and the you'll-never-be-as-strong-as-me tone in my cousin's or uncle's or Dad's voice. There's just the trail and the rhythm of the trail. It feels so damn good to be walking.

Out of Lukla and down a set of stone stairs and through a granite archway, we walk. The trail contours a hillside, with steep forests of pine on my right and a field of ankle-high emerald plants on my left. Are those potato plants? They're sprouting in even rows from the coffee-colored earth. A woman with a creased face scrapes at the ground with a hoe. A gray mutt yelps at a soaring gorak. The scene could have been nearly identical forty-nine years ago, but the millipede of hikers on the trail has a modern flair. We pass Europeans with neon pink and green and blue and purple clothing. There's a group of Australians with floppy-brimmed sun hats and laidback accents—"No worries, mate." Up ahead there's a group of Japanese trekkers more than thirty strong, each person with a camera and a pair of trekking poles. The group is walking four wide, beating the trail with their boots and sending up clouds of dust and destroying any semblance of solitude. Now they squeeze between two boulders and stop in the middle of a wire suspension bridge to snap photos of the turbid waters beneath them. This isn't wilderness. It's a pulsing artery of tourism and commerce and everyday life. The beat of the trail goes *cha-ching, cha-ching, cha-ching.*

It's not just us tourists, though. It's all the people that support us too. A porter with a stack of plywood goes by, then another with a twenty-gallon propane bottle, another with three cases of Fanta, and another with an enormous bag of hay. Whatever the load is, a single strand of rope or woven fabric called a "tumpline" runs beneath the load and then across the porter's forehead. No shoulder straps or waist belts like we have on our backpacks, just a tumpline. I watch one porter lean forward dramatically and hoist a load of two duffel bags onto his tumpline. I can feel the pain in my neck. He walks fluidly up a set of rough-hewn stairs, faster than I can, relying on a T-shaped cane for balance. Then he stops at the top of the stairs, props his cane beneath the bottom of his load, and simply leans back into a straight-up position so the cane's supporting the weight. Thirty seconds and he's ready to continue. He leans forward and jets off out of sight around a bend.

Dave's like, "Give the porters a wide berth, everyone. Be careful not to trip somebody with a trekking pole or loose shoelace. An injury could ruin their livelihood forever, so be aware of your surroundings."

A porter zooms past on my right and, holy shit, he's carrying a whole stack of ten-foot hardwood beams. I catch Lam Babu's eye and ask him, "How much do you think that weighs?"

"Hmm. Maybe two hundred pounds," he says, making a more-or-less gesture with his hand. "For building a new guesthouse in Namche."

What's the heaviest pack I've carried? Eighty pounds on Aconcagua? I think I complained the entire time, and the next day I felt like I'd been squeezed through a pasta maker. I swear I'll never complain again. Never.

A young woman sends me a furtive smile from a doorway. A prayer wheel spins clockwise. I take the khata from around my neck and tie it in a daisy chain to a strap on my backpack.

The beat of the trail goes on.

Twenty minutes later I follow Dave down a rocky, uneven section and turn around to take a photo of Dad and, hold on a sec, what the hell's wrong with him? All wobbly and pale and offbeat, he's barely picking up his feet, just dragging his boots along like he's wading through surf. I can tell how hard he's squeezing the cork handles of his trekking poles because his knuckles are turning white. *Thump.* The rubber toe of his boot hits a rock and then, oh no, he's falling. He's falling and there's no stopping him. I picture it all in a flash—he'll break a hip or tear a meniscus or hit his head on a boulder and his trek'll be over before it even begins. A helicopter will evacuate him to a dingy hospital in Kathmandu, where he'll get an infection and gasp his last breath. The ancient hospital bed, the red streaks running up his leg toward his heart, and the distant glaze in his eyes when he says good-bye. It's happening. Then he stabs a trekking pole into the trail and flexes that giant left arm of his and, thank heavens, he's not falling anymore. He stumbles over the rocks, makes it to the flat, and shoots me a look that says, *Why are you stopping?*

Acid burns my heart. What've we gotten ourselves into? Today's supposed to be one of the easiest days of the trek, and there's no way we'll make it to Base Camp without an injury if Dad keeps walking like this. I can tell from the squint in Dave's eyes that he's thinking the same thing. Everyone must be thinking the same thing. Bringing Dad along on this trek was a terrible idea.

But it's not like we're going to turn around after the first hour of hiking. No. We've got to make it to Phakding at the very least. It's all downhill from here.

Lam Babu whispers in Lhakpa's ear and the skinny boy takes up a position directly behind Dad, less than a few feet back. Maybe Lam Babu is thinking that Lhakpa can grab onto Dad if he falls. Like that'll make any difference.

I take my place in front of Dad, parting crowds of oncoming trekkers, porters, and yaks like I'm a secret service agent fending off reporters. Without a word, Dad follows my footsteps.

"Do you want me to carry your pack?" I ask. We're all carrying day packs and they're supposed to have nothing more than a warm layer, a bottle of water, a few snacks, and perhaps a camera, but Dad's day pack looks unusually large. It's bigger than mine.

"No," he replies in a defensive tone. "The pack's light. I just need to keep going slow."

"Okay. No rush," I say.

We walk on. Dad follows me in a sort of controlled stumble, every step a fall that he arrests a split second before impact.

We walk across a suspension bridge and I look beneath my feet through a gap in the aluminum decking and there's the Dudh Koshi, frothy and churning and twisting, the color of a glacier. We make it to the far side where a group of trekkers waits. One of them has a swath of sunscreen in his peppery beard and he says, "Mr. Whittaker? Mr. Jim Whittaker?"

"Yes. I'm Jim," Dad says and puts out his sweaty hand.

Sunscreen Beard grabs Dad's hand and melts. "Oh my God! You're a hero of mine, Mr. Whittaker. You've been a hero of mine since I was a little kid. I've wanted to come to Mount Everest ever since I read about your climb. I finally made it to Base Camp this year. I can't believe I'm meeting you here on the trail."

Dad leans against a concrete stanchion a little gingerly and says, "Good for you for getting out here. It's beautiful, isn't it?"

"Oh, it's incredible." He turns to the other trekkers in his group and says loudly, "This is Mr. Jim Whittaker, everyone! The first American to climb Mount Everest."

All of a sudden they're surrounding Dad and wanting to shake his hand and have their picture taken with him. Dad's all smiles and bows, giving attention to each admirer, maybe because he appreciates the chance to take a break without having to ask for one. Or maybe the attention invigorates him. Dad has toned down his machismo as he's aged, but sometimes when he's in a room full of mountain climbers or social climbers or other Whittakers, it'll come back. Then it's easy to imagine him at the peak of his fame, an icon of American power and virility, the ultimate alpha male. I'm probably lucky he was fifty-five when he had me because I'm not sure I would've survived an upbringing in an even hotter crucible of achievement. My daddy issues are bad enough as it is.

Dave and I watch Dad pose for photos. "He sure is wonderful with people," says Dave. "I like that. So many of these other Everest heroes won't give a stranger the time of day."

"Yeah, he's always been like that. Unless, of course, they mistake him for Uncle Lou," I reply.

Dave gives me an I-know-what-you-mean chuckle.

"So why are you here in Nepal?" asks Sunscreen Beard.

"We're here to toast a rum and Coke at Base Camp. It's been almost fifty years since my climb and I want to say hello to the mountain one last time before I check out," says Dad.

The trekkers erupt in laughter. "If you don't mind me asking, how old are you?" asks Sunscreen Beard.

Dad bugs out his eyes and says, "Eighty-frickin'-three!"

Jaws plummet.

"You've got to be joking. That's unbelievable!"

Dad stands up straight and taps a fist against his chest. The crowd's hanging on his every word. "Made weak by time and fate," he says, pausing for effect. Then his booming voice rises to a crescendo to finish Tennyson's lines. "But strong in will / To strive, to seek, to find, and not to *yield*."

In Phakding, we stay at a guesthouse named Joe's Garden. The nearby river is roaring constantly, which reminds me of being at the ocean cabin, our off-the-grid family getaway that Dad built in the late '60s on the remote Washington coast, where the sound of crashing waves never ends. Here, jagged treetops ring the walls of the valley. Daylight is fading in the western sky. I bang my knuckles against rough wood—*rap, rap*.

"Come in," Mom says.

A window lets in twilight from high on a plastered wall, and a single LED bulb in the center of the ceiling casts a dull blue glow onto bare floorboards. Dad and Mom have pushed together the two single beds so they can sleep next to each other. How cute. Dad's propped up in one of them, reading John Grisham by headlamp. He looks pretty warm and comfortable in his brand-new sleeping bag. Mom's peering at the screen of her camera, scrolling through today's images.

"How you doing?" I ask.

"Not too bad, son," says Dad, looking at me through his reading glasses. "I think the downhill's actually worse than the uphill. My knees don't handle it very well."

"Yeah," Mom interjects, "and we're still not *acclimatized* yet. Dave and Melissa and Kent all live at altitude. We're the only ones who came from sea level. Not to mention we're still jet-lagged." There's more than a hint of annoyance in her voice, like she really wants to say, *Give us a frickin' break here. We're old and this is hard.*

"I know. I know. I'm feeling a little bit behind too. Just remember you can go as slow as you need to. The Namche Hill's going to be pretty tough tomorrow, but we have all day. We're not in a rush," I say. I'm trying to be calm and positive and I think it comes out sounding pretty level.

"Sometimes it feels like we *are* in a rush," says Mom.

"I don't want to hold you guys up from getting to the climb, dammit," says Dad, which is the exact wrong thing to say.

"Jim! For heaven's sake! That's exactly what I'm talking about. You're not holding anyone up," says Mom. She looks at me for reassurance.

"I don't think it's a big deal if we're a day or two behind. You guys are the centerpiece of this trek, so don't worry about that," I say honestly. As long as Dad and Mom are here, I don't have to confront the mountain alone.

"Yeah," says Mom. "Thank you."

"I'm sure Lam Babu has someone who can carry your pack. It would probably help," I say and immediately regret it.

"No. The pack's really not the problem. I don't even notice it," says Dad, as I knew he would.

Mom shoots me a get-a-load-of-this-guy glance and shrugs like she's resigned herself to having lost all control.

"All right, don't feel like you have to go fast. We're not in a rush," I say.

"I'll give it a shot tomorrow," Dad says stoically. In the blue light, with his back resting against cracked plaster, Dad looks about as worn down as I've ever seen him, worse than when he was going through the cancer treatments, worse than when he was recovering from the double knee replacement. He takes a deep breath and exhales slowly and says, "If she goes, she goes."

"C'mon, Dad. You got this," I say. I want to make him feel better, so I sit down next to him on the bed and put my hand around his bicep and squeeze. "Ten thousand stainless-steel bands. Right?"

Dad smirks slyly and I feel his bicep go taut. "I don't know," he says, "more like ten thousand boiled noodles."

13.
BLAME THE FIRE

What's that shallow wheeze behind me? I turn my head to look at Dad—forehead dripping, hands squeezing cork handles, eyes focusing on the next step. He doesn't look any better than yesterday. He's still wobbly and his breathing sounds worse, like he's exhaling through a harmonica. I slow down and listen. A yak bell gongs. A prayer flag rustles. Pant legs swish. A porter passes on my left carrying a wooden crate with three bowling ball–sized chunks of granite. I can't hear Dad's heartbeat, but I imagine it's a jackhammer. Can he make it up the Namche Hill today? My watch says 9,430 feet, which means it's about 2,000 vertical feet to the lowest terrace of Namche Bazaar, but there's still miles of undulating trail ahead until we get to the base of the hill.

Up ahead one yak team is coming down and another's going up and—*boom*—horns and tongues and shaggy coats collide. It's a total mess and there's no way we're getting in the middle of it, so we stop and watch. One herder whacks hides with a bamboo switch. The other herder yells, *"Tsoh! Jah!"* his voice echoing through the valley.

Dave says, "Remember to always step to the uphill side of the trail when yaks go past. They can be pretty oblivious, and when they're loaded with duffels they don't really realize how big they are. You don't want to be caught on the downhill side of the trail and get crowded off a cliff. Trekkers die every year like that, so just be aware."

Thanks, Dave. Now I'm thinking about death and blood and the Khumbu Icefall, and I'd rather not think about that stuff until we're up and down and off the mountain. Actually, I'd rather not think about that stuff at all.

I turn to Dad and ask, "How did you sleep?"

Mom is the one who responds. "Not very good. I was awake most of the night. Still getting adjusted to the time change and altitude."

"Yeah, me too," says Dad. He coughs through a raspy lump in his throat.

"All right," Dave interjects. "The first part of the trail is pretty easy today and then we have the Namche Hill, but we'll take it piece by piece."

"We need to go *slow*," says Mom, emphasizing the final word like a teacher hammering a lesson into a student. But Dad doesn't have the capacity to go slow, not really, and I think being in the Himalaya just makes him want to go faster.

I hike around the corner of a slate-roofed building and look past a fluttering emerald *darchor*. Dave's waiting next to a boulder the size of an Airstream. It's covered in angular letters carved into the gray stone and then painted white. Every inch is decorated. It's like a page in an ancient tome. Gombu told me they're called "*mani* stones" because the letters spell out a traditional Buddhist mantra—*om mani padme hum*. When I asked Joss, he said it translates to "the jewel is in the lotus," or something like that, but when I asked him what it was supposed to mean, he just gave me a look that said, *You'll have to find out for yourself.* I've seen plenty of mani stones before and there'll be hundreds more ahead, but this one's really big and ornate. Maybe the carvings are new or the paint is fresh. It looks cleaner than the boulders that I saw at Tengboche and Thokla Pass when I was last on this trail. One path leads around the left side of the boulder and another leads around the right.

Dave reminds us to go around mani stones on the left side and spin prayer wheels clockwise. "It's not really a matter of what you do or don't believe. It's about respecting the local customs. We're climbing Mount Everest, so we need all the good juju we can get."

I'm not sure what I believe. I'm not religious, but I'm not unimaginative or unsentimental either. People will tell you the world works a certain way, that they've got it all figured out, but I'm pretty convinced there are still things in this world that nobody understands. I've seen what happens if you don't pour a shot of rum overboard when you're crossing the equator, or you don't put a coin under the mast, or you depart for an around-the-world voyage on a Friday. Thirty-five-foot seas and seventy-knot winds: that's what happens. Superstitions aren't superstitions if they actually work. Walking the correct path around mani stones definitely can't hurt.

I drag my fingers across the letters, sharp edged and surprisingly warm. I feel like I should be wishing for something, like I've just tossed a coin into a fountain or blown an eyelash off my finger or seen a shooting star. What do I want to wish for? What's the most important thing on my mind? The words form in my head without much thought. *Please let Dad make it to Base Camp alive.*

Through a gap in a barbed-wire fence and up a flight of muddy stairs, a promontory overlooks tin-roofed guesthouses and the growling rapids of the river. Trekkers and porters are lining the edge of the trail and they're all looking at something across the valley. A billowing tower of yellow smoke rises from the forest, obscuring the sun. The smoke filters the sunlight into a rich orange color that's painting the trail and the plastered buildings and the foamy river. A gust of wind rips down the valley and there's a deafening crackle like the sound of those glittery fireworks you see on the Fourth of July. Fins of flame jump from tree to tree, eating green branches in seconds, climbing the hillside. I've never been this close to a forest fire. It can't be more than half a mile away. Is the heat I feel on my cheeks coming from the fire or the sun? At least it's on the opposite side of the river, but aren't we supposed to cross a suspension bridge before we climb the Namche Hill?

Another gust and the fire rushes up the hillside and curls against a cliff band like a wave slamming against a sandy shore. Then it falls back. The fins of flame can't reach the roots of the trees at the top of the cliff band. The fire shrinks down beneath a cape of yellow smoke, waiting for the wind to change.

Here, in sight of the effervescent river, there's a visible haze in the air. I take a deep breath and it tastes of charred wood. A guy in a limeade jacket asks, "Are you guys on your way up?"

"Yeah. We're hoping to get to Namche today," I reply.

He screws up his eyebrows and says, "The hill's really smoky. We just came down and it wasn't fun. Tons of particles and garbage in the air. I could hardly breathe."

"Thanks for the info," I say, but in the back of my head I'm thinking, *We're totally screwed.*

12:31 p.m., which means we've already been hiking for more than three hours, but we're still on the flats below the Namche Hill. It's lunchtime. Once we're on the hill, there won't be any guesthouses until Namche and who knows how long it'll take us to get there, so we might as well stop here in Jorsale for a snack. There's an empty guesthouse on the west side of the river, the same side where the fire burns. I drop my backpack in a grassy courtyard and take a seat in a plastic chair. I look down the valley at the cloud of yellow smoke punching the sky.

Kami sets two thermoses with wooden lids on the table and says, "One ginger. One lemon."

Dave extracts a travel-sized bottle of Purell from his jacket pocket. "Pass it around. Keep one of these little bottles on you at all times. I try to remember to use it after I shake hands and before I eat. There are tons of germs floating around up here."

Dad takes a careful sip of lemon tea and sighs. Dave asks the question that's on my mind too. "How're you feeling, Jim?"

"I'm feeling okay, but I'm still not completely acclimatized yet and I still haven't slept much in the past few days," says Dad. Mom's nod says she feels the same way.

Dave furrows his brow like he's puzzling through a chess problem. We're basically sitting at the bottom of the Namche Hill and from here the trail goes strictly up. There's no respite from the steepness. Dave mulls it over. "Okay. I see two ways we can go about this," he says. "We can stop here for the day and tackle the Namche Hill tomorrow, or we can stick to our original plan and go for it today. If we take an extra day here and have a good day tomorrow, that's okay. We'll have to change some reservations and stuff, but that's not a big deal if we make those changes in advance.

On the other hand, if we go today and don't make it and have to turn around, that could pretty much end the trip."

Anger wells up in me like a hot spring. I almost say, *Shut up, Dave. Dad's gonna make it. You have no idea how strong and determined he is.* I don't say it, though, because I'll be sharing a tent with Dave for the next two months. Instead, I bite hard enough to feel my jawbones pop through my cheeks.

Dad nods silently. There's no way he'll want to wait. It sounds too much like defeat. It feels like we're already giving up and we're letting doubt take hold. But if we have to turn around on the hill, it will mess up our reservations at every busy guesthouse along the trail, we will be separated from the porters carrying our duffels, and we will have expended a ton of energy getting nowhere. It would probably take at least two extra days to sort it out. This is peak trekking season in Solukhumbu, and by that time there might not be anywhere left for us to stay. Maybe waiting *is* the best option. From the look on Dave's face I can tell that's what he's thinking, and from the look on Dad's face I can tell he's torn. He doesn't want to be the one to admit that he needs to stop. He'll probably say something like, *I don't want to hold you guys up*, and then Mom will freak and this whole thing will explode in seconds. But he doesn't say anything. Nobody says anything. There's just an awkward silence. Suddenly, our group of proud mountaineers is haltingly shy.

Melissa's voice breaks through. "Hopefully it rains this afternoon, like it usually does here, and the fire dies down by morning. I think it'll be less smoky tomorrow and we can start early, so we'll have all day. It makes sense to me if we stay here for the night," she says.

I could hug her. She's phrased it so it doesn't sound like defeat. It sounds logical and unemotional, like the obvious choice. Blame the fire. Blame the smoke. This isn't *our* fault. It's the mountains telling us we need to stop.

Dad's eyes fill with relief. "Good," he says. "Tomorrow it is."

14.
LIKE A BROKEN DRUM

After two weeks of hiking, the American Mount Everest Expedition entered the region of Solukhumbu, where the trail traced the Dudh Koshi through foggy evergreens and magnolias and rhododendrons, angling north toward Mount Everest. The men were lighter and tougher already. Their torsos had left behind ice cream and bacon and extra butter. Their legs had shed all remnants of sofas and office chairs. Their feet, blistered and waterlogged for days on end, had hardened to crocodile skin. Dad had become known as "Big Jim," partly because there was more than one person named Jim on the expedition, and partly because he was six feet five inches tall and 215 pounds with the chest of a silverback gorilla. Watching Big Jim shoulder his backpack every morning and do push-ups in the dirt every afternoon, you couldn't miss the implacable power in his limbs. As James Ramsey Ullman put it, "And in Jim Whittaker, striding on through the miles, one could feel the concentrated power of a locomotive."

On March 7 the men climbed away from the rushing Dudh Koshi to the terraces of Namche Bazaar. A rainstorm had dogged them for days, but now it suddenly dissipated. The fog melted into a brilliant sky. Way off in the distance and mostly hidden behind the icy battlements of the Nuptse ridge, a triangle grazed the heavens. Mount Everest. The summit was so far away that it seemed diminutive compared to closer mountains. Nevertheless, it was an image that had been haunting their thoughts for months and years. Big Jim put his head down and kept on hiking.

I stick my head out the bedroom window into the perfume of dawn—river mist and pinecones and cold dirt and distant glaciers. Night must've squelched the forest fire because the choking haze is gone from the horizon and the sky is the color of Paul Newman's eyes. The landscape is all sharp and pointy—peaks and treetops and tin roofs and a lightning rod and a bare flagpole and the horns of a grazing dzopkyo. But softer things hide amongst the harsher geometry. A bead of dew hangs on the pink petals of a magnolia. A gorak's weightless feathers curve against gravity. A prayer wheel rests still next to the serrated letters of a mani stone. The dzopkyo's slobbery tongue drips onto its bell. Looking closely, you see that the world's made of contrast.

In the dining room I find Dad and Mom eating eggs and *rösti* and drinking coffee. I slide onto a bench across from them and grab the Purell and squeeze a clear dollop onto my palms and rub until the sticky's gone. Then I snag a lonely piece of toast. Dad has shaved and it makes his face look younger. I ask him how he slept.

"Like the bottom of a stove," he says. "Great!"

That's a good sign. Maybe he's turned a corner. Maybe.

I bite into whole wheat and crunchy Jif, but all I can taste is a big fat gob of stress.

I stuff my PrimaLoft hoody in my pack and toss in a full water bottle and I'm ready to go. Dad shuffles into my bedroom and asks, "What would you think if I had someone carry my pack?" He's whispering conspiratorially and glancing over his shoulder, probably on the lookout for Kent's camera.

"I think it's a great idea. I'll talk to Lam Babu," I reply.

"Are you sure? Do you think that will be okay?" he asks again, wincing.

"Dad. Yes, it's okay. Absolutely. Lemme see your pack?"

Dad passes it to me and lets go of the straps and, Christ, I nearly drop it. It's at least three times heavier than mine. "Jeez! What'd you put in here?" I ask.

"Two water bottles and some extra clothing and some snacks. That's it," he says.

"Must be a lot of Snickers bars."

Dad shrugs and then says, "Thanks, son. I'm really glad you're here to walk next to me."

"Me too," I say. I can't hold his gaze because I'm not used to this type of softness, but I add, "You got this."

"I'm just going to go slow. I'll get there, but it might take me all day."

"Good thing we have all day," I reply, and I'm trying to sound casual, but maybe a little concern seeps through.

If it takes Dad all day to climb a single hill, can we really justify going higher? The Namche Hill's certainly not the steepest or the last obstacle on the path to Base Camp, but I guess many a dream's been broken there. How will our dreams turn out?

We've got the trail to ourselves for once. It's quiet and empty like the doldrums after one of those tropical squalls, when the rain falls so hard it flattens the wind waves to glass. We hike across a suspension bridge that's cemented to a fifty-foot crag of river-choking stone. Then we start to climb. We climb up three flights of hand-carved granite steps and through a glade of evergreens and the trail pinches tightly on itself, the first switchback. Dave's in front, leading the procession. Then Dad and, a few feet back, Lhakpa, who's carrying Dad's pack. I'm next in line and behind me it's Mom, Lam Babu, and Melissa. Kent runs up ahead and crouches in the dust and lets our boots stomp past his lens, only a few inches away. My legs settle into Dave's pace. We're on our way.

"Hey, Leif?" says Mom quietly as I'm rounding the first switchback.

"Yeah? What is it?"

"Why don't you get behind Dad and give him a little more space. I don't think he likes having someone walking so close. It makes him feel rushed. Get in there between him and Lhakpa. Let him find his own rhythm."

"Okay. Are you all right back here?" I ask.

"Oh yeah. I'm fine as long as you and Dad don't go too fast," she says. She's got to be joking, but maybe not because her tone is completely deadpan. Does she know something I don't know?

I maneuver in front of Lhakpa and turn around and raise my hand, palm forward, silently telling him to stay farther back. He surprises me with a how-dare-you look, but decides to allow my contravention.

I fall into step behind Dad and watch his feet closely. He's definitely smoother today. Maybe he just does better when he's going uphill. Maybe he's like me and he gets this urge to attack the trail. Still, he's not breathing like he should. He's focusing too much of his energy on his legs and feet and he's forgetting to breathe, so I suck a loud draft of air into my lungs and shove it out forcefully, pursing my lips like I'm trying to blow out a candle five feet away or ignite a suffocating fire—*shooosh*. It's plenty loud for Dad to hear. He hesitates for a moment and turns his head halfway around and glances at me. *That's right, Dad, it's me behind you. I'm here and we've got all day and you better not forget to breathe.* I purse my lips and push out another *shooosh*. Dad smiles wryly. Without a word, he turns his eyes toward the steep trail ahead and draws in a single enormous breath.

Because I'm a Whittaker, people assume my parents required me to be a climber from a young age, but that's not the case at all. Dad and Mom rarely talked about climbing at home. They didn't *prevent* me from learning how to climb and, these days, Child Protective Services would probably arrest them for their completely hands-off style. Sometimes I wish they would've forced me into a climbing gym at age five. Imagine how strong I'd be now. Then again, I might've ended up hating mountains. I remember the first and last time I went climbing with Dad and Mom. They took Joss and me up Pinnacle Peak, a spire of gray rock shaped like a witch's hat on the edge of Mount Rainier National Park. I couldn't have been more than six and I hated the feeling of a backpack on my shoulders. For the first hour, as we traversed green meadows, I complained unceasingly about my sore feet. I didn't understand the appeal of a ball-less, bat-less, basket-less, goal-less sport. I was bored and uncomfortably sweaty and hungry. There was nothing fun about it.

Intolerant of my bad attitude, Dad tried to distract me with a few basic mountaineering techniques. First he showed me the rest step. "It'll save you a lot of energy. Lower your heel and lock your back leg and rest on your bones instead of your muscles," he said. He demonstrated the flamingo-like motion and watched as I imitated it.

Next he taught me about the guide pace. "It's probably a lot slower than your top speed," he said. "Find a pace that you can maintain for hours and stick with it. Count the rhythm in your head. Soon it'll be instinctive. You won't have to think about it."

He described pressure breathing. "Force the air out through your lips. It'll help empty all the oxygen out of your lungs so when you inhale it's a much deeper breath," he said. He demonstrated pressure breathing, producing an awesome gasp that felt, compared to my tiny wheeze, like it might blow down the very mountain on which we stood. Hiking right behind Dad, I practiced these new techniques, mimicking his exaggerated breathing and herky-jerky steps.

It was midday when we came to a broad saddle, a drooping section of ridgeline between Pinnacle Peak and its neighbor, Plummer Peak. There, Dad opened his backpack and pulled out a bright-red rope. He tied the climbing rope around his waist. Mom smoothly paid it out while Dad, shirtless, scrambled up a few hundred feet of rock to the summit. I watched, entranced. Dad was massive. He moved quickly and confidently, muscles hardly working, like a machine doing what it was built for. To me, it was obvious that if he wanted to, he could crush the rock with his bare hands and he could yank the clouds into his lungs and he could levitate, beyond the confines of physics, like a superhero or a god. Watching him climb, I was certain that I would never be as strong as he was.

Dad pushes a tornado through his lips, puts his head down, and begins to hike. Sheets of golden light shoot through channels in the trees. Dad's boots thud steadily. A chipmunk scurries up a trunk. Three gray jays jet out of a thicket and fly away, chirping like they're annoyed. The needles of a trailside juniper shudder as Dad hikes past. He's finding a rhythm now. Any stranger can see it. Step. Breathe. Step. Step. Breathe. Maybe he's acclimatized or maybe he just prefers the uphill. I stop and watch him cruise around another switchback and, man, it's easy to imagine the locomotive from forty-nine years back.

We're gaining on another trekking group and they must hear Dad's pressure breaths and footsteps coming up behind them, because they shift to the side of the trail to let us pass. They're all in their thirties and forties and they're sweating through their clothing, and here comes this eighty-three-year-old man breathing down their necks. Dad nods and smiles at each of them and he's like, "Every step is health, fun, and frolic." One guy's got a defeated look on his face like his entire life's been leading up to this hike and now he's getting passed by an octogenarian. I love it.

Dad's legs churn and he bounces around another switchback and past a rock wall, and every step eases the tension in my shoulders and in Dave's eyes and in Lam Babu's face.

I turn around and glance at Mom. She's focused on her feet and she's moving just as well as Dad, her two heavy cameras swinging from a harness. She looks up for a second to get her bearings and our eyes connect and I jerk my head toward Dad. But she's seen it all before. She's not surprised. She shrugs in a matter-of-fact sort of way, unhitches a camera from her harness, and snaps a photo of me in one of the sunny sheets. Dad is such a lucky guy. He'd be so much older if it weren't for Mom's tricks. I mean, how did she know it would help to have me walking and breathing behind him? We're ticking off switchbacks one by one and Dad won't tolerate a break.

We stroll across Namche Bazaar's lowest terrace and I glance at my watch and, holy cow, it's been only three hours and twenty-seven minutes since we left Jorsale. Even for a young and fit hiker, three and a half hours is an excellent time. Dad passed the test with flying colors. Our team beams with a collective smile as Dad spins a line of prayer wheels clockwise and steps into the village of Namche Bazaar.

Tears stab against the backs of my eyeballs, but Kent's camera is on me, so I try to hold them back. Instead, I grasp Dad in a vigorous hug.

"You crushed it, Dad. You absolutely crushed it!" I say.

"Thanks, son. I needed your help," he says. His tenderness is unfamiliar. I guess the mountains bring it out. I guess the mountains make it okay.

Together, we look up at a village carved into a mountainside. A gorak alights on a string of faded prayer flags strung between two rooftops over our heads. Sharp white mountains cut into the sky on all sides.

"What do you think?" I ask Dad as he gazes at the mountains.

"It's like a broken drum," he says, and even though I know what's coming next, even though I've heard him utter this phrase a million times before, his words are a balloon tied to my heart. "You can't beat it."

15.
SLOW DOWN AND LOOK

Yaks stomp. Trekkers click their cameras. Reflections shimmer off the surface of eddies. I flip my Maui Jims down and plug my earbuds in and the trail's suddenly more organized and familiar. My iPod chooses "Smack My Bitch Up," which makes me want to hike faster but doesn't jibe with the prayer flags and prayer wheels and pine trees and purple flowers on the side of the trail. I skip forward. The next one is this hip-hoppy track by Blockhead. Joss must've put it on here. I remember we were talking about making a ski movie and Joss said he'd pick this song as the soundtrack for his segment. I can see why. It's catchy and bouncy and for a second I can picture Joss floating through pillows and blowing up powder. Then I'm back to Nepal, back to Dad's boots kicking up dust in front of me. He's chugging along like he can hear the music too.

Up ahead, Dave halts. "Grab a sip and a snack," he says. "We've got another five hundred vertical feet to Tengboche. Now's a good time for a break before we hit the last hill."

A who-do-you-think-you're-talking-to look flashes across Dad's face, but he stops nevertheless. I grab a Snickers and twist it in half. He sees it and his eyes jump, so I pass him the bigger half. He chews twice and it's gone and he says, "Take ten. Expect five. Get two," and motors away through the sunlight.

I glance back at Mom. She rolls her eyes.

We crest the top of the hill and the view opens up like one of those aerial shots in an IMAX film that makes the audience a bit queasy. There's Lhotse and Nuptse and Ama Dablam, and Everest with its trademark plume and inky rock. The view must be even better from the second-story windows of the monastery. When we trekked here in 2003, I remember Gombu telling me that Tengboche is the spiritual center of the Khumbu Valley. The monastery was rebuilt in 1989 after a fire mostly destroyed it and now it's a stately white-and-red structure with a red tin roof and ornate eaves. A gateway leads into a courtyard and the gate is covered with blue and green and yellow and red carvings of many-armed gods and goddesses and tigers and fish and lotus flowers and bowls overflowing with food. Next to the gateway, there's a room with a prayer wheel that's taller than I am and bigger around than one of those ancient Douglas firs on the trail to Mount Olympus. It's heavy too. You can't just stick out your hand and pull it as you hike by. You've got to stop for a minute and really put your back into it, but once you get it going it'll keep spinning and spinning, sending its prayers out in every direction like drops of water off a shaking dog.

What did this place look like in 1963?

It was snowing hard, so Dad and his teammates decided to rest and wait for the weather to improve. They took acclimatization hikes on nearby peaks and reorganized their equipment and visited the monastery one afternoon. The high lama was suffering from a severe toothache. Dave Dingman and Gil Roberts were doctors, not dentists, and they hesitated to remove the tooth because of what the lama and monks and citizens of Tengboche might think if the procedure went wrong. Antibiotics didn't help, however, and they finally agreed to remove a rotten tooth. They extracted the worst of four troublesome ivories and crossed their fingers. A few days later, the lama invited the expedition members to dinner. He was no longer in pain and he spoke garrulously while Gombu interpreted. The lama talked of Chinese rule in nearby Tibet and of the Dalai Lama's exile. He wondered what would change if China completed a road from Tibet to Kathmandu. Would Buddhism disappear?

This place is special somehow. It's a feeling. It's like the landscape's alive or conscious or recording the things that happen here. All these stories are tied up in it and you've got to pay attention if you want to hear them.

Dad leads us off the main trail to the west, behind the monastery, on a faint path that contours along a secluded ridgeline. Joss and Gombu were here the last time we visited this place. I recall the pink rhododendron petals and the white stone shrines and the names inscribed here.

I duck in amongst the branches to visit them. It's shadowy and still, so I take off my shades and pause the tunes and put my arm around Mom. Dad touches each shrine. He's gentle and slow. He goes to Jake's shrine—"Long Live the Crow."

I think about the enormous grief Dad must be carrying after having survived so many of his loved ones. He's seen scores of his friends and partners killed. In the case of his young climbing partners—like Jake Breitenbach and Leif Patterson—the deaths had little reason or explanation. The mountains took them. Maybe that's why Dad and Mom didn't teach me more about climbing: they know exactly how dangerous the mountains can be.

I think about the Khumbu Icefall—the tottering chaos of seracs and crevasses—and my breath is instantly gone. It's just pure emptiness in my stomach and chest and throat now.

"We should build one for Gombu and put it here," says Dad without facing us. "Wouldn't that be nice?"

Gombu died less than a year ago at his home in Darjeeling at the age of seventy-five. I remember when Dad broke the news to me. He knocked on my bedroom door early one morning and peeked his solemn face inside. "Gombu passed away. My old friend and partner is gone," Dad said, tears welling up.

Nawang Gombu, the nephew of the famed Sherpa Tenzing Norgay, was twenty-seven years old when he joined the 1963 American Mount Everest Expedition. He was already one of the most skilled and experienced Sherpa in the world. Gombu's parents moved their family to the Khumbu Valley soon after his birth in Tibet's Kharta region, northeast of Mount Everest. When he was a teenager, Gombu was sent to study as a monk at Rongbuk Monastery. He detested the strict rules and harsh punishments, so he ran away from the monastery after a year and crossed a high mountain pass back into Nepal, where he asked his uncle Tenzing for work on a climbing expedition. At seventeen he became the youngest member of the 1953 British expedition, which, for the first time in history, put human footprints—Tenzing's and Edmund Hillary's—on the highest point on planet Earth. Gombu, for his part, carried two loads of oxygen to a high camp on the South Col, earning the Tiger Medal from the Himalayan Club and the Queen Elizabeth II Coronation Medal for his efforts. Gombu later trained in Switzerland to become one of the first instructors at the Himalayan Mountaineering Institute in Darjeeling. After moving there and beginning his lifelong work, he continued to participate in Himalayan expeditions, including a 1954 American expedition to Makalu, a 1959 expedition to Cho Oyu, and the first Indian expedition to Mount Everest in 1960, during which he climbed to within seven hundred vertical feet of the summit before bad weather forced him to turn around.

Gombu was a valuable member of the 1963 team because of his past experience on Everest, his technical skill as a mountaineer, and his abilities as a translator. Besides his native Sherpa language, Gombu spoke Hindi, Nepali, and English. Throughout the trek and climbing expedition, Gombu helped resolve disputes between Americans and Sherpa. His insights into native customs and etiquette must've been priceless to the team as they passed through the Khumbu Valley at the mercy of friendly landowners and porters. His knowledge of the climbing route was invaluable.

But, perhaps most importantly, Gombu was driven. "No man among us, Eastern or Western, burned with a greater desire to reach the top of Everest; and we were all convinced from the beginning that he would stage a magnificent performance," wrote James Ramsey Ullman.

Maybe Dad and Gombu sensed a similar drive in each other. They became quick friends and this friendship blossomed into a lifelong partnership on the steepest pitches of Mount Everest.

In my memory, Gombu is a face that's always smiling and a rumble of laughter and a pair of gentle hands thicker than a dictionary. Gombu spent many summers working as a guide for RMI on Mount Rainier. We often visited him and he would sometimes carry me on his shoulders in the huckleberry meadows around Paradise. I remember him pouring spicy "rocket fuel" on his omelets and naming each peak on the Himalayan skyline during our trek in 2003. As I watched Dad's and Gombu's affectionate interactions forty years after their historic ascent, it was obvious they had an unbreakable bond.

"Next time we come back to Nepal, we'll make a memorial for Gombu," I say, and saying it makes me wonder if Dad would want a shrine built here when he passes away. Will this be Dad's last trip to Nepal?

"I'd sign up for that," interjects Dave, who's standing close by on the edge of the clearing.

"He was a prince of a man," says Dad.

A warm gust blows toward Mount Everest.

Below Tengboche the rhododendron trunks are broader than my thighs and the canopy blots out the sun. This forest is ancient and primal. There's not a building in sight. A skin of lime-green moss covers a bumpy field of boulders. The trail is only wide enough to walk single file, and it's empty for once. We're miles from honking horns and hazy streets and plastic bags and folding signs that offer the adventure of a lifetime. It feels wild.

I wouldn't mind taking my time to enjoy it, but Dad's eager to get to the next guesthouse. Mom must notice the wildness too, because she slows her pace and stops to take photos of those miniature purple flowers. I follow Dad around a bend in the trail and lose sight of her.

Up ahead, a herder escorts four yaks through the dank forest. He's wearing thin flip-flops and patched jeans and a tattered black T-shirt with an AC/DC logo on the front. He's carrying this pencil-thin switch in his right hand and swaying back and forth rhythmically as he follows his yaks downhill like a dinghy pulled behind a ship set adrift. I wouldn't mind having more of what the herder has—his carefree speed and lack of a destination.

A cell phone rings. I know it's a cell phone because the cell phone I purchased in Kathmandu makes the same sound—an artificial harp playing an upbeat riff. The herder pulls a phone out of his patched jeans and holds it to his ear. He talks animatedly in Nepali, ignoring the yaks. The yak in front stops to eat a patch of grass on the edge of the single-file trail. The other three yaks halt too, unable to squeeze past the traffic jam. When the herder realizes what's happening, a wave of anger rushes over his face.

"Jah!" he screams, but the yak in front doesn't move. The herder picks up a rock and, keeping the cell phone to his ear, pitches it at the grazing yak. It whizzes past the yak's nose, missing by a hair. The yak flinches and calmly rips a few more bites of grass and then moseys onward.

Maybe wilderness is a perception.

"What's Denali like?" I ask Dave. He's been to the summit on more than twenty different occasions.

"Denali's fun if you can watch TV every night," says Dave, flashing his crooked smile.

"Whadya mean?" I ask.

"Oh, there's a lot of bad weather and rest days. You get cooped up in the tent. It's important to bring some episodes of *Mad Men* or something to watch," he says.

"You bring your iPad?"

"iPad, Kindle, iPhone. All of it."

"Nice," I say. "So it's like Everest, then?"

"Yeah, pretty much. Only shorter and without all the people."

I give him a snorty laugh.

In 1963, Al Auten, AMEE's communication officer, used a single-sideband transceiver to communicate with the outside world. Throughout the trek, the team rarely used it because it took hours to set up and the signal often failed to reach Kathmandu. In one instance, they tried to reach the American embassy in order to ask for a helicopter evacuation of a badly burned local woman, but after hours of trying, Auten was unable to establish a connection. He instead had to relay the message through an Australian ham operator. It worked and a helicopter eventually carried the woman from the village of Junbesi to a hospital in Kathmandu, where she recovered.

The connection improved when the team reached Base Camp. Auten and a ham operator in Kathmandu, Lieutenant Colonel William Gresham, had arranged to speak on March 20 at 5:00 p.m. Auten's voice came across loud and clear in Kathmandu that afternoon with an update from high altitude, as it would at prearranged check-in times for the remainder of the expedition.

Though radio communication between Base Camp and Kathmandu was reliable, it did not allow the men to communicate with people back home. Instead, the men corresponded via handwritten letters sent to Kathmandu on the backs of runners. A runner's fastest downhill journey was eight days and the record for the uphill leg was twelve days. Once the letters were in Kathmandu, it took between a few days and a few weeks for them to be delivered to American addresses. Without a way to speak directly to loved ones, most of the team members suffered from a type of loneliness that's hard for me to imagine, but they were also forced to interact with the landscape and with each other in a way that's impossible today.

Nowadays, cell phone and wireless internet service extend all the way to Base Camp. In 2011, Ncell, a privately owned GSM mobile operator, installed a tower at Gorak Shep, a small village on the edge of the Khumbu Glacier close to Base Camp. Using a prepaid SIM card and a USB wireless adapter, climbers can connect to the World Wide Web from the comfort of their tent.

When we were in Kathmandu, for less than thirty dollars I bought everything I need to surf the web and call home. I have more minutes and data than I can possibly use, even if I spend the entire expedition watching kitten videos on YouTube and calling Freya, the girl with the cape of silky hair and the inexhaustible excitement in her eyes who I met playing Ultimate a few years ago.

We've been off and on since then and she's studying photography at Colorado Mountain College now. Will our relationship survive my trip to Everest? I'm hoping so. Calling her from my tent at Base Camp will certainly help.

The phone and internet card won't function above Base Camp, but Dave's carrying a satellite phone too, which will have reception all the way to the summit. There's no escape.

I just sat down in the dining room at Rivendell, a popular guesthouse in the village of Deboche. Kent comes in and asks me if I'm ready for my interview. "I want to get you fresh off the trail," he says, motioning for me to follow him downstairs.

"How's my hair?" I ask Melissa, who's curled up on one of the benches reading a months-old fashion magazine.

"Dapper as usual," she says, waving me away as she sips ginger tea.

Two tripods and two video cameras are pointing at a plastic lawn chair in front of a granite wall. I plop into the chair and Kent hands me a lapel microphone and I attach it and make sure my zippers are closed and every layer of Eddie Bauer clothing is hanging properly from my body. Kent asks me to talk into the microphone while he adjusts the sound levels. I'm not exactly sure what to say—am I just supposed to gush about myself?— so I ask him if he's talked to his wife and two young daughters recently.

"I spoke to them last night," he says. "It's hard to get the girls to focus on the conversation. They just hold the phone up to their ear and keep talking to each other or playing or something. I don't think they quite realize how far away I am and what I'm doing."

"They know you're on Everest, right? But they don't understand what that means," I say.

"Yeah, exactly," says Kent, and then spins his finger in the air. "Keep talking. Keep talking."

"I remember when my dad called home from the Peace Climb in 1990. I must've been about five. It was Earth Day and there was this big event in Port Townsend. A bunch of people were around to do a beach cleanup or forest cleanup or something. Afterward, they all came over for a potluck and to hear my dad call from Mount Everest. I guess it was a big deal but I had no clue. He'd spoken to President Bush earlier in the day. I was kind of mad at Dad for being gone, I think. When he called, Mom picked up the phone and put it on speaker so everyone could hear. He thanked everyone for the cleanup efforts. He said he and his team had collected many tons of garbage off the mountain and buried it or burned it. Everybody cheered. Mom took it off speaker and talked to him for a few minutes, and then Dad asked to talk to my brother. Joss spoke into the phone while everyone watched. It was my turn next, but I refused to take the phone. I was too shy. I really wanted to talk to him, but I didn't like everyone watching. I remember shaking my head and wrapping my arms around my mom's leg and hiding my face. Everybody laughed. They probably thought I was cute, but I think I cried from embarrassment. The worst part was I didn't get to talk to Dad. So don't be too hard on your daughters. I guarantee they miss you."

"Wow. Great story. Can I get you to tell that to me again now that I have the sound adjusted?" says Kent.

"Sure. I guess. Are you ready?"

"One second." Kent hops from camera to camera and double checks the focus and exposure. He presses each shutter release and slides a pair of headphones over his ears and then points his finger at me. "You're on."

"So you just want me to tell the same story again?" I ask.

"Sure. And any others you can think of. Basically, I want to know exactly what it was like to grow up as Jim Whittaker's son," says Kent.

"Oh. No problem," I reply. "But I'm not sure you're going to have enough tape."

I'm back in the dining room after acing the half-hour interview when Mom rushes inside, fresh off the trail, and says, "Oh my God! Did you see the musk deer?"

Musk deer are kind of like the saber-toothed tigers of ungulates. They've got these bunny-like ears and muscular hind legs and enlarged canine tusks that are easily broken and constantly regrown. They look like they're from a bygone prehistoric era. The male deer produce the musk, a rare and highly sought-after substance that's used in perfumes and medicines. They're protected in Nepal, but they're often trapped and killed by poachers. The species is widely considered to be on the edge of extinction.

"No! We were trying to get here too fast, I guess. We must've missed it," I reply.

"Oh, it was beautiful. Hidden back in the rhododendrons. I saw it for only a few seconds before it bounded off. Wow!" says Mom. I love that Mom finds so much wonder in a single fleeting glance of something mysterious.

"Did you get any photos?" I ask.

"I don't think so. It was too quick," says Mom. She's practically out of breath.

She tells the story again and again to anyone who hasn't already heard it. Each time she embellishes it a little more, until the musk deer is a mystical creature able to disappear on a whim and reappear, seconds later, in an entirely different place. Who knows? Maybe there *are* magical things alive in this world, present and visible to those who are willing to slow down and look.

16.
REST DAYS

On Friday, we'll stroll the valley and move close enough to Base Camp to get there in a long day of hiking, but today it's chess or Scrabble or cribbage with a cup of tea and a bowl of popcorn. I've heard it can take weeks for your body to learn how to capture the elusive Himalayan oxygen molecule and use it more efficiently. It's a gradual mutation, not like when Bruce Banner gets angry or when Peter Parker gets bitten by the radioactive spider. The heart beats faster. Red blood cell production skyrockets. Capillaries form denser webs in muscle tissue. Breathe and breathe and breathe like it's a drug. If you climb too fast, your body can't keep up, so there are mornings, like this morning, when we wake up without a destination.

The dining room is at the end of a shadowy hallway to the left of the kitchen, through a set of yellow double doors. I slip inside into a wave of heat coming from a rotund cast-iron stove. Dad and Dave and Mom are sitting around a coffee table with plastic mugs of steaming java. Dad's gnawing on toast with strawberry Smucker's, which is nice to see because he hardly touched his chicken chili last night.

"What do you want to do today?" I ask Dave. "Scrabble? Chess?"

"Maybe later. I think we should go for a little walk this morning. It's good to move the legs, get a bit higher," he says.

"I was kind of looking forward to catching up on my reading, but I guess I can come along. What were you thinking?"

Dave hardly acknowledges my sarcasm. "Go out the back door and start walking uphill," says Dave.

"When do you want to leave?"

"Meet here at ten?"

"Okay. How long are we going? Backpack and stuff?" I ask.

"Bring water, a snack, and a layer. We'll see how far we get."

Out the courtyard through a break in the waist-high rock wall, there's a pattern of trails laid over the umber hillsides. We left the blue pine and birch and juniper and rhododendron behind yesterday, and now the land's the skin of a russet potato. White mountains and turquoise glaciers peer down like they're scientists and we're rats. The river fans out into branchy fingers, some of them broken off at the ends.

A dog barks incessantly. A yak bell clangs.

Dave's boots go *thud thud thud*.

Is he angry? He's speeding up and attacking the trail, but I'm not going to let him get away. Hell, he's nearly twice my age and I haven't been this fit since two-a-day basketball practices, before the surgery. I can keep up with this old man any day of the week. Nobody beats a Whittaker to the top of a mountain.

My head's a nail hit with a hammer. Slowing down will make the pain go away, but Dave shows no signs of tiring. 17,321 feet and 12:53 p.m. We've been hiking for almost three hours and I admit it's been years since I've been this high or felt this worked. I'm all sweat and dust and pain. Throbbing in my temples. Burning in my feet. Aching in my lungs. There's no spring left in my legs, just numbness. A gorak coasts overhead and caws and, damn, I wish I could fly like that, catching currents, effortlessly harnessing invisible layers in the sky.

Instead, I'm racing Dave up an unnamed spire, a knee or ankle or toe of a much taller mountain, and I'm losing. He's over the crest of the nearest hill and running across a flat bench and making it look so fucking easy now. He's hardly working and still accelerating as he crawls up the final talus slope toward the spire. The hammer pounds me again. Giving up would be the easiest thing in the world. I'd be done with this pain and embarrassment a lot quicker that way. I kick a lichen-covered rock and nearly tumble, but my other leg sticks out instinctually and holds me up, so I have to keep going. I wish I'd fallen.

Then I'd have an excuse. I could tell myself I was unlucky. The truth is I'm just weak and pathetic.

Breathe once, deeper than before, then gun it with all you have left.

A lone yak stares at me like it's never seen anything so crazy.

Dave's waiting at the top with this punchable look on his face. He's all calm and casual and hardly breathing and I'm hyperventilating and I can feel my heartbeat in the tips of my fingers—*dum dum dum dum dum.*

"Nice job," says Dave. "How do you feel?"

"I feel terrible. How do *you* feel?" It comes out sounding like I'm annoyed by his patronizing tone, which I am.

"I have every advantage, Leif. This is what I do," he says.

Maybe Dave's mutations are permanent. That's got to be it. He lives in Taos and ski patrols on 12,481-foot Kachina Peak. Every year he climbs Everest and Denali and Mount Rainier dozens of times. He's already acclimatized.

"Except age," I say.

"Hey, watch it! I'm only forty-eight. What are you? Twenty-five?"

"Yep. But it's not helping much."

"Stand over there and I'll get a picture of you with Ama behind," he says.

A week ago, Ama Dablam was this wrinkled thumb sticking out from a fist of glaciers, but the trail's gone past it and around it and now we're looking at the backside, a pyramid of hanging ice.

People are always changing, but mountains change too.

I sit on the rocks next to a string of weather-beaten prayer flags while Dave snaps the photo.

"How high are we?" I ask.

"My watch says 18,154."

"Higher than Base Camp."

"Quite a bit," says Dave.

A sip of water and half a Twix and the throbbing's going away.

A sloop-shaped cloud collides with Ama Dablam. A shiny black beetle crawls over my knee and disappears in the rocks.

"Ready to go down?" asks Dave.

My heart's a string of firecrackers.

I just nod and blink and he's gone down the slope, running away in a full-blown sprint, smaller and smaller, a tiny figure in a humongous landscape. A tail of dust spirals behind him. There's nothing I can do except run after him.

We pop through the wall and into the courtyard, where laundry hangs stiffly from clotheslines and a trekker lounges in a plastic lawn chair, engrossed in the latest James Patterson formula, something about treasure and sex and murder and a sunken ship.

"Good day hike," says Dave, patting me jovially on the back.

"Yeah. That was fun," I say, but I'm bent over at the waist and my hands are on my knees and there's no way that anybody would look at me and think I'm having fun.

"Order a snack if you want. We're a little late for lunch. I might get some popcorn or something."

"I might take a nap."

"Good idea. Remember, it's a rest day," he says.

I feel like punching him again, but instead I just say, "Right."

My bedroom's dark and cold and empty. I'm drowning in sweat and I'm shivering uncontrollably, so I crawl into my sleeping bag and curl into a ball. Shivers run through my muscles from head to toe. The shivers course between my shoulder blades and beneath the scar on my spine. I shiver and shiver and shiver. Maybe these are growing pains. This is me changing, my heart and lungs and blood getting stronger. I'm mutating and that's kind of cool, but does it *have* to hurt so much?

I lay my sweat-soaked head on the pillow and try to relax.

Lam Babu passes me a khata and says, "Put the rupees here"—he lays a 500 against an end of the silk—"fold like this"—he accordions the scarf—"and give it to Lama Geshe"—he pinches the folds with both hands and bows slightly, presenting the package to an imaginary monk. Lam Babu says it doesn't matter how much money we include, but if this is anything like the American collection plate, then I know there's a direct correlation between decimal places and the efficacy of the blessing, so it's probably safer to go big—1,500 oughta get me up Everest, don't you think? Then again, I wouldn't mind an easy descent too. Better make it 2,000. Dave and Melissa and Kent and Mom are folding their own khatas. Dad said his stomach was feeling a little funky, so he decided to stay behind at the guesthouse. A red-breasted bird alights on a stone wall and Lam Babu motions for us to follow him inside.

I duck a neck-height lintel and walk into a dim and musty corridor. Glancing through a door to my right, I see a middle-aged woman peeling potato skins into a plastic bowl. To my left there's a hallway of unpainted plywood walls and a set of dark wooden stairs. We walk straight ahead into an open room much brighter than the others. Windows and padded benches line two walls on the far side. It smells of incense and black tea and it's quiet except for the sound of our boots knocking on patches of hardwood floor between threadbare carpets. Lama Geshe sits cross-legged on a bench in the left corner, resting his back against a windowpane. Afternoon sunlight streams in behind him, silhouetting his hunched figure. A quarter-inch layer of peppery hair adorns the rim of his mostly bald scalp. His dark eyes droop a little at the bottom and deep wrinkles fan out around their edges, but otherwise his skin's surprisingly smooth. If I had to guess his age, I'm sure I'd be way off. He's got to be at least fifty and I doubt he's older than seventy, but I could be wrong because his boyish smile makes him look fifteen and there's ten lifetimes of wisdom in his eyes.

To his right there's a table littered with photographs and T-shirts and books and strips of paper. To his left there's another table. A pile of red strings and a brass bowl filled with uncooked white rice rest there. A collage of summit photographs entirely covers one wall. Climbers in down suits and enormous boots gaze out at me, their arms raised in various gestures of celebration. I recognize the summit of Mount Everest, but there are others—Cho Oyu, Ama Dablam, Anna-purna, K2, and Makalu. Signatures and notes are scrawled in felt-tip pen. Some photographs look brand new, like they were given to Lama Geshe this season, but others are wrinkled and faded. How long has

Lama Geshe been here? Was he around when Dad and Gombu passed through? He grins and laughs huskily and waves his arms, welcoming us in.

We form a line in front of him. Dave bends over at the waist and hands him the khata with two hands. Lama Geshe pinches one end between his fingers and flicks it into the air and the white silk catches the sunlight. The khata unfurls and the rupees land on the bench next to him. Then he runs the khata through his fingers and wraps it over Dave's neck. Dave says, "Thank you, Lama Geshe," and then takes a seat on a pew-like bench. Lama Geshe repeats the ritual with each of us until we're all scarved and seated.

He begins a guttural chant, grasps a handful of rice from the brass bowl, and tosses it aimlessly into the air. Rice taps my face and legs and I hear it bouncing against windowpanes and across the hardwood floor. Lama Geshe's chant is a hypnotic bass line that I feel in my guts. I let it flood into me and imagine myself standing on an apex of snow. Verse after rumbly verse, a rapid coda, and Lama Geshe pauses the chant. Then Lam Babu says it's time for our individual blessings.

Dave stands in front of Lama Geshe, his palms pressed together in front of his chest in a sign of prayer, and bows. Lama Geshe reels off another chant and then untangles one of the red strings from the pile and wraps the middle of it around the back of Dave's neck. He joins the ends of the string beneath Dave's chin and ties them together with a simple overhand knot, chanting all the while. Before Lama Geshe releases Dave's new necklace, he pulls on the red string, bringing Dave's head down toward his own. Their foreheads gently touch. He chuckles and lets go of the string and hands Dave a strip of paper.

Lama Geshe performs an identical ritual for Mom and Melissa and Kent. Now it's my turn. I stand in front of Lama Geshe and he looks up at me and his eyes sparkle. He says something to Lam Babu and Lam Babu translates, "Lama Geshe says you are very tall."

"I am," I say. "Too tall for the door." What am I supposed to say? He's sitting cross-legged on the bench and I'm towering over him, a corn-fed giant, so I bend farther at the waist.

Lama Geshe chants again. He takes a red string and reaches it around my neck. He ties the ends together and I get ready for him to pull me gently down and then, whoa, he yanks hard. Really hard. *Crack.* Our foreheads smash together, but Lama Geshe doesn't flinch. He holds me there, our foreheads touching, and I feel the skin-to-skin heat. Our eyes meet and he's got this giddy look on his face as if to say, *The joke's on you.* Is he messing with me? I smile back to show him I have no problem laughing at myself and he bellows with raspy giggles.

I feel very blessed.

The inscription on the strip of paper says:

"A request to all sentient beings on this planet . . . Give up all intentions to harm others from your heart and do your best to benefit them all. If each and every one feels the universal responsibility to do so, we will enjoy the feast of peace!"

Lam Babu receives the final blessing. He tells us to carry the strip of paper and the red string to the summit of Mount Everest. The string represents the protection of Lama Geshe's compassionate embrace, and this protection will remain with us as long as the string remains tied around our necks. Later I'll hitch the khata to my backpack and slip the strip of paper into the ziplock with Dad's journal. Now I grab beneath my shirt for the string and feel the gold chain of the Saint Christopher medal. The string's tangled around the chain, which would probably offend about half the believers on planet Earth, but I bet if Buddha and Saint Christopher met at a low-key shindig on the banks of a river, they'd discover that they have all sorts of things in common. If anything, the string and the chain will be stronger together. My guess is that, deep down, they're just the same. And here on Mount Everest, I'll need both. I fiddle with the string. Lama Geshe's overhand doesn't feel very secure and I'd hate to lose it, so I twist the string around my fingers, tie two more knots, and snug them tight.

Thursday's another rest day, which, I've learned, really means the opposite, so I'm not surprised when Dave says, "Let's go find something steep." Through a draw between two ribs of parched grass there's a boulder, about twenty feet tall, with an overhanging face on one side and a diagonal crack on another. Dave says it's a great place to remind our bodies how to move on technical terrain. Hiking's a workout, but having air beneath your feet is a more delicate game. We don't have crash pads or rock shoes or ropes, so we stick to the slabby side with the crack. The Himalayan sky is all wispy clouds and ominous calm like something ugly is coming.

I clamber halfway up the shallow crack because it's easy and fun. Then the holds disappear. I look between my toes at the hard ground ten feet below and, sheesh, it feels like a thousand feet. I squeeze a handhold tighter than I need to and survey the rock above. This boulder's well within my abilities, but one loose hold could mean a broken ankle. That would be an idiotic way to go out.

In the corner of my eye, I see Dave traversing around the base of the boulder. He's never more than five feet off the ground. Smart.

Dave must see me hesitating because he says, "Don't fall."

"Thanks for the reminder," I yell. It's easier to go up than down. I shove my right toe into a crack and twist my foot and take a deep breath and step up. Repeat the same motion three more times and I'll be at the top. See? It wasn't that bad. I scramble off the backside and jump a few feet to the ground.

"How was that?" asks Dave.

"Fun," I say, like nothing happened, but I bet Dave detects a hint of adrenaline in my pupils because he's seen the same look in many an eye.

He gazes at the rock. "Do you think they bouldered here in 1963? It's the perfect place."

Dad has a story about practicing on a boulder in his big Lowa Eiger boots. This could be the same boulder. I can imagine the team puzzling through the problems and flexing their arms, preparing themselves for the Khumbu Icefall and the Lhotse Face and the West Ridge. Tom Hornbein and Willi Unsoeld and Barry Bishop took turns pioneering different routes. Some of the Sherpa joined in, displaying enviable natural talent. Dad and Lute Jerstad, the ice experts on the team, tried the boulder wearing high-altitude mountaineering boots. "Man, they were clunky," I remember Dad saying. "Willi was a really good rock climber. So was Jake. But the boots were stiff and heavy. Terrible."

They were here all right, playing like we are, free of deadly consequences for a while.

After three more times up the boulder, my arms are pretty spent. Dave hops off, satisfied. We stroll slowly back toward the guesthouse.

"I'm sure people ask you this all the time, but don't you get tired of climbing the same routes over and over again?" I ask Dave.

"I guess not. People keep telling me the South Col isn't a challenge anymore. Or that it isn't pure. Or that it isn't truly climbing for one reason or another. But I don't see it. It's still a damn hard challenge to *me*. It's certainly beautiful. The mountain still has a lot to give me and I have a lot to give *it*," he says.

"Would you ever want to climb a route like the West Ridge?"

"Maybe when I was younger, but probably not even then. I'm built for these big glaciers, heavy loads, and long expeditions. When I get on that vertical stuff, my legs start to shake. When I climbed the Pacific Ocean Wall with Jimmy and Conrad, it took me most of the trip to get used to the exposure, the feeling of having no control. I hated it until the last day. Then I was finally having fun and it was over. I wrote an article about it in *Outside* magazine. The subtitle said something about panic attacks, cold sweats, and an order of Depends."

"But what about the pressure to go out and do harder, more dangerous routes? I mean, every article in every magazine these days is about an ascent that only a few select people could ever hope to do. The stories are always about coming close to death or committing to a fifty-fifty move. I even have climbing friends who tell me they no longer enjoy hiking or easy scrambles because there's no risk. I've never understood that," I say.

"Then you're probably wired more like me. Like I said, this mountain's always a challenge and it's always risky, no matter what route you take. It's enough for me. Let the armchair climbers say what they want. They can't know until they've been here. This is an entirely different game," says Dave.

"Do you think it's irresponsible to attempt the West Ridge? Is it too much risk?"

"Jeez, what's with all the questions? Are you writing a fucking book or something?"

Dave knows I'm a writer and I don't mind when he joshes me about it. His joking somehow makes the idea of writing a book seem more appealing, as if it lends credence to the idea. "I'm just interested in why people choose to climb what they do," I say.

"I'm kidding," says Dave. "I think the question of risk is difficult because most people think climbing Mount Rainier or bungee jumping is too much risk. We're comfortable doing those things—well, maybe not bungee jumping—but I wouldn't attempt the West Ridge. It's not worth it to me. Are you really willing to die for it? Probably not. But Hornbein and Unsoeld certainly took that risk in '63. I mean, they had to know they might not come back alive."

"I think that was part of the appeal," I say.

"Man, they were tough back then," says Dave, shaking his head. "It's almost embarrassing how easy we have it now. Your dad *never* complains. Most people want to tell you why it's hard for them. He never says a word."

The departing sun dips into a blanket of gossamer clouds, painting the mountains in rich light. Behind Dave, I see Nuptse shrouded in flamingo-colored alpenglow. Humungous cornices hang from its ridge, forming shadowy roofs and dramatic angles. Snakelike flutes of wind-molded snow crawl down the mountain's flanks, ending in stained aprons littered with fallen chunks of black debris. I glance at Dave and nod my head toward the mountain. He rotates his shoulders and looks at Nuptse. Without a word, he finds his camera in his backpack and strolls to a nearby mound of grassy earth. He snaps picture after picture as twilight gradually slips away.

"Haven't you seen this view a million times before?" I ask as I walk up behind him.

"Yeah, but it's always a little different," he replies, staring at Nupste without blinking. "And it's rarely like this."

17.
TREASURES AND VALLEYS

The next day I weave through a playground of boulders in the bottom of a bathtub-shaped valley between Pheriche and Lobuche. Twenty-thousand-foot monsters rise on all sides. The Himalaya are everywhere now—to the left, right, behind, and definitely above, very high above. Which peak is that ahead? Cholatse? Arakam Tse? I climb it with my eyes, searching for a feasible route. Here's a mellow couloir, but it dead-ends at a blank face of snow-etched stone. There's a doable ridge, but higher up it tumbles away into a billion feet of vacant air, so that's not a great option. I don't see an *easy* way up. You've got to binge-drink risk and not be afraid of the hangover if you want to climb a mountain around here. It's safer not to look at the big picture. One foot in front of the other, that's what it takes to climb mountains, according to Dad, so I twist-tie my eyes to my midtop hiking boots and try to forget about what's ahead.

Speaking of Dad, he's not looking like himself. His legs have gone all wobbly again and his face is the face of the evil emperor from *Return of the Jedi*. He's wincing every couple steps and sweating through his baseball cap. We hike over a frothy creek and he bangs his boot against a clump of coffee-colored dirt, catching himself with a trekking pole. He's breathing like a tuckered-out retriever and I've got to make him stop without letting him know that it's him we're stopping for, so I say, "Hey, I need to stop for a minute. I've got a rock in my shoe."

Dad sits on a scoop of granite next to the trail.

"Are you feeling all right?" I ask.

"No. I was up all night running back and forth to the bathroom. My stomach's really upset," he says, his wrinkled hand pressing into his belly.

Oh no. Did he forget to use Purell after shaking hands with an admirer? Did the chicken chili disagree with him? Did he brush his teeth using tap water? The body's a delicate ecosystem here at fifteen thousand feet and even the tiniest invader can wreak havoc.

"Are you taking anything? Pepto-Bismol? Imodium?"

"Yeah, and the antibiotics Dave and Melissa recommended," he says.

I'm relieved he told Dave and Melissa about it because they're both EMTs and I'm sure they know more than I do. "Cipro or whatever?"

"I think so," he replies. I catch Dave's eye and he nods a yes.

I offer Dad cashews, but he grunts, "No. I just need to keep going slow."

A stray mutt yelps at the clouds, the sound shrill and menacing.

We stop for a snack at a lonely guesthouse that sprouts from a switchback— blue tin roof, granite walls, and peeling plaster against a backdrop of sheer ice and jagged rock. Dad pulls a roll of toilet paper out of his backpack and walks off to an outhouse—really just a hole in the ground with three stone walls propped around it.

A chipmunk pilfers a crumb from beneath the table.

A chill gust streams around the backs of my ears.

Hopefully it's just a one-day thing and Dad'll feel better tomorrow.

Hopefully the antibiotics work.

Out he comes, a face of ash. I rip off a rectangle of carrot cake Clif Bar and hand it to him. He chokes it down like it's a shot of vinegar. "It's better if I just keep moving," he says, nodding toward the trail. Then he walks off, trekking poles *scritch-scratching* against rock.

"Jim! Wait for us!" yells Mom, but he's already focused on the path ahead and he doesn't turn around to acknowledge her.

Dave and I grab our backpacks and run after him. We assume our customary positions in front of him and behind him. I release one giant exhalation to let him know I'm there and to remind him to do the same, but his breaths are staccato and frantic, out of control. What about his heart?

We're nearly to Thokla Pass, which means we're nearly done going uphill for the day, and then Dad dashes to the side of the trail and hides behind a boulder. Returning, he buckles his belt and says, "I feel a lot better. Let's go." Then he's charging the hill like nothing's happened. He's trying to shrug it off and act like it's not a big deal, but it's a huge deal. I feel my concern reflected back in Dave's and Melissa's and Lam Babu's eyes.

Nevertheless, the rhythm of the trail goes on. It doesn't stop for anyone.

Thokla Pass is covered with coarse, heather-like shrubs and hundreds of crude stupas, square, shoulder-high towers made of stone the color of an October storm. Adorned with tangled nests of khata and faded prayer flags, they dot the stark plateau like so many tombstones, tokens of remembrance for fallen climbers. I want to walk amongst them and pay my respects. I also can't bear to watch Dad suffer for a second longer. Lobuche is only a few minutes away; Dad will make it there without my help. I tell him I won't be far behind. He nods in understanding and hikes away without looking back.

Everyone except Melissa and me disappears around a bend in the trail. We meander our own paths through the stupas. Many have plaques and epitaphs. I recognize some names. Scott Fischer, 1996. He was made famous posthumously by Jon Krakauer's best-seller, *Into Thin Air*. Dad and Mom took me to the funeral in Seattle. The service was outside, somewhere close to the water. Most people wore white instead of black. It was a sunny spring day. The air was heavy with the scent of decaying seaweed and cedar. Dad and Mom shook hands with various friends, all of them sunburned and lean. They introduced Joss and me to Ed Viesturs, who'd recently returned from Everest.

Dad pointed at thick, blood-filled veins on Ed's forearm and said, "From being at altitude for so long." Then Dad asked, "How's everybody doing up there, Ed? Are they strong?"

"Yeah, they're strong," replied Ed. "Hell, Jim, some of 'em are even stronger than I am. But that's not the problem. They just don't know how to breathe."

Dad nodded knowingly, but I didn't understand. How could a person not know how to breathe?

I walk to the next stupa. Alex Lowe died in an avalanche on Shisha-pangma in 1999. He was widely considered to be one of the best all-around alpinists in America at the time of his death, and probably one of the best in the world. The avalanche began when a serac unexpectedly collapsed almost a mile above him. Alex and his two partners, Conrad Anker and David Bridges, were on a relatively flat section of glacier when Alex spotted the avalanche. The men realized it was heading directly for them. They ran, but had no chance of escape. In places, the debris field was five hundred feet wide and twenty feet deep. Miraculously, Conrad survived. The force dragged him more than sixty feet across the glacier. He sustained two broken ribs, a torn shoulder, and a few deep lacerations on his head. Alex and David were gone.

The next stupa is for Babu Chiri Sherpa, who held two incredible records on Mount Everest. In 1999 he spent twenty-one hours on the summit without oxygen and in 2000 he made the then-fastest ascent of the mountain in sixteen hours and fifty-six minutes. His death was as unlikely as it was tragic. One day he walked to the edge of Camp 2 to snap photos. He had stood in the same place dozens of times. It was his eleventh Mount Everest expedition and he was intimately familiar with the terrain and the hazards. Something happened. Perhaps a snow bridge collapsed. Perhaps he slipped. Somehow he fell into a crevasse and that's where he died, cold and in pain, only several paces from the nearest tent.

I'll never be as strong a climber as these men were. They were gifted. They were unrelenting. They were the best. But I guess I've got one thing going for me: desire. I bet my desire is as strong as anyone's. I *want* to climb Mount Everest and I *will* climb it. As long as it lets me.

More stupas dot the crest of a knoll off to my left. I untie the khata from my backpack. The silk brushes my neck as I walk over. These stupas are old and weatherworn without names or epitaphs. Moss and lichen grow in cracks between the stones. Trekkers snap photos in front of the famous names, but nobody is over here, which is fine with me because I feel like being alone. I find a cleft on the far side of the knoll and kneel in front of a tower.

I've read that Buddhists believe there are secret treasures and sacred valleys hidden in the world. The treasures are called *terma*, important teachings that have been concealed in the landscape for future discovery. They're supposed to be buried in the ground or hidden in a crystal or concealed in a tree or submerged in a lake or secreted in the sky. Terma are also thought to be hidden in the minds of religious adepts, where they wait until conditions are favorable for revelation. The sacred valleys, called *beyul*, are kind of similar: they are places where a person can enter deeply into nature and interact with the mind's unvisited regions and learn to see the world differently. Entering a sacred valley is believed to enhance the virtues of wisdom and compassion. Beyul are also refuges for followers of Buddhism in a world turned to evil. People who try to force their way into the sacred valleys may encounter misfortune or even death. Those who enter with good intentions will benefit from the protection of the land and of the deities embodied therein.

Any magazine or website will tell you climbing mountains is about dodging hang fire on a sketchy roof or whipping seventy-five feet to your last piece of questionable gear or free-soloing a greasy dihedral in Indian Creek, but you rarely read about people climbing to see the world differently. My knees are in the dirt of a sacred valley and I'm not sure what I believe, but I know how powerful this place can be. I've heard the thundering groan of an avalanche. I've looked into the Khumbu Icefall and felt a strange presence staring back at me.

I pull the khata from around my neck and place it at the foot of the stupa and pin it down with a stray rock. *Please protect me.* There are all sorts of ways to see the world and I'm open to the possibilities.

18.
NOT A BAD PLACE TO CHECK OUT

When he's in the right mood—usually after a few too many rum and Cokes—Dad tells stories about his early years as a climber. One of my favorites is about Mount Index, a 5,948-foot fang of rock in the Cascades where Dad learned the meaning of a "deadpoint."

Dad and Lou were teenagers when they attempted the North Tower of Mount Index. At first, the climbing was easy and they scrambled up a few moderate pitches until they reached a vertical wall not far below the summit. It was Dad's turn to lead. He set off on solid rock with Lou in a hip belay. Lou wasn't anchored to the rock in any way. He sat braced with his legs against the wall and the climbing rope wrapped around his waist. Dad, tied to the other end of the climbing rope, pushed higher.

As he went, Dad noticed a crack in the wall. He thought the crack might accept a piton, but pitons cost thirty-five cents in the 1940s and Dad didn't want to waste one. After all, the climbing was easy, so he went past the crack without placing any sort of protection.

He moved around and above an overhang, climbing to within four feet of a prominent ledge. There he ran out of holds. In his haste, he had climbed into a position he couldn't reverse. His right hand and foot gripped tiny holds while his left hand and foot dangled in the air, searching for nubbins that weren't there. He had made a mistake and now he was stuck.

Lou was at least fifty feet below. If Dad peeled off the wall, he would fall fifty feet to Lou's position and then another fifty feet until the rope caught him. If this happened, there were only two possible outcomes. Either Dad would pull Lou off the wall with him, killing them both, or the rope would break and Lou would be left without a twin brother. There was no possible way to survive a fall. Nor was it possible to climb back down.

"Louie!" screamed Dad, "I'm stuck!"

"It's okay. I've got you," his brother called back, but Dad knew it wasn't true.

His muscles tiring and his legs trembling, Dad did the only thing he could. He jumped.

With all the energy he had left, Dad flung himself upward, reaching for the ledge four feet above. For a split second, his body was no longer in contact with the rock. He was flying upward through the air, the energy from his acrobatic motion propelling him higher and higher.

At the apex of his jump, Dad came to the deadpoint. His body was no longer rising but not yet falling. For the tiniest of moments, Dad was suspended in midair, entirely still, just before the force of gravity took control. And in that moment he stuck his hand to the ledge. There was no letting go. He kicked against the rock, pulled himself over the ledge, drove a piton into the wall, took a deep breath, and yelled for Lou to follow him up.

Today's April 11 and we've been in Lobuche for two nights, so Dad should be feeling better by now. Should be. He pours Heinz on his fried potatoes and stabs one with his fork. Sunrise streams through the foggy windows at his back, silhouetting his stubbly jaw and noggin. Melissa tops off his mug with coffee. Mom rubs a lens with the hem of her orange top.

Dave breaks the silence. "Well, do you feel like giving it a shot today, Jim?"

"Yep," he says. "I think I'm a little better and I don't want to hold you guys up. If she goes, she goes." He's trying to sound nonchalant, but it comes out with more than a hint of I'll-make-it-no-matter-what. I know how much Dad wants to get to Base Camp because I know how much *I* want him to get there. He's suffered a ton already and he's probably taken years off his life. It would be such a shame to fail now, less than a day's hike from Base Camp, especially knowing that if it weren't for the micro-scopic armies infiltrating his gut, we would've made it there already.

We burst out of the guesthouse into a lifeless world of ice and rock. No more pretty green trees or sweet dampness or tiny purple flowers. The air up here's like the air in the Mojave on a frigid November night. There's the faint *koosh* of the river and an animal odor like what wafts from the empty stalls at the county fair. Dad merges onto the trail without a word, his eyes focused solely on the footsteps ahead. The screen on my wrist says we're at 16,154 feet, which means it's about 1,400 vertical feet to the city of tents on the lateral moraine. That's like half the Mount Townsend trail, but so much different because we're already way higher than any mountain in the Lower 48. I double-knot my laces and cinch my hip belt tight and cruise after Dad.

Between head-high ripples of land and around a prow of rock and across an empty flood plain, we hike. Given the way he's focusing on his steps and breaths, maybe Dad *can* make it to Base Camp. He's placing his boots precisely in the dusty lugged imprint of Dave's Vibram soles. I walk behind, ready to catch him if he falls and remind him to fill his seven-liter lungs with air. Step. Breathe. Step. Step. Breathe. He's got a rhythm. Maybe he can make it.

A ten-person team in matching black-and-orange soft shells zooms by on our right. Eight yaks lumber past on our left, yellow duffels hitched across their heaving spines with ratty purple climbing rope. Kent strafes the line of trekkers with his camera, bracing his elbows against his ribs to reduce the shake.

There's a big hill up ahead and the path changes from a straightaway into a zigzagging mess like a liar's polygraph results. Dad's all rhythm and focus, and then he takes his eyes off his feet and looks up at the hill and, fuck fuck fuck, he's lost it. His eyes go squinty and he drops his trekking poles and dashes off the trail. Dave and Mom and Melissa all look as grim as doctors assessing a dying patient. They're worried that Dad would rather kill himself than give up and they're probably right. He'll keep going until his lungs fold up like an origami crane and his heart tears to shreds. It's just how he is. I wish they'd make a pill that'd cure Dad in seconds. I wish Joss were here so we could bear Dad's sickness together.

Dad pulls up his pants and returns to the trail and continues hiking without giving us a chance to talk.

If I had to guess, I'd say we're about halfway up the barren hill and Dad's off the trail again, relieving the pain in his stomach. He reappears and gives Dave a let's-get-going wave, but Dad can barely move. His rhythm's completely gone. A dozen steps and he stops, unable to catch his breath. A line forms behind us because the trail's a rutted channel and there's no way around. Another dozen steps and Dad stops again. His breathing is rapid and shallow and, for Christ's sake, I can't stand to watch this any longer, so I step in front of him and say, "Dad, it's not worth it. We don't have to go any farther."

Our eyes connect and he gives me this look that drills right down into my core and I'm certain I'll never forget this moment. Dad knows he can't make it to Base Camp, but he wants to continue nevertheless. It's a look of stubborn perseverance. For whatever reason—maybe it's just pride or some desire to teach me a lesson—Dad won't allow me to stop him.

"Let me get to the top of this hill," he says. "Then we'll see."

This hill's an arbitrary apex. There are more hills after it and much bigger hills surrounding it. It doesn't even have a name and it's not particularly beautiful. It's just this lonely mound of glacier-carved earth, but to Dad I guess it's something more.

I get out of his way and he hikes past me, breathing three or four times per second.

Grunts. Breaths. Footsteps.

We reach the crest of the hill and Dad dashes off the trail a third time. Mom comes up behind me and says, "We have to stop this, Leif. With the diarrhea I don't think he's been able to digest his heart medication. If we talk to him together, we can stop him." Everyone except Dad is close enough to hear her. A hot poker scrambles my insides as I look from face to face. Dave nods his approval, heartfelt support marking his eyes. Melissa grasps my shoulder warmly and Kent has already turned off his camera, letting this moment go unrecorded. Lam Babu, Kami, and Lhakpa quietly stand by, ready to provide their assistance as if Dad is family to them too.

Dad hobbles over to us and takes a seat on a boulder. Mom and I stand in front of him. His rapid breathing hasn't slowed. I think I can hear the thumping in his chest—*ga-gung, ga-gung, ga-gung*. He might have a heart attack right here, and if he does there's almost nothing we can do. No ambulances or hospitals up here. Not even close. A helicopter evacuation would take hours. If Dad's heart gives out right now, he'll die with his back on the trail, eyes staring upward at the distant white mountains.

"Dad, we can't go on any longer," I say. "It isn't safe. It isn't worth it."

"Honestly, Jim, we need to turn around," says Mom. Her voice cracks.

"How high are we?" he asks like he didn't hear us.

"About seventeen thousand feet," I say. Base Camp is less than five hundred vertical feet higher, but there's decades of undulating trail still ahead.

Dad lets his eyes play over the landscape, taking in the mountains—Pumori, Lingtren, Nuptse, and Chomolungma. "This wouldn't be a bad place to check out," he says.

God dammit! How can he even mention such a thing?

"You're not checking out yet," I reply sternly. "We're going back to Lobuche."

Dad looks at me. In the few seconds before he speaks, his whole demeanor shifts. The hard resoluteness. The indestructibility. The man who's taken care of me my whole life, who's never shown a sign of mortality or weakness, is, for the first time, willing to let *me* take care of *him*.

"Do you think that would be okay, son?" he asks.

Would Dad keep going if I told him to? Probably. He'd either make it to Base Camp or die along the way. No matter how much we both want him to get there, it isn't worth Dad's life.

"Yes. It's okay, Dad," I say. "Let's turn around."

Later, I tuck Dad and Mom into a cozy room in the guesthouse and go outside amongst the boulders, lichen, and hoof-beaten earth. My journal's in my pocket but I'm too torn up to write, so I just walk slowly across the valley, trying not to think about an indestructible man broken down, needing help. The sunset half hides behind the blackened fingers of Lobuche Peak and I do my best to enjoy it, pretending there isn't a hand squeezing tighter and tighter around my heart with every beat. The original plan was for Dad and Mom to spend a few nights at Base Camp with us before trekking back to Lukla with Kami and Lhakpa. Instead, my parents will catch a helicopter to Kathmandu tomorrow and the rest of us will hike to the end of the trail, the foot of the Khumbu Glacier. Not that much has changed, so why do I feel this sorrow and fear? My legs are empty and disconnected. I sit on a mound of dirt and the Himalaya suddenly blur. Alone in the gargantuan landscape, I can no longer hold back. I think about how time is relentless and how one bad bug is enough to take Dad away. I think about a future without him and the blurriness thickens. Maybe I feel like this because now I'm pretty much on my own. I wipe my eyes on the fleecy collar of my jacket and the peaks are sharp again, but the clarity lasts only for a second.

19.
CARES LIKE AUTUMN LEAVES

The landing pad is just a circle of rocks in front of the guesthouse, like an oversized fire ring. The morning's bright and still, good flying weather. Mom and I are standing in a patch of sun and Dave's talking to Lam Babu on the opposite side of the landing pad and Kent's got a tripod set up, aiming his camera at the rising golden orb. Dad walks down the guesthouse steps and sets his backpack next to the landing pad and puts his hands in his pockets, smiling. He looks happier and lighter. He still hasn't shaved, so the outline of his face is soft and gray. I'm like, "He looks better," and Mom says, "I think the Azithromycin is helping."

"Did he start that last night?" I ask.

"Yeah," says Mom. "Dave and Melissa called the Himalayan Rescue Association. They run the medical clinic at Base Camp, and I guess the doctors said that Cipro hasn't been very effective in this region lately. The local bugs are growing immune to it or something, so they suggested he go on Azithromycin. He finally stopped waking up to go to the bathroom at midnight and then we managed a few hours of sleep."

Why didn't Dave and Melissa consult the HRA sooner? Why didn't Dad start taking Azithromycin three days ago when he first mentioned feeling sick? It doesn't matter. It's too late for that. The helicopter's already on the way. Still, Dad's got this visible verve and energy now, and maybe we don't have to give up. Maybe if we rest in Lobuche for a few more days, Dad will be ready to hike again.

Mom must be able to read my thoughts because she says, "Don't let us forget how hard this was, Leif. Slap some sense into me if we ever talk about coming back here. Dad and I are too old for this."

"I will," I say. "We were so *close*. I wish we could've made it."

"I know, but this is the right thing to do," says Mom.

"Yeah. It is. Isn't it?"

"Absolutely, son. It isn't worth your father's life. And no matter how good he looks this morning, he's still really sick. He's just hiding it and trying to look positive. You know how he does that," she says.

I do know, but part of me wishes Dad wouldn't hide stuff like that because seeing him all energetic makes saying good-bye even harder.

Kent aims the camera at Dad. "Is there anything else you want to say before you depart for Kathmandu?"

Dad clears his throat and speaks with his trademark Whittaker gravitas, voice booming as he quotes John Muir. "Climb the mountains and get their good tidings. Nature's peace will flow into you as sunshine flows into trees. The winds will blow their own freshness into you and the storms their energy, while cares will drop off like autumn leaves."

Thuda-thuda-thuda.

It's the sound of a helicopter rising from low in the valley. The blue-and-gold bird coasts in over the top of us and sets down in the middle of the circle, rotor wash sending loose dirt and pebbles flying in all directions. Through the helicopter's windshield I can see the pilot. He's wearing a starched white shirt and a black leather jacket and aviator glasses with gold rims and black leather fingerless gloves. Lam Babu runs up to the pilot's door and then motions frantically for Dad and Mom to get inside.

I grab Mom and squeeze her hard and say, "Call me when you get to the Yak and Yeti."

"We will, but don't worry about us. Just have a good climb," she says.

Dad hurries over and hugs me and yells above the whine of the engines, "Love you, son. I'm so proud of you." But before I have a chance to reply, Dave's dragging him and Mom toward the helicopter by their elbows. Dad and Mom crawl inside the fuselage. They're seated and buckled and Dave's about to close the door when Dad grabs his arm and says something to him. I can't hear it over the whine, but whatever Dad says makes Dave smile. He pats Dad on the knee and gives him a thumbs-up and shuts the door. Dave runs over, crouches next to me, and screams, "Cover your face!"

The earsplitting whine crescendos. The helicopter thrusts a powerful draft of air against the ground, stripping bits of loose dirt. I wrap my elbow around my nose and mouth, but I keep my eyes on the blue-and-gold machine. It lifts off the ground and hovers for a few seconds and then banks sharply downhill, floating through the crisp air like a gorak sailing on the currents. I can see Dad's face looking back at me through the window. That's him, holding up a hand, waving good-bye.

The bird shrinks to a speck and we're left with a magical silence.

Gorak Shep is the last village before Base Camp, but it's not really a village. It's just three tin roofs and twelve granite walls and a cell tower scraping the blue. Off to the north is a perfect dell of tan sand. When Dad and his teammates passed Gorak Shep on their way to Base Camp, the dell was at the bottom of a frozen lake and the foot of the Khumbu Glacier extended to the outskirts of the village. By the time they were on their way home, the frozen lake had transformed into a crystal oval of water. Flowers sprouted from the moist soil on the lake's boundaries. It's no longer a lake and there are no flowers here. It's as sad and desolate as the postapocalyptic world of *Mad Max*. My dusty footprints cleave the sand. I hike faster and faster because breathing hard helps keep my mind off the emptiness inside.

At the far end of the dell, the trail crosses beneath a twenty-foot-tall boulder. The boulder has become a popular canvas for remembrances of dead climbers. There are names and dates and inscriptions on every side. Dad and his teammates were the trendsetters. They commissioned the first inscription. A local stonecutter chiseled into the rock:

IN MEMORY OF

JOHN E. BREITENBACH

AMERICAN MT. EVEREST EXPEDITION

1963

I let my fingers brush across the letters, rounded and smooth and warm from the sun. I could stop here for a while and think about Jake, but I'd rather not think at all. Right now I just want to move. My heartbeat matches the pace of my feet.

We hike around penitentes and past frozen tarns and between two Stonehenge-sized boulders that are like the posts of a natural gate. There's the West Shoulder of Mount Everest gleaming and glinting on my right, and there are Nuptse's frozen gullies, but I can't see the Khumbu Icefall yet. On the southern edge of Base Camp, we hike past groups of matching three-person tents and nylon domes. It's all slippery ice beneath the gravel and cobbles and boulders, so you've got to watch your step. We must be getting to the middle of camp now because there are more tents here than I can count. Every available feature—platform, dell, mound, and ramp—is occupied with tents. I follow Dave through a narrow alley between canvas walls and step over a guyline and there's a flag with the RMI logo hanging loosely against a banana-yellow dome.

Dave drops his pack on the rocks and turns around and sticks out his hand. "Hell of a job, Leif," he says as we shake.

"Thanks. You too, man. First stage complete," I say and I'm trying to hide the emptiness I feel, but maybe a tad seeps into my voice.

"That was the hard part," says Dave. "The rest is a piece of cake."

I take a seat on a boulder and look across the city of tents and there it is, the frozen wreckage of the Khumbu Icefall. It looks exactly the same as it did when I saw it last—a terrifying expanse of crumbling moats and minarets, 2,200 feet tall from trough to crest. I was half expecting it to speak to me like it once did, but it's not saying a word. All I can think about is how this moment would be different if Dad and Mom were here. There are no rum and Cokes and there's nobody that looks at Mount Everest like an old friend. There's just this searing emptiness—and a churning, growing discomfort. What is that? Is it fear? Is it loneliness? I don't think so. I don't feel like this because I'm afraid of the Khumbu Icefall or because Dad and Mom aren't here. I don't feel like this because of the Saint Christopher medal and red string around my neck, or the recession of the glacier, or the people who've died here, or the scar on my spine, or because the next two months'll be the hardest challenge of my life. No. It's not that. The pain in my belly is coming from an entirely different source. I think I'm actually sick.

One giant heave and my stomach turns inside out and I gasp for air.

20.
HELL OF A NITE

Thank God we each have our own three-person tent at Base Camp because I'm sure nobody wants to share a tent with me, not right now at least. Melissa's tent is right next to mine and I feel bad for her because she's been listening to my tosses and turns and groans and retches for the past three hours, three months, three years, or however long I've been sick. It comes in waves. One minute I'm floating on my back in a Caribbean tide pool and then I feel the ocean slithering over my skin and then undertow rips me into the deeps. The wave vacuums up all the water in sight and me with it, building into one of those heavier-than-a-planet curlers that Laird Hamilton loves to shred. I crawl into the vestibule of the tent, toothy gravel biting my hands and knees, and *gaaah*, the wave crashes. White noise. Darkness. A half-conscious sense that I'm being pulverized, tenderized, twirled, and raked viciously across the reef. I'm not inside my body, but I'm not outside either because there is no inside or outside. There's just a heap of wet hair and clammy skin and abs contracting violently and the faint idea that it'll all be over soon, one way or another, alive or dead. Then it *is* over. The wave pushes me into the shallows. I peel open my eyelids and, gross, a pool of yellowish, greenish, reddish sick glistens in the gravel with the remnants of the other hundred, thousand, million waves that've hit me. I fall back into the tent and listen to the gurgle of my gut.

I unscrew my Nalgene and risk a tiny sip. Melissa filled the bottle for me and she must've added a powder because the liquid's teal and it tastes like something you'd find in a back-of-the-store fridge at 7-Eleven. What is that? Gatorade. And it's my favorite flavor too: Glacier Freeze. I know for a fact that it doesn't taste even remotely like a glacier, but the tooth-decaying mass-marketed emulation is almost as good. Almost. Do I risk some food as well? Maybe just a couple Saltines to coat the torn lining of my stomach.

Half an hour floating on my back, thinking about how weak I am, and the tide pool's slithering again. Here comes the undertow and the buildup and, ugh, I crawl into the vestibule. This wave's all enriched flour and high-fructose corn syrup. This wave's teal.

I can imagine a trillion better ways to begin an expedition to the highest peak on planet Earth.

Seriously, though, how long have I been sick? Half an afternoon and one whole night. The waves are finally over, but this isn't the end. It's the beginning of another stage and this next stage is like a river.

Thank God our camp has a toilet tent. In fact, there are two—Dave calls them the "pee tent" and the "poop tent." The pee tent's there for privacy. You're supposed to urinate directly onto the rocks on the floor of the pee tent. The poop tent's outfitted with a crude boxlike contraption set on a knee-high tower of rocks. The box holds a seat over a twenty-gallon plastic drum. Dave says a porter or yak driver will remove this plastic drum at regular intervals throughout the expedition and carry it down valley to a location near Lobuche, where the waste inside the drum is buried. The porter or yak driver who comes to remove the drum is referred to collectively as the "goo man." I feel bad for the goo man, but thank God for the poop tent.

I've been wearing a rut in the moraine between my tent and the poop tent. Otherwise, I'm curled into a ball on my Therm-a-Rest. My gut's churning and pinching and gasping and there's nothing I can do to make it feel better. I've tried everything.

Kumar, head chef and leader of our Base Camp support staff, sets a plate of food on the rocks inside my vestibule—potatoes, carrot salad, and a salami sandwich on a buttery bun—but there's no way I can stomach that. Instead, I swallow a tab of Azithromycin followed by a tab of Imodium followed by a chewable tab of Pepto-Bismol. Staring at the nylon ceiling, I think about Dad.

I've obviously got the same bug he had. How in the world did he manage to hike? This thing's ruthless and unending and completely debilitating. There's no I'll-give-it-a-shot or I-just-need-to-keep-going-slow. Nothing like that. I couldn't hike one mile if the existence of the universe depended on it. Climbing a mountain is absolutely out of the question.

Day three of Leif Whittaker vs. Tiny Green Men and I think I'm winning the battle, if not the war. The waves are gone and the river's slowed down to a four-a-day trickle and Kumar's food is looking appealing, but how much collateral damage has been done? Tomorrow is the *puja*, which means five more days until the Icefall. Am I really ready for that? Will I ever feel normal again? Will I ever be strong enough to climb Everest? I have serious doubts. I hate that I'm sick and everyone else is fine. I would've had trouble keeping up with Dave and Melissa and Kent before the sickness, but now I haven't got a glacier's chance in a fossil-fuel world.

I should've stayed home and never met with Neil Fiske and avoided Everest entirely. That's what I'd been doing for years and it worked out well enough. What the fuck was I thinking? Back home, Chris and Anna will be walking North Beach with Luna trailing them, toting a pole of driftwood in her jaws. Danny'll be concocting a creamy dessert in a cast-iron pan with local blueberries and honey. Spencer'll be on his second pint of scotch ale, waxing philosophic about natural building materials and permaculture to a circle of paint-spattered shipwrights. And what about Freya? She'll be crawling between her jersey sheets and squeezing a pillow between her knees and, *mmm*, I could be that pillow right now. But I'm not. Mountaineering's such a *stupid* sport.

Shut up. Stop thinking like that. Find something to distract yourself.

I pick up Dad's journal from '63. It's probably just Dad writing about how strong he was—doing training hikes near Tengboche with a sixty-pound backpack, sending a seventy-foot wall in the Icefall, or kicking steps for thousands of feet on the Lhoste Face—but I pull it out of the ziplock and begin to read.

For the first ten pages, Dad answers the daily questionnaire with mostly high numbers on the one-to-five scale. His mood's a five. His sleep patterns are a four, the team dynamic a five, his general health a five. His notes are all brief and positive. He describes how the porters coerced him into drinking chhaang one night or how he ends each day of hiking with a set of sixty push-ups. It's exactly what I'd expect from Big Jim Whittaker in his prime. He was unstoppable. For a man like him, the summit was a foregone conclusion, but I'll never be like that.

I turn the page and, looky here, Dad's answers are mostly low numbers on March 3. His mood's a two. His sleep patterns are a one. His general health's a two. The note beneath this questionnaire is different than the others: "Had a hell of a nite last nite. Woke up sick at 10:30 and threw up all over the tent. What a mess. Then got sick in a pot about five more times during the nite—dry heaves at the last."

I imagine the waves pummeling Big Jim Whittaker and, all of a sudden, I feel a hell of a lot better.

21.
OLD AND HAPPY

The lama wears baggy maroon pants, an ochre The North Face puffy from the early nineties, and a felted beret-like cap. He's sitting full lotus in front of the many-tiered puja altar that our Nepali teammates built from stone before we arrived. It's in the center of our camp, equidistant from the dining tent, communications tent, and kitchen. Lam Babu is sitting on his right, beating a handheld circular drum with the knobby end of a hook-shaped stick—*bdoom . . . bdoom . . . bdoom*. On the bottom tiers of the altar are brass bowls of uncooked rice and woven platters filled with Twix and Snickers and Crunch and Hershey's and popcorn and boxes of Coke and Fanta and Sprite and San Miguel beer and a few giant aluminum kettles. On the upper tiers are these ornate, pear-shaped pastries of dense brown dough with discs and curlicues of butter pasted on for decoration, and also a few photos—Kent with his wife and daughters, Melissa with her husband, and Chhering with a smiling old lady who's got to be his mother. On the ground, piled around the foot of the altar, are helmets and ice axes and boots and harnesses and anything else we want to get blessed. The participants—our fourteen-person team of Americans and Nepalis, plus a handful of folks from neighboring camps—are sitting on boulders and pads in a loose horseshoe around the altar. Lastly, there's an unopened fifth of Khukri XXX Rum that's been wrapped in a khata and placed on a central tier directly in front of the lama.

I lean over and whisper in Dave's ear, "Where did that bottle of rum come from?"

"Your dad," he says. "He bought it in Namche so we could have a toast when we got here. Before he left he gave it to Lam Babu and told him to bust it out on a special occasion. I guess that's today."

"Aw. That's awesome," I reply.

"I *thought* you'd like that"—tapered grin and amused eyes—"oh, and by the way, be ready to zip your camera in a pocket when the food fight starts."

"Food fight?" I ask.

"Yeah. You'll see."

The lama begins a guttural chant in an unfamiliar language as he leafs through a stack of ancient paper sheets with dark calligraphy. The drumbeat syncs to the lama's voice—*bdoom . . . bdoom . . . bdoom.*

I've heard the puja described as a request to the local deities and the mountain for safe passage, good weather, and permission to climb, which sounds like a great idea to me. Our Buddhist teammates won't go through the Icefall until the ceremony's been completed. It's as much a part of Everest protocol as acclimatization, and every team at Base Camp takes part. April 16 must be an auspicious date because drums and chants echo from every corner of the moraine. The atmosphere's a cross between guided meditation and Carnival.

While some of us were trekking, the other half of our team was constructing Base Camp—transporting equipment from its winter storage place in Gorak Shep, arranging provisions, organizing loads to be carried up the mountain, and generally being far more productive than us hikers. Soon after our arrival, Dave introduced me to everyone, but I was preoccupied with my own pathetic existential crisis, and beginning to feel sick, so I probably didn't make the best impression. Today's my chance to remedy that.

Lam Babu is the overall leader of our Nepali climbing team. An Everest veteran who's been working in the Himalaya since he was a young man, he now occupies an organizational role. He will probably not go all the way to the summit, although Dave says he will be along for most of the ride. Second in command is Chhering—drill-bit hair, Hollywood cheeks, and the wiry limbs of a marathoner. Kaji and Pasang round out the climbing team. Kaji's older—I'd say late thirties if I had to guess—with a stringy black beard and a calm demeanor. Pasang's the kid of the group.

I doubt he's ever had to shave, but there's a fire in his chocolate eyes that foretells all kinds of passion and conviction. Kumar, our head chef and also the leader of the support staff, is taller and thicker than the rest of the Nepali men. Kumar has four assistants—Yubaraj, Raju, Cancha, and Jetta—who will fill various support roles during the expedition. Sadly, we said good-bye to Kami and Lhakpa when we arrived at Base Camp. They were employed only for the trek and are, I imagine, already back home, or perhaps in Lukla, where they will join another trekking team and repeat the cycle.

Finally, Mark Tucker, a.k.a. Tuck or Tucky, is our expedition coordinator, which I take to mean that he's an inimitable cog in the climbing-Everest machine. Nothing works without him. Tuck's a bulldog in appearance—neck thicker than my thigh, shoulders that'd make a one-hundred-pound backpack look like a purse—but his giddy laugh is a communicable disease and I was infected from the moment we met. He was one of twenty climbers to reach the summit of Mount Everest during the 1990 International Peace Climb, which was heralded by the *Guinness Book of World Records* as the most successful Everest climb in history. Originally from Huntington Beach, California, Tuck boasts that he was the first Southern Californian to stand on top.

Our teammates' hardworking ethic is evident in the detailed construction of Base Camp. They've transformed what was once an uneven square of ridged and pockmarked moraine into a meticulously landscaped home, complete with flights of stone stairs, perfectly flat tent footings, and a central courtyard. They must've carried and repositioned many tons of rock in order to construct camp , and I already feel indebted to them to an extent I will probably never be able to repay.

Base Camp is replete with western luxuries. Besides our personal sleeping tents, there's a 120-square-foot, eight-foot-tall communications tent with a removable floor, folding tables, and a VHF radio. Above the radio there's a laminated photograph of a surfer catching a turquoise wave. Half a dozen portable solar panels and a bank of twelve-volt batteries power the system, which is efficient enough to charge computers, camera batteries, iPods, and even a small pump that pushes water from a thirty-gallon drum into the shower tent. That's right. Shower tent. The pump sends water through a propane on-demand heater and into a showerhead tied to a metal tent pole. East of the shower tent is Kumar's kitchen tent, a rectangle of granite walls roofed with two layers of blue tarp. Benches line one side of the rectangle and a four-burner propane stove stands in a corner. A knee-high island built in the middle stores a wide range of cooking implements and serving dishes.

Finally, no camp would be complete without a dining tent, the center of all conversation, leisure activities, and food consumption. Ours is a yellow army-style tent with a white canvas interior and a layer of dark carpet on the floor. Inside is a rectangular dining table covered with a flower-print tablecloth and topped with clear plastic. A dizzying array of condiments, sauces, and snack foods occupies the center of the table—everything from ranch dressing to Heinz ketchup to Jim Beam barbecue sauce to Goldfish and Triscuits. In one corner there's a set of mobile plastic shelves, which contain board games, decks of cards, books, over-the-counter medications—Advil, Imodium, Pepto-Bismol—and two full water coolers. In another corner, there's a cabinet-sized propane heater. Two energy-saver lightbulbs hang from the ceiling, power cords running down a corner pole, underneath the foot of a wall, and across camp to the battery bank in the comms tent. To keep our spirits high, Tuck has decorated the corners of the dining tent with bouquets of colorful fabric flowers.

And at the very center of camp, in between the dining tent, cook tent, and comms tent, the tiered puja altar rises from the moraine.

Bdoom . . . bdoom . . . bdoom.

Kumar, Pasang, Kaji, and Chhering are working on the *tharshing*, a ceremonial flagpole. On the aluminum pole they zip-tie an American flag, a Nepali flag, and an Eddie Bauer flag. To the top they attach fresh juniper boughs and seven strings of new prayer flags. The lama's chanting tops out like a chorus and the tharshing springs into the air. Kumar secures the base while Pasang, Kaji, and Chhering tie the ends of the flags to boulders on the perimeter of our camp so that the seven strings of color radiate from the center like bicycle spokes. Blue-white-red-green-yellow. Blue-white-red-green-yellow. I've heard it's bad luck if the tharshing is damaged and it's good luck if a bird alights on top. Sure enough, here comes a gorak. It zooms through the blue and plants its talons in the juniper like it's extracting a prized trout from a glistening lake. It hovers there, wings spread, half arrived and half departed, while the *bdooming* and chanting continue.

Yubaraj nests some dry boughs in a crevice next to the altar, pours some clear oil over them, and strikes a match. He blows into the fire, nursing it to life, blocking the wind with his bare hands. Smoke drifts over us and I yank a sweet toke into my nostrils and, flash, I'm helping Dad smoke salmon, native style, the meat stretched onto cedar racks in the backyard, a crackly bonfire flaring up. It's weird how smells evoke memories and how memories evoke emotions and how quickly you can go from feeling alone in the dumps to feeling surrounded by friends.

Raju walks over with a beach ball–sized kettle. Dave and Kent and Tuck shake their heads *no thanks*, but Melissa raises an empty stainless-steel mug. Raju tilts the kettle and chhaang plunks out in clumpy spurts. It looks like the Ivar's clam chowder you get on the Seattle ferry at 9:15 p.m., the inch or two that's been coagulating in the warmer since noon. My large intestine performs a Quad Cork 1800 and I say, "No, *dhanyabad*," to Raju. Melissa sips daintily and smirks across the circle at Chhering and Kaji. They giggle like schoolmates and Raju fills their mugs to the brim. Kent pops a can of San Miguel and I snag a bottle of Coke. Raju circles with a platter of snacks. I partake in a fun-sized Crunch and a sour-apple Jolly Rancher and a handful of popcorn. Chuckles. Cheshire grins. This isn't a somber ritual. It's supposed to be fun.

The lama grabs handfuls of rice from a brass bowl and flings the grains into the air as he chants. Tracers of rice curve and knuckle through space. The bowl is passed clockwise and we each take handfuls. The chant swells and Lam Babu nods and we underhand the rice toward heaven. The grains bounce silently over our equipment and into our drinks and across the family photographs, imbuing each object with a blessing.

Lam Babu hefts the bottle of Khukri XXX Rum, untwists the cap, and fills it with the amber liquid. He dips his pinkie finger into the rum and touches it to his lips and then shampoos the rest of the capful into his hair, absorbing the blessing. The lama performs the same ritual and then the bottle revolves around the circle. It's half empty by the time it reaches me. Dad would be proud. I drop a few shots in my Coke, swirling the alcohol with the soda. I raise it in the direction of the Khumbu Icefall and think about Dad and Mom. They'll be poolside at the Mandarin Oriental in Bangkok right about now, which wouldn't have sounded half bad to me a few days ago, but today there's no place I'd rather be than here, balanced on the cusp of an adventure. One throat-burning swig and I'm ready to embark.

Chhering and Kumar come around with plates of *tsampa*. Dave and Kent and Mark and Melissa grab as much of the heavy flour as they can cup in their palms, so I slide my camera in its case and hide it beneath a rock and take some tsampa too. *Bdoom . . . bdoom . . . bdoom.* The chant builds and builds like a vibey bass line and you can just feel the climax approaching. Here it is. The Nepalis shout *swooo!* and we hurl up powdery clouds like LeBron James sprinkling the courtside crowd with chalk before tip off. It lands in our hair and on our shiny Eddie Bauer parkas and we're suddenly a team of spastic bakers, flour spilling all over the place.

Dave plants his dusty palm on my forehead. "May you grow as old and as happy as this flour makes you look," he says, and rubs the white dust across my brow.

I smear a streak of white down the bridge of his nose. "Same to you. You're already pretty old, but you can always look older."

"Hey, watch out. You'll look like me before you know it."

Then Chhering dyes my hair in tsampa and Lam Babu brushes it on my cheeks and Kaji paints it on my eyebrows with a delicate finger, and I do all the same things back to them. It's kind of intimate, touching another person's face, but hell, we're about to sweat and breathe and sleep and risk death together, so there's no point in being shy. People say hardship forms the strongest bonds and I guess that's true, but teams are formed through everyday stuff too—pizza parties and dugout banter and postwork pints.

As if on command, our team draws together into a semicircle, arms over each other's shoulders, an interconnected string of elbows and chests and hips with independent feet. In unison, the Nepalis start to sing. Their shrill voices fly through the thin air, unimpeded and proud. The semicircle pulsates inward and outward like a lung being filled and emptied and filled again. I follow their lead and let myself get taken away. We stomp our boots and thrust our heads into the center. It's a repetition. Stomp-stomp-kick, stomp-kick, dive toward the middle, and then draw back and start all over again. I don't understand the words of the song, but there's a pattern to the phrases and tones, so I hum along quietly until I've figured it out. Then I let my voice rise with the others. At least for a second, it feels like we're not Americans and Nepalis anymore. We're not guides and chefs and porters and sirdars and filmmakers and privileged sons. We're just a group of snowy-haired mountaineers with a singular goal.

Bdoom . . . bdoom . . . bdoom.

The Khumbu Icefall waits.

PART FOUR
CLIMB ON

22.
DON'T FALL

Beep-beep, beep-beep. Peel the lids and it's frigid black. Where's my headlamp? I rummage in the mesh pouch and feel my knife, cough drops, Buff, and there it is, the plastic pod with the rubber button. A shaft of white cleaves the black. A bright disc sweeps across the nylon. My watch flashes 2:03 a.m. *Beep-beep, beep-beep.* I press START/STOP and feel the cocoons in my core metamorphose into full blown butterflies. My tent's a capsule of safety and outside it's all hanging glaciers and spindly seracs and crevasses that are deeper than the Mariana Trench. I mean, I could *die* today. Literally.

When I asked Dave how long it takes to get through the Icefall, he said, "Depends on how fast we move." I've read that Sherpa routinely do it in under three hours and some clients take as long as ten. Ten hours inside that crumbling maze? Not me. I've been worried about this day since I first saw the Icefall, and I'll push my heart to explosion before I dillydally beneath those collapse-without-warning towers. It'd be so much easier to stay here and read *Jitterbug Perfume*, basking like an iguana in my nylon greenhouse, but then I'd have to live with that not-knowing feeling forever, which might be worse than a quick death. So I slide out of my sleeping bag and jam my feet into astronaut boots.

Rice porridge with brown sugar, two strips of bacon, and a cup of gritty coffee make me human. Dave and Kent and Melissa and I sit in the dining tent, harnesses racked, helmets strapped tight, transceivers at 100 percent power. Tuck's here too, even though he's not climbing. He serves me two more strips of greasy bacon, winks, and says, "Eat up. You're gonna need it."

Outside, a juniper fire smolders in a crevice, the smoke mixing with our foggy exhalations. Dave crouches and takes a pinch of tsampa in his outstretched hand and lets the grains slide between his fingers onto the flame. Glowing branches sputter. Melissa seizes a fistful of rice and launches it toward the stars, brilliant this morning because the moon's just an eyelash. Hard grains bounce silently and disappear in shadows. Kent points his camera at the altar and tries to capture the stars in the frame, and I step in front of his lens and silently wish for safe passage and good luck. Today deserves a little prayer because each step's an act of faith and each breath's a resounding commitment.

I bend over to strap my crampons to my boots. First the left, then the right, and I stomp a few times to make sure they're secure. When was the last time I wore crampons? Aconcagua? Baker? No. I remember now. It was a month ago, when I was training in the Buckhorn Wilderness, an hour's drive from my parents' door. There's that hatchet-splitting-kindling sound that I know and love so well. It's the same melody my spikes have crooned on every glacier I've ever climbed. Everest is bigger and scarier and less familiar, to be sure, but it's just like two Rainiers stacked together. Dave double checks my doubled-back harness and I double check him too. A nod, a breath, and we're off and running.

It's fast, but it's not Dave's rest-day pace, at least not so far. Step. Breathe. Step. Step. Breathe. Today's both training and test. I'll show Dave I can hack it.

Movement is what keeps us safe. It's not a complex algorithm. It's simple math. More time in the Icefall equals higher chance of death. We tell ourselves, like all climbers do, that it's safer at night, when the seracs and bridges aren't melting, and that's probably true to a certain extent, but the deeper truth—the truth that inevitably cancels out all other considerations—is that the Icefall's unpredictable. We're climbing through and into and on top of nature's proof of chaos theory. There's no way to know if two boxcars of ice are going to crush me today, or if they're not. I've read that the Icefall is tumbling and twisting and crashing down at a rate of four feet per day. Our presence here doesn't change that. The Icefall doesn't care who I am. We can't control it and we can't predict it. The only thing we *can* control is how fast we move, which means I'd better stop thinking about Russian roulette and keep my attention on my feet.

Step. Breathe. Step. Step. Breathe.

Over Dave's shoulder I glimpse a connect-the-dots of headlamps— other climbers tracing the route through the Icefall. Maybe Dave's expecting us to be hares instead of tortoises because it looks like we're starting behind most of the other teams. Dave's headlamp picks out the bamboo wands and orange tape that mark the faint bootpack, where hundreds of sharpened points have abraded the ice. We're traveling perpendicular to a series of runnels and ridges. We've been moving for about half an hour and this must be the section Dave and Tuck call the Up-Downs because it's like a giant washboard. I follow Dave, right on his heels, through the bottom of a runnel, past a frozen pool, and up a fifty- foot hill, spiny and brittle on the crest. Then we're down the opposite side and into another dip and Dave's like, "These Up-Downs are hell on the way out. You're thinking, *It's all downhill from here*, until you hit these things. Your legs'll be Jell-O after that."

I used to think climbing Everest meant starting at the bottom and ascending until you reached the top, but to get accustomed to the lack of oxygen at high altitude, we have to do a series of acclimatization rota- tions. An old climbing adage pretty much explains it: climb high and sleep low. The idea is to go successively higher, forcing our bodies to cope with thinner and thinner air, but always return to a lower elevation to sleep, rest, and recover. We're supposed to complete three rotations before our final summit bid. Each rotation is four or five days followed by a similar period of rest at Base Camp, which means the entire process should take about a month. Dave said our goal with this first rotation is to get through the Icefall to Camp 1 and spend a few days climbing back and forth between Camp 1 and Camp 2. Then, if we're all still alive, we'll run through the Icefall back to Base Camp where the oxygen molecules aren't quite so far apart.

I'd rather not think about the way down yet, but Dad always says the summit's only halfway, so I guess it's not a bad idea to corkscrew your mind every once in a while and think about the landscape in reverse.

Melissa and Kent are nipping at my heels. Melissa's all business, eyes focused on the next move, breath synced with her steps like she's playing a tune that she memorized as a child. Kent jogs to the side and crouches, a red dot flashing on his camera as I trudge past trying to look smooth. Who's that coming up behind us?

"Helllooo, RMI team." It's Chhering, Kaji, Pasang, and Lam Babu. In their oversized backpacks they're carrying tents and pickets and ropes and stoves and shovels and fuel and sleeping bags and food, not to mention all their own layers and liquids and climbing hardware and anything else they need for a rotation to Camp 2 and back. Ego says my pack's forty pounds, but if you hung it on a scale, it'd maybe break thirty. Maybe. How heavy is Chhering's pack? Sixty? Eighty? One hundred? It's embarrassing that Chhering's toting the tent I'll sleep in and the butane I'll burn and the Idahoan instant mashers I'll eat, but people are experts at denying awkward truths and I'm no different. He jogs past, forehead level with my sternum, and I'm reminded of what Dad would sometimes say about Gombu: "Most Americans hardly noticed him. They couldn't believe such a small man had climbed Mount Everest. Then Gombu took a deep breath and his chest blocked out the sun." A flash of color, a furtive glance, and the men are gone before I have a chance to say *thank you, thank you, thank you.*

I watch Dave climb a twenty-foot wall of pockmarked ice. He reaches the upper deck and waves for me to follow. A fixed line dangles, white and pinkie thin like the lines you see spooled on the deck of a seiner. I squeeze the cord in my leather-gloved palm and bang my toes into glacier. Relax your heels and suck in your hips and pull down hard. I get to where Dave should be standing, but he's already gone, stomping toward the next obstacle.

Another Sherpa team scoots past. I count twenty-seven, but they're moving so fast that I probably miss a few. One guy's wearing tennis shoes under his crampons. Another's wearing an Adidas tracksuit with fly gold piping. One guy has a swami-belt harness sagging down his hips and another has this eighties splash-of-color parka that'd be worth a barista's monthly salary, plus tips, if you sold it at a vintage shop in Ballard. They're all hefting packs like Chhering's, but it hardly affects their motion. I'm wary and purposeful with each step, but they trot over the glacier like it's a sidewalk. I recall watching Tahitians spearfish, free diving amongst the coral and hovering for minutes, limp limbed and at one with the fluctuations of the current, waiting patiently for an obese grouper to meander into their sights. I could spend lifetimes learning to move like they do and I still might not get it right.

"Dave Hahn, Dave Hahn, Dave Hahn. This is RMI Base Camp checking in." Tuck's voice crackles from the speaker that's clipped to Dave's shoulder strap.

Dave turns his chin toward it and presses a thumb into the PUSH-TO-TALK button. "Hey, Tucky. We're approaching the Little Bowling Alley. Making good time. We'll check in with you when we get to the Football Field."

"Yeehoo!" says Tuck. "Keep up the good work. Base Camp out."

Then Dave's pushing again—step, breathe, step, step, breathe—around an icy cube and along a flat-topped rib that leads to a canyon. Half an hour in and this must be the Little Bowling Alley.

Sir John Hunt, leader of the 1953 British Mount Everest Expedition, ascribed names to various sections of the Khumbu Icefall. Hunt called one dangerous section Hellfire Alley and another Hillary's Horror. He named the worst section the Atom Bomb Area. The Icefall has obviously changed since then—melted, collapsed, and reformed—but Dave's a student of history and he reveres mountaineering tradition, which is probably why he too has ascribed nicknames to sections of the Icefall. Dave's labels also serve a practical purpose. There's no true map of the Icefall because it'd have to be redrawn every week, but there are some general landmarks and they're the quickest way to describe our position. I bet they'd be especially handy to direct rescuers in an emergency. Tuck knows we're above the Up-Downs now and on the edge of the Little

Bowling Alley, so if the thousand-pound fin looming over my right shoulder were to suddenly collapse, at least he'd be able to find my body. After all, we're not the bowlers in this metaphor.

Dave throws his leg over a six-foot aluminum ladder and goes down into the canyon, crampons *ting-tinging* the rungs. He gets to the bottom and peers up at me and says, "Don't stop for lunch in here"; then he's gone in a jiffy, rolling through the canyon and out of my headlamp's range.

Melissa and Kent are stomping up behind me along the flat-topped rib and there's no time to think about all the bad things that could happen, so I clamber down the ladder and let the rhythm take control.

Step. Breathe. Step. Step. Breathe.

White nylon slides across goatskin gloves.

Dawn tinges the horizon.

Modern steel bites ancient ice.

Prior to 1963, eight expeditions had solved the puzzle of the Khumbu Icefall, but Dad and his teammates found no old ladders or ropes or footprints to guide them. There were no clues to indicate which way the other teams had gone. The American Mount Everest Expedition would have to pioneer a route from the beginning to the end of the maze.

With that goal in mind, Dad, Willi Unsoeld, Lute Jerstad, Nawang Gombu, Nima Tenzing, and Pasang Temba set out on a balmy morning in late March. They crossed crevasses on logs cut from nearby pine forests and chopped steps in the ice and hacked down threatening seracs and marked junctions with wands. The team had brought six sections of aluminum ladder with them to Nepal, but these were saved for use on vertical walls. Towers of ice much taller than the men prevented them from seeing the best route ahead, so Norman Dyhrenfurth, Will Siri, and Ang Dawa ascended the flanks of the Lho La pass and found an elevated viewpoint. From there, they watched the climbing team through binoculars and listened on walkie-talkies. When the climbing team came to a Y or fork or dead end, they would radio Norman for advice. Left, right, or straight ahead? Heeding Norman's directions, the team made excellent time as morning transformed into a sweltering afternoon.

After about five and a half hours, they reached a thirty-foot wall between two crevasses. Unstable houses of ice hovered over the wall, threatening to collapse, but the men couldn't find a safer way around, so they anchored a fixed rope there in order to make the ascent easier and quicker for subsequent teams. At about 19,300 feet, they established a cache of equipment and supplies, which they called the Icefall dump. Severely dehydrated and content with their efforts, they returned to Base Camp and collapsed into their tents. Dad wrote, "I drank three full quarts of water, coffee, tea, and juice before going to sleep but was still so dehydrated I didn't have to get up to pee all night long."

Dad had it rough. Nowadays there's a team of badass Sherpa that builds and maintains the route through the Khumbu Icefall every season. They're called the "Icefall Doctors." When we paid them a visit Dave brought along a duffel full of still-in-the-plastic Eddie Bauer puffies as a token of gratitude for the hazardous job they perform. Dave told me they're a highly respected group. The Sagarmatha Pollution Control Committee, a local NGO, collects a route fixing fee from every foreign climber who goes through the Icefall, and uses this revenue to employ the doctors. The doctors begin their labor in the Icefall at the beginning of April, weeks before anybody else. On a daily basis, they replace melted-out anchors, lengthen bridge crossings, or forge entirely new additions to the route after collapses and avalanches have altered the landscape. Some of them have been performing this task for more than a decade. Any and every climber who passes through the Khumbu Icefall relies completely on their work.

I plod through a frigid corridor and around a glacial interpretation of The Thinker and there's Dave looking back at me, his right crampon latched onto the first rung of a horizontal ladder that's laid over a crevasse.

"Use your ascender *and* tether for the first few ladders. After that you'll probably feel comfortable enough to just use the tether," says Dave.

"Sounds good," I say, but in the back of my head I'm thinking, *I'll never feel comfortable in here.*

The aluminum ladder's about six feet long with square rungs, all gashed and dented. Toward the middle there's a rung that's been bent into a sharp V. It looks like an inexpensive ladder. You'd find a similar one at Ace Hardware, except it'd be brand new. Six millimeter cord parallels the ladder on each side, anchored to pickets that've been hammered into the ice to the hilt. They look solid, but how many melt-and-freeze cycles have gone by since they were placed here? They'll probably support my weight if I fall. Probably.

Better not to think about it.

Trust the Icefall Doctors.

Safety is a necessary delusion.

Dave reads my expression and says, "Just don't fall." He steps to the front of the ladder and bends over and clips his ascender onto the right-hand railing. He clips his tether onto the left-hand railing and I can tell he's doing it for my sake, demonstrating how I should follow. "Give me some tension on these lines," he says.

"Like this?" I ask, gripping the cords and leaning back.

"Yeah, just keep them tight. It makes it a lot easier, especially on a wobbly ladder," he says. "Stay clipped in behind the anchor until I'm across. Then I'll give you tension from the opposite side," he says.

"Okay."

"And try to avoid that busted rung. Better to step over it," he says, pointing at the V.

"Gotcha."

"Oh, and hey, Leif?"

"Yeah?"

"*Don't* fall," says Dave. He smiles crookedly and maybe he's trying to take the pressure off and calm my nerves with humor, but it has the opposite effect. Pins and needles tickle the back of my neck.

"Thanks," I say, "I appreciate the advice."

First-rung-to-second-rung, second-rung-to-fourth-rung, fourth-rung-to-sixth rung, sixth-rung-to-ice, and Dave's across.

"All you," he yells from the opposite side.

I squeeze the rope and lock steel to aluminum and, look at that, my twelve-and-a-halfs are long enough to span the gap between two rungs. The connection's surprisingly secure. It's like I'm fastened to the ladder. Thank God I have big feet.

Three vertiginous steps and I'm perched above the crevasse's stomach and, for some stupid reason, I look down. Turquoise stripes shimmer. The bottom's a toothy jumble. That's where I'll land if I fall. That's where my legs'll shatter and where my blood'll stain the glacier. It'll hurt, bad, but I probably won't die. Probably not. I recall the log in Elk Lake and the sting of the rusty water. *It's not going to kill you,* I tell myself, even though I know this time it could.

Three more steps and I'm standing next to Dave.

The sun rises. Golden light erodes the furrowed horizon and plasters Pumori. It changes into a glistening and majestic cone, defiantly shouting for its own piece of glory amongst the taller peaks that surround it. The sky's empty of clouds and full of mountains. There's another ladder twenty feet ahead and another not far after that. I switch off my headlamp and stow it in a pocket and follow Dave to the next ladder. First-rung-to-last-rung and then it's my turn again. I dead bolt my crampons to the metal and relax. This time it feels a tiny bit easier to jump in.

23.
PICK YOUR BRAIN

Seven more ladders and three more walls and there's a miles-wide bowl of ice boulders the size of frozen Ford Fiestas and Toyota Tacomas and eighteen-wheelers piled on top of each other in precarious heaps. This must be what Dave calls the Popcorn because of what it would look like if you peered down from a helicopter *thud-thud-thudding* at twenty-two thousand feet, but the view from here is more like a wrecking yard out of the sixth ice age. According to the bamboo wands and nylon cord, the route goes beneath the arm and bucket of a rimey backhoe before floating across a stack of refrigerator-sized kernels. What's beneath it all? The entire terrible thing looks like it's suspended in midair. If one kernel shifts, the stack will shift with it in a groaning reorganization of weight and pressure. We'd better be long gone when that happens.

I clamber over a waist-high chunk and launch myself across an airy gap between two kernels. The landscape resists all patterns, but we're trying to impose our rhythm nevertheless. Step. Breathe. Step. Step. Step. Breathe.

Dave goes, *"Psh,"* so I look past his sweaty back to see what he's *psh*ing at and, oh shit, there's a big group of guided climbers ahead of us and their pace is, for lack of a better term, glacial. I count ten clients and one foreign guide and two Sherpa in the group. They're roped up in traditional glacier-travel style—one rope team of seven and another rope team of six. It's easy to tell who's a guide and who's a client because the clients are in Gore-Tex from head to toe and the guide's stripped down to a long-sleeve tee, chest hair escaping his collar, and he exudes this air of confidence and self-importance. It reminds me of the old joke: How do you know when there's a mountain guide in the room? They'll tell you.

One of the clients—cardiologist? corporate attorney? CEO?— must've been careless when he was attaching his crampons this morning because they're visibly loose. The rubber soles of his boots are sliding around on the steel with every step and the dangling straps are liable to trip him like untied shoelaces. We're right behind him now. Beads of sweat pop out of his neck and drip onto his collar. He tilts his head down, appraising the viability of further climbing. He doesn't look very fond of what he sees.

I'd like to tell him he should turn around, that there's no way he's going to make it to the summit alive, but this guy's probably paid a boatload of money—$70K? $100K?—so I guess he shouldn't be prevented from killing himself, as long as he doesn't kill me too. Besides, am *I* really much better than *he* is? When Dave and Chhering look at me, do they notice the same weakness and ineptness that I see in this guy? Being Jim Whittaker's youngest son doesn't grant me a stronger claim to this place, but at least I know how to put on my crampons.

"It's like a funeral procession," says Dave. He shoots me a horrified look and then cranes his neck to peer ahead, searching for a suitable place to pass.

Ten minutes and we reach a section with no ladders visible ahead. Dave unclips from the fixed line and accelerates, so I do the same. We redline it. Step. Breathe. Step-step-step-step-step. Breathe. My heart's a steam whistle. This has got to be my threshold pace.

We slide in front of the group and, phew, Dave taps the brakes. I let my heart throttle back and then I ask Dave, "Do you see that"—inhale, exhale, inhale—"type of thing often in here?"

"What do you mean? Roping up like that?" he asks.

"Yeah. And their size? And"—exhale, inhale—"how slow they were going?" I ask.

"Well, I rarely see people roped up in here. Very rarely. But, you know, different strokes." Dave shrugs a shoulder, puts an upturned hand in the air near his armpit, and raises his eyebrows. It's one of Dave's trademark gestures and, as far as I can tell, it means something like *don't blame me*.

"It doesn't make sense," I reply.

"I know. I know . . ." he says, trailing off.

"Are teams usually so big?"

"Actually, I think that was just *part* of their team. The other half of them are probably already at Camp 1 or still waiting at Base Camp to begin their first rotation. That's definitely not the biggest group I've ever seen," says Dave.

I want to ask more questions, but I don't have the breath, so I think about Dad instead. Did Dad and his teammates ever imagine that, forty-nine years later, there'd be hundreds of summit hopefuls rolling the dice in the Khumbu Icefall?

They never had to contend with slow-moving groups, but they couldn't sprint through the Icefall either. On the second day of climbing, Jake Breitenbach, Dick Pownall, Gil Roberts, Ang Pema, and Ila Tsering set off from Base Camp in two rope teams, their bodies and minds focused on pushing the route farther and improving the path that had already been established. A morning of slashing steps and resetting anchors burned out their shoulders, and it was 2:00 p.m. by the time they reached the final thirty-foot wall that led to the Icefall dump. Out in front, Pownall ascended the wall while Ang Pema and Jake Breitenbach waited close behind. The second rope team of Gil Roberts and Ila Tsering was still about forty feet back when the world exploded.

It's hard to imagine the sound of a crumbling serac. Was it like a crack of thunder or a deep growl like an approaching F-15? Ang Pema and Dick must've heard it best. White debris cascaded down on them, tumbling and crunching. Dick was buried up to his chest and Ang Pema was even deeper, wedged upside down. Gil and Ila Tsering hacked desperately at the glassy rubble until they freed Dick and Ang Pema, but the rope between Ang Pema and Jake trailed into a tapered canyon that was now flooded with twenty feet of impenetrable ice. Jake didn't have a chance. There was no saving him. Gil cut the rope. A frayed nylon end slipped away into the white.

Dad rushed up to meet them and slung the injured Ang Pema around his neck, piggybacking him to safety. Then he went back up and hacked for an hour at the debris around the severed strand of rope, but there was no sound or sign of Jake. A stark silence hung over the Icefall. He was gone.

Tears. Grief. Anger. The men searched for meaning and reason and fault, but they'd done nothing wrong. The mountain had shifted without warning or emotion, and one of their friends had been killed. Some looked for solace in a bottle and others contemplated the risks. Was climbing Mount Everest worth it? Jake's absence made this question painfully tangible. That he had died doing what he loved didn't make it easier to accept. The men examined their own motivations and wondered if the expedition could ever be enjoyable again after such tragedy.

Of course, quitting was not an option, at least not so early on. Too much time, money, energy, and passion had been invested to give up now. Nor would Jake have wanted that. The men would have to climb through the same hazard that had just killed their teammate. Three days later, they dutifully continued, carrying loads of supplies to the dump in preparation for stocking higher camps. Climbing went on, as it had to, but some of the men wondered if the joy of climbing could ever return?

We've made it to the A-Bomb Area. A forty-foot-tall freestanding tower of ice hovers directly over the climbing route, threatening to collapse. It's still early and the sun's not baking the Icefall yet, but the tower's crisscrossed with cracks and fissures like those sandstone sea stacks near Cape Elizabeth. It's probably been here for years and it hasn't fallen so far, but I bet if you yanked out a brick of ice from just the right place, it'd all come down in an instant. Jenga, Jenga, Ja-ja-ja-jenga.

Dave and I are practically running now and we're out from beneath the A-Bomb tower in less than a minute, but there's another problem: the next section's called the H-Bomb Area. Twin seracs, each as tall as a ten-story building, hang menacingly over the left side of my brain. Dave unclips from the fixed line and speeds up even more. Maybe he's thinking the fixed line slows us down in here. We're always having to unclip and reclip at anchor points, which wastes valuable seconds, so I guess it's safer to risk falling in a crevasse than it is to risk being caught beneath the buildings when the demolition charges go off. Sprinting's the safest method of all and that's pretty much what we're doing. Step. Breathe. Step-step-step-step-step-step-step-step. Breathe. We sprint directly beneath the twin seracs across a field of frozen rubble and, no fucking way, another group of climbers is blocking the route. Six clients, two guides, and two Sherpa are meandering along like they're on a tour at the San Diego Zoo. I'm about to scream, *Get the fuck out of the way*, but Dave just zooms calmly past them, brushing shoulders as he cruises by. I follow right on his heels, straining my ears for creaks or booms. We're nearly past them when one of the clients—a bald guy with an uncanny resemblance to Paul Giamatti—reaches out and grabs Dave's arm.

"Dave Hahn?" he asks with an I'm-your-biggest-fan tone. For some reason he strikes me as a hedge-fund manager.

Dave stops in front of Hedge Fund and looks down at the man's hand like he wants to break multiple fingers. "Yes. I'm Dave. Do I know you?"

"Not really. Well, we were in Antarctica at the same time last year. I was on a different team," he says.

"Oh really?" says Dave. Hedge Fund's hand is still on Dave's arm and Dave glances up at the twin seracs and I wouldn't be surprised if Dave bops the guy on the nose and sprints off.

C'mon, c'mon, c'mon! Do it, Dave. We need to move.

"Yeah. Listen, I want to pick your brain about Mount Vinson. I didn't summit last time. When's the weather best? Is it better in December? Because in January, it was tough," says Hedge Fund.

"I'd love to sit down at Base Camp sometime, but we're in the middle of the Khumbu *Icefall* right now," says Dave.

Oh for Christ's sake! Just *go*, Dave. The fuse on the H-Bomb's burned down to a nub and we're still standing here, directly beneath a thousand, million, trillion pounds of ice. Go, go, go, go, go!

The hand releases and Hedge Fund's like, "Oh, okay. Yeah. I just had a few questions. No big deal. Like, what boots do you use up there? My feet got cold last time."

But we're already sprinting again and we're not stopping.

"Get in touch when we're back at Base Camp. I'm at the RMI camp," yells Dave over his shoulder.

"No problem. I'll come over for tea or something. When do you guys usually have dinner?" asks Hedge Fund.

But Dave just keeps sprinting until we're free of the twin seracs and out of Hedge Fund's sight.

Step. Breathe. Step-step-step-step-step-step-step-step. Breathe. I'm surprised there's enough juice in my legs. This is Dave's rest-day pace and my lungs are burning like I'm breathing through a snorkel, but I'm keeping up nevertheless.

Four days after Jake's death, Dad, Gombu, Willi Unsoeld, and Lute Jerstad climbed into uncharted territory. At about twenty thousand feet, just before the Icefall smoothed out into the tongue-shaped basin of the Western Cwm, they came to a seventy-foot wall of ice with a five-foot-wide crevasse at its base. It was the Icefall's final defense and there was no way around. Willi Unsoeld aimed his gaze at Dad and said, "Well, Jim, you're the ice climber."

Dad racked a dozen coat hangers on his harness and hurdled the crevasse, sticking to the opposite wall with his ice axe and crampons. He screwed a coat hanger into the wall, clipped the rope through it, and began his ascent.

An hour later, his preconceptions about Mount Everest had been shattered. He'd expected Everest to be essentially a taller version of Rainier, but now his frantic gasps proved otherwise. Dad had made it about halfway up the wall when Willi hollered, "Jim! You're turning blue! Come on down. It's my turn."

Willi took two more hours to surmount the wall. It was a super-human performance, and when he finally reached the top he let out a tremendous yodel that carried with it the rising spirits of his teammates. The deadly Icefall was behind them and the wonder of the Western Cwm waited ahead. With Nuptse on the right, Everest on the left, and Lhotse directly ahead, the Western Cwm was like the ward of earth's grandest castle. It was a calm and peaceful place that was completely protected from the prevailing winds, which is why the Swiss expeditions of the 1950s gave it a different name: the Valley of Silence.

During the next week the team solidified the route through the Icefall, carried loads of food and equipment to Camp 1, and prepared to thrust higher into the middle of the Cwm. On March 31, an advance team of Barry Prather, Gil Roberts, Dad, and a group of Sherpa ventured into the gradual terrain, threading the needle between crevasses. At 21,350 feet, on the Cwm's northwestern boundary, they founded Advance Base Camp (ABC), which would be their home until their task was done. After the death of a teammate and an extremely taxing effort in the Icefall, it was a liberating moment. Their eyes rose toward Everest. That evening, as the blanket of night crept up the Lhotse Face and the stars sparkled in an ethereal sky, Dad radioed Base Camp. Every member of the expedition could hear the thrill in his voice when he said, "I think maybe I'll take a moonlight stroll up to the South Col tonight."

Sugar Hill is a fifty-degree slope of sugary snow that disintegrates beneath our crampons as we climb. The route's a shoulder-deep laceration and each climber that passes through—each set of footprints—cuts deeper into the slope. What'll it look like by the end of the season when thousands of boots have eaten it to crumbs?

I crest Sugar Hill and walk across a platform the size of a tennis court, and there's Dave looking over the lip of a crevasse, so I come up next to him and look down too and, sheesh, that's the biggest crevasse I've ever seen. It's at least sixty feet deep and one hundred feet across, and it looks like the only way to get past is to descend into the murky depths and balance on a series of frozen plugs like stepping-stones and climb out via a set of vertical ladders on the opposite wall.

Dave mutters under his breath, "The Damn Deep Ditch."

Ten load-carrying Sherpa in identical green jackets, two climbers in matching yellow down suits, and four other individuals are clogging the plugs and ladders. At first glance, I can't tell which direction—up or down—the throng's moving. The entire scene looks more like a royal court dance than a life-threatening obstacle at 19,400 feet. Off to my left is an immense hanging glacier that's clinging to the West Shoulder of Everest. They call it the Horseshoe Glacier because of its two branches of ice with a hollow section in the middle. We're not *right* beneath it, but if one of those branches were to calve off, the ensuing avalanche could take out the entire upper half of the Icefall, and us with it. We won't truly be safe until we're through the Damn Deep Ditch and into the Western Cwm.

But I'm not particularly worried anymore. I don't know why. It's just a feeling. There's no point in dwelling on the dangers I can't control.

Tangerine sunshine floods the glacier. The light's too intense, so I pull out my Maui Jims and filter the Icefall through polarized lenses. Everything's suddenly more vibrant. My boots turn from straw to electric yellow. Melissa's soft shell flashes from sweet pea to peppermint leaf. A mild wind rises from low in the valley and I feel my heart go higher with it. We're almost free of the Khumbu Icefall now. A few more obstacles and we'll be into the Western Cwm. Maybe the lack of oxygen's affecting my brain because the anxiety and fear I felt at Base Camp this morning are gone. A childlike sense of enjoyment washes over me.

Dave turns around to address me. "Don't let anyone get between us in here," he says, nodding toward the Ditch.

"No worries. If anyone tries something, I'll push them in," I reply.

"You feeling all right?"

"I feel great, man. This is fun! It's like a jungle gym," I say.

"Uh-huh," says Dave, peering up at the Horseshoe Glacier. "It'd sure be fun if it couldn't kill me so bad."

"It's a little scary," I say, but I'm not really scared anymore.

"Once we get to the other side of this thing, it's an easy walk to Camp 1," adds Dave.

"Sweet. Game on!" I say.

I lock my crampons into the rungs of a ladder and clip my tether to a railing. My ascender dangles from my harness, unused and unneeded. Dave hops like Huckleberry Finn from plug to frozen plug, crossing the Damn Deep Ditch with style. I scurry after him, flexing heel to toe without thinking, my body flowing naturally over the cold surface. This is how I like to climb.

24.
BLOODSTAINS

Three rubberized duffels, a dozen bamboo stakes, and a rat's nest of rope. That's Camp 1, at least so far, until we open the duffels. I plant my axe and slide out of my backpack and Dave's like, "Nice work, Leif." High fives and shit-eating grins for Kent's camera. Then half a liter of raspberry Emergen-C and six margarita Shot Bloks to preempt tomorrow's stiffness.

"How long did it take us?" I ask.

Dave peels back a sleeve and looks at his watch. "About four hours. Not bad. We'll probably shave some time off that on our next rotation, but not bad for our first trip through," he says. In the back of my head I'm thinking, *Shave some time? I doubt it.*

I take in my surroundings. The glacier's a pattern of ripples—crests and troughs, tents and footprints. Red tent, blue tent, one tent, two tent. The International Mountain Guides (IMG) camp is off to my right and the Alpine Ascents International (AAI) camp is a few ripples ahead. IMG has the orange Eureka! tents and AAI's usually in the yellow The North Face ones. Who else is up here? There are dozens of outfitters and we're all competing for the same territory. The safest location's toward the middle of camp, equidistant from two gargantuan hazards: Nuptse's hanging glaciers on the right and the West Shoulder's hanging glaciers on the left. Colorful wands reserve blocks of ice for one team or another. There's a pecking order, as any magazine or book will tell you. I've read *Into Thin Air* and *Outside* and the web forums, so I'm fully aware that hidden inside these tents are people who won't hesitate to step on me if that's what it takes to get to the top. I know that the cooperation and teamwork that existed on Everest in 1963 are ancient history. But I don't really care. We're smaller and faster and better than they are. I *like* our little corner of the Cwm.

My eyes follow a trail of footprints that leads beneath the radiant ice and burnt yellow rock of Nuptse. That's got to be the route to Camp 2. I'm tracing it with my gaze when this unbroken ribbon of ice catches my attention. It's a continuous line of vertical glass that knifes through Nupste, all the way from the floor of the Western Cwm to the summit. That must be the Crystal Snake. I remember reading about the route in *The World's Most Significant Climbs*. How the hell did Damian and Willie Benegas, the famed Argentine twins, manage to haul themselves up that thing? I can't imagine. I literally have no idea how you'd even begin to climb that ribbon of crystal. A shitload of ice screws? Forearms made of exotic Argentine hardwood? The telepathic mind meld that comes from being twins?

I sweep the landscape from right to left. There's the Lhotse Face and the Yellow Band and the Geneva Spur and, oh wow, a pyramid of cast-iron rock that's cleaving a cloud bank in two. That's it. That's the last ten thousand feet of Mount Everest. It looks so damn *close*. I recall the first time I saw it from the barren promontory above Namche Bazaar when I was eighteen. It was like looking at the moon and I couldn't believe Dad had climbed it. But now the view is different. It's like looking at Olympus from the Blue Glacier or Rainier from the Paradise parking lot. It's well within my reach. Hell, I could make it up there in a single day.

Fire and vinegar run through my veins and I say, "Dave, let's do this. I'm ready. We can make it up there this afternoon!"

"Whoa, whoa, whoa," replies Dave. "Slow down, youth. We still have another *month* of climbing before we're ready for that."

Dave's right. I don't want Everest to be a repeat of Cotopaxi, where my climbing partner, Tyler, and I acclimatized for a single night before our summit attempt. We were thousands of feet from the top when the headaches, nausea, and fatigue hit, but it was my first big climb after the surgery and I wanted to prove myself. Tyler read my determined expression and said, "I'm really tired and really cold, but let's keep working." A few hours later we stained the summit crater with bile while three college-age girls snapped selfies and giggled cheerfully, completely unaffected. I'd proved myself all right.

We got away with it in Ecuador, but Everest isn't as forgiving. It'll kill you pretty quick if you stare at the summit too long and lose focus on the little stuff—every ladder rung, calorie, footstep, and deep breath.

I jab a bamboo stake into the ice and tie a trucker's hitch in the guyline and ratchet it down until the pea-soup wall of our Eddie Bauer tent is *djembe* tight.

"Dave Hahn, Dave Hahn. This is RMI Base Camp. Please respond." Dave's radio crackles to life.

Dave extracts the extendable mic from his pack. "Go ahead, Tucky."

"Bad news," says Tuck. "There's been an accident in the Icefall not far from C1. Sounds like a Sherpa fell off a ladder. One person. Garrett and Lakpa Rita and Damian are already responding, but they might need another hand, so I said I'd check with you and Melissa. What's your status?"

I think about the Sherpa with the swami-belt harness and the guy with the sneakers under his crampons and the way they tiptoed over the ladders without the slightest hesitation or concern.

Dave turns to Melissa and says, "They're probably going to need you," but she's already dumping extra clothing and fuel and food and her sleeping bag and Therm-a-Rest out of her backpack into a heap on the snow.

"Yeah, Tuck. Melissa'll be on her way in a few minutes with medical and I can follow her with the Sked and oxygen and crevasse kit if they need it. Any more information on location?"

"I think it's one of the last ladders before you get to camp. On your side of the Damn Deep Ditch."

"Copy that"—Dave makes eye contact with Melissa—"Melissa can assess when she gets there and let me know what's needed." Melissa nods and tosses a medical kit and a water bottle into her backpack and zips the lid closed. I don't think they've worked together before, except for maybe a few climbs of Mount Rainier, but good guides have an unspoken code.

"Roger," says Tuck. "We'll keep our fingers crossed down here."

Melissa shoulders her backpack and says, "I'll be on our frequency, Dave."

"Is there anything I can do to help?" I ask because I want to show Melissa, Dave, and Kent that I'm not a feeble client; I can contribute to the team.

"Just get my stuff off the snow and finish anchoring the tents," she says over her shoulder as she speed walks away, disappearing behind a ripple. I feel a little sheepish. I'd prefer to do something more heroic, but playing basketball taught me that part of being a good teammate is setting screens and diving for loose balls, not just throwing down thunderous dunks. I find Melissa's Therm-a-Rest and blow it up.

Dave rummages through duffel bags. He asks me to throw anything unnecessary out of his backpack, so I unpack his mug and book of *New York Times* crossword puzzles and extra socks and Kindle while Kent finishes tying guylines to bamboo. Dave loads up the Sked stretcher and oxygen bottle and crevasse rescue kit. It's a cumbersome load and he huffs when he shoulders it, about twenty minutes after Melissa left. Geared up and cinched tight, he takes three steps toward the Damn Deep Ditch and then Melissa's voice comes over the radio.

"Dave Hahn from Melissa."

"Go, Melissa."

"We're not going to need the Sked or oxygen, Dave." She's breathing hard between words. "But we could use a sleeping bag to package. An old one that nobody needs, that can get ruined."

Dave squeezes his lips together and shakes his head, grief smudging his face.

A new voice comes over the airwaves. "Hello, Dave and Melissa. This is Ang Jangbu. We have extra sleeping bags at the IMG camp at Camp 1. We don't have anybody up there right now, but if you go to our camp and look in the tents you will find one you can use."

Dave shoots me a that's-your-job look, so I run, run, run across the ripples to the village of orange Eureka! pods. The first tent's empty, but in the second tent there's an old synthetic-fill sleeping bag that reminds me of the rectangle in my parents' garage. I snag it by a loop and run, run, run back to Kent and Dave, because running numbs the sorrow and cuts off the doubt.

As Dave is attaching the sleeping bag to his pack, a young Sherpa trudges up and says he'll take it to the accident scene. Dave passes it off, radios Melissa that it's on the way, then sets down his giant pack and sits on top of it to wait.

Lankier shadows and richer light mean morning has flipped to afternoon. Melissa reappears, finally. She trudges into camp and drops her pack and chugs a whole liter of water. I stay silent, not wanting to pry, but then the story just comes out of her and there's no need for questions: "He was working for Peak Freaks. Somebody said he lost his balance on the ladder and I guess he wasn't clipped into the fixed line. That crevasse is like fifty feet deep, and I think he went headfirst. It was probably quick. Lots of blood. Damian and Lakpa Rita went down into the hole. Being heroes like usual. Garrett did a great job with the haul system. There were *so* many people down there. Everyone was trying to help."

Maybe the magazines and web forums've got it wrong. Maybe it's not just cutthroat guides and hedge-fund managers and underappreciated Nepalis up here. Right now it feels more like we're one big community and we've just lost a member.

Sitting on the snow in front of her tent, Melissa squeezes a wet wipe in her fingers and dabs at a red splotch on the sleeve of her green jacket. She dabs and dabs and dabs until the wet wipe is red too, but the splotch still won't go away.

I sit down next to her. "How you doing?" I ask.

"I'm okay. Thanks for asking. It's been a long day," she says.

Dab, dab, dab. White knuckles and a shivering hand.

"It won't come out, huh?" I ask.

"No," she replies, her voice heavy. "It's no use. You know how blood is."

25.
SLEEP MORE WHEN YOU'RE SLEEPING

A rhythmic *thuda-thuda-thuda* wakes me. My throat's itchy and my lips are cracked and an auger is boring into my temple. Frost, ripstop walls, a half-full pee bottle, a boot liner in a mesh pocket, a downy feather, and the realization that the dream I was having about swimming end to end in a lukewarm pool was, in fact, a dream. Next to me, close enough to smell, Dave coughs the butter from his lungs and props himself on an elbow.

"Time to get up?" I ask. Each letter's a chunk of pumice scraping my larynx.

"If I were you, I wouldn't get out of that sleeping bag until the sun hits the tent," he replies.

Thuda-thuda-thuda.

Dave unzips a door and peels back a corner, and in the crescent of light I see a red, white, and blue helicopter glide past. The engine revs and then levels off. Right about now a team of guides will be lifting a frozen corpse wrapped in a sleeping bag. One, two, three, and they'll heave together and slide it into the compartment. The rpms skyrocket and the skids lift up and, *thuda-thuda-thuda*, the helicopter levitates through the crescent again, diving for Base Camp.

"Nice piece of flying," mutters Dave. "Those B3s are pretty amazing. A few years ago they would've had to lower the body through the Icefall."

"I guess this way is safer for everyone," I say.

"Except the pilots."

"Yeah, but aren't those flights becoming pretty routine?" I ask.

"Nothing's routine at twenty thousand feet."

A nonorganic egg-yolk sun cracks out from behind Nuptse, bathing our tent in warmth. Cue the climbing scene.

Sweaty feet in frozen boots. Harnesses digging into hips. A trekking pole in one hand and an ice axe in the other. Minty lip balm is a pleasant garnish to the fading taste of Quaker's instant apple and cinnamon. Inhale crystalline air. Clang our axes together in a sort of pregame huddle and we're off, crampons *chunk-chunking* away. We go wand to wand across a powdery apron, beneath the Crystal Snake, and down an eight-foot ladder into a channel running along the bottom of a crevasse.

Dave reminds me, "We're not trying to go as fast as we *can* on this first rotation. We're just trying to get stronger." We'll spend three nights at Camp 1 on this first rotation and then return to Base Camp for four days of rest before starting the sequence over again. Ideally, on our second rotation we'll make it all the way to Camp 3, about twenty-four thousand feet. By the time the expedition is over in early June, we will have climbed and descended more than one hundred thousand vertical feet, over three times the altitude of Everest, which is probably why Dave's reminding me to take it slow.

Out of the channel and back to the surface of the glacier, and I glance up to my right and my typewriter heart misses a key or two. Whitecaps of ice hang from Nuptse—nothing more than little radar blips from here, but how big and loud will they be when they collapse? Dave toes the accelerator, thank God, and we're out from beneath the hang fire and into the middle of the solar oven that's the Western Cwm. We strip to our base layers and gob sunscreen on our faces and I chug half a liter of melted snow. Then we're moving again, slogging over furrows and wrinkles until we reach a big yawner with a double ladder. The end of one ladder overlaps another. Purple climbing rope lashes them together. Dave shuffles confidently to the middle of the ladder and, uh oh, it flexes horizontally. Dave hesitates, even though Dave never hesitates. He freezes in the center for one, two, three, four, five seconds. A deep breath and he's tightroping again, very delicately, like he's that crazy guy from *Man on Wire*. Safely on the other side, Dave leans against the fixed lines, giving me tension.

Three steps in and I can tell this ladder's different. The rungs are round instead of square and they're farther apart too. The one-crampon-to-two-rungs pattern doesn't work. And this ladder is more slackline than ladder. It's wobbling and swaying and it's getting worse as I get closer to the middle. The moment you think you've got it all figured out is always the same moment the world changes.

Don't look down, don't look down, don't look down.

I look down.

Fuck fuck fuck fuck fuck.

Featureless walls and depthless black. There's no surviving a fall from here. I freeze.

My quads are shaking a little like they do after a thousand lunges. *C'mon, Leif. It's easier to go forward than backward. Dave did it, so I can do it too.*

I inhale and walk across, and I don't exhale till I'm standing next to him.

"That was a bad one, huh?" says Dave.

"Scary . . . as . . . hell," I reply.

"It needs some diagonal stabilizing lines. Hopefully they'll install those soon because we'll be crossing this ladder more than a couple times in the next few weeks."

Melissa approaches and Kent balances on the lip of the crevasse, his camera framing her as she steps to the middle. Dave and I are photo-bombing the shot. I stick my chest out and put my weight on my back leg, trying to make the act of standing appear as badass as possible. I'm not exactly sure what Eddie Bauer is planning to do with this footage—blog segments? festival film? back-of-the-store highlight reel?—but Kent's ever-watchful lens reminds me that all my mistakes, naive comments, and unzipped zippers will be archived forever in sparkling HD. Priorities change when you're in front of the camera: look good, have fun, safety third. I flex my biceps and grin.

Melissa and Kent make it across without incident and the climbing scene continues.

Back sweat, forehead sweat, armpit sweat, and sweat behind the ears. The bootpack splits the Cwm in two, Nuptse on the right, the West Ridge on the left, and the Lhotse Face in our crosshairs. Threads of cirrus swirl overhead. The jet stream's probably buffeting the South Col right about now, but here, five thousand feet below, it's as still as a museum. We climb through a gateway of towering penitentes and along a frosty moraine and there's Camp 2 in front of us, a pile of duffels and a pyramid of orange oxygen tanks. My watch says 21,371 feet, which means we're way higher than Mount Vinson and Cotopaxi and most of the other peaks I've climbed. In fact, the only time I've climbed higher than this was on Aconcagua. No wonder my body feels like an empty paper sack.

Sour Patch Kids, ranch Corn Nuts, string cheese, "abundant apricot" fruit leather, three miniature Hershey's Krackels, and half a can of pizza Pringles make me whole again. They say altitude suppresses appetite, but I guess that's only if you're eating Dinty Moore beef stew, smoked oysters, freeze-dried crabmeat, and powdered eggs like Dad did. I can stomach Cheetos and Slim Jims pretty much anywhere.

Dad spent a month at or above Camp 2, a.k.a. ABC, before making his summit push, which is nothing short of crazy when you consider what's known about high-altitude physiology today. Dad chose to stay for two reasons: the team needed someone to push the route higher and he didn't want to go through the Khumbu Icefall again. If Dad had known he'd lose twenty-five pounds in four weeks, would he have thought twice? During their time at ABC, Will Siri subjected the men to a variety of tests. They produced blood and urine samples on a regular basis and even did exercise experiments to record variations in blood pressure, heart rate, and respiratory rate. They were one of the first expeditions to catalog the results in detail, and their research built the foundation for modern climbing strategies. Now we know the body simply can't recuperate at this altitude. Life's a gradual deterioration up here and getting lower is the only way to reverse it.

After half an hour breathing Camp 2's thinner air, we head down, through the gateway and along the wavy basin and across the wobbly ladder. Ninety minutes and we're back to the frozen ripple where our nylon pods wait.

If this acclimatization rotation goes like it should, tomorrow morning will be almost identical to today, but first it's hot drink after hot drink and the SLEEPY TIME playlist on my iPod. I'm sucking down my third mug of spiced cider as Jay Farrar croons "Windfall": "Ketchin' an allll-night staaa-tionnn, somewhere in Louisiana, it sounds like 1963, but for now-ow-ow, it sounds like heavennn." The world's a tangled string of meaningful connections. I've heard this song hundreds of times, but never in a tent at 19,800 feet with Everest looming and stories from 1963 floating in my head. Now the lyrics have a different meaning. I wouldn't be surprised if the next time I hear them, I think about today. For a split second, it does feel like heaven.

Dave taps me on the shoulder and mouths, "Chess?" so I hit PAUSE and he lines up the magnetized pawns. A dozen moves and I already know my king will die, but I play it out anyway because there's daylight to burn.

"Checkmate," says Dave.

I say, "Good game. If I beat you, I'd be worried."

We shake hands like proper competitors and Dave says, "You'll get me one of these days."

"Maybe at Camp 3 when your brain's turning blue."

He pulls out his book of *New York Times* crosswords and flips to a Monday puzzle. He's using a pencil, so I say, "Pencil, huh? Aren't you supposed to do them in pen?"

"At sea level, sure. They're easy down there," he says.

I guess it's easy to erase wrong answers on a crossword puzzle, but wrong answers on the mountain are written in permanent ink.

I press PLAY and let my shoulders sink into my Therm-a-Rest. The haunting voices of the Be Good Tanyas make my eyes heavy and . . .

. . . I'm suffocating! I jolt upright into darkness and hyperventilate.

Breathe-breathe-breathe-breathe-breathe-breathe-breathe.

A termite's tunneling into my skull.

Calm down.

It's okay.

You're at Camp 1 on Mount Everest and that feeling of sinking into quicksand was nothing more than a dream.

I fall back on my Therm-a-Rest and pull the mummy bag around my head and think about how, once I get to the summit, I'll be able to say, *Actually, I have followed in his footsteps.*

I press PLAY again and my breathing begins to slow and . . .

. . . I'm suffocating! Breathe-breathe-breathe-breathe-breathe-breathe-breathe.

Calm down.

It's okay.

You're at Camp 1 on Mount Everest and it's still night, so you don't have to get out of your sleeping bag, not yet.

I roll over and empty my bladder into the water bottle marked "Leif's Pee." I screw the lid tight and zip all my zippers and think about mint-chip ice cream and hot tubs and freshly cut grass tickling my bare feet and . . .

. . . I'm suffocating! Breathe-breathe-breathe-breathe-breathe-breathe-breathe.

You're at Camp 1 on Mount Everest and night's getting brighter, so there's probably no reason to try to fall back to sleep.

I switch on my headlamp and find my handkerchief and blow a knot of coagulated blood out of my nose. Real pretty. Is this what it takes to live up to my old man's legacy? What a raw deal.

Dave stirs in his sleeping bag and asks, "How'd you sleep?"

"Not very good. I guess I got a few hours," I reply.

He shoots me a quizzical glance and says, "You oughta sleep more when you're sleeping."

Dave finds his red lighter and thumbs the flint. *Ksshh.* The stove's blue flame is almost invisible. Onto the stove goes a pot and into the pot goes snow.

We're starting all over again. It's supposed to be easier the second time around, but I'm not sure I'm any stronger or smarter yet.

Breakfast, sunrise, the pregame huddle, and we hike beneath the whitecaps into the Valley of Silence.

Twenty-four hours later, we're running down toward the Damn Deep Ditch and I peer into a fifty-foot crevasse and there's a streak of blood staining a wall. It's a flash of gruesome color standing out amongst so much tumbling white. I hesitate at the edge of a ladder and Dave yells, "Keep moving. Slide right on by. We don't want to hang out in here," so I shut down my brain and keep on running, through the Damn Deep Ditch, down Sugar Hill, beneath the H-Bomb Area, out onto the Football Field, across the Popcorn, and along the Little Bowling Alley to the edge of the Up-Downs.

Base Camp's so close. It looks like it's five minutes away, but the path goes up and down, up and down, forever.

Up.

Down.

Up.

Down.

Up.

Down.

Then it finally does come to an end, and we set our backpacks next to the puja altar. There's a hollow, aching pain in my legs and I'll probably be crippled for the rest of my life, but the air's noticeably thicker at 17,500 feet, so maybe I'll heal. Maybe.

Tuck walks out of the dining tent to greet us. "Yeeehooo! Nice job, boys and girls!" he says, high-fiving each of us in turn. "How was it?"

"Not too bad," says Dave, "except for the H-Bomb Area. That thing sure is scary."

"Clench your butt and get through there quick," says Tuck. Then he turns to me and asks, "How 'bout you, big man?"

"Oh, you know. Piece of cake," I say, but in the back of my head I'm thinking, *How many more times can I go through there and survive?*

26.
LUCKY AND GOOD

Between the puja altar, the kitchen, the dining tent, and the comms tent, that's where the horseshoe pit goes. Tuck's boring into the moraine with an old ice screw and a thermos of boiling water. Jetta and Cancha, Kumar's kitchen assistants, join me with a five-gallon bucket and a shovel to collect Base Camp's finest gravel. A shovelful here, a shovelful there, and the bucket's overflowing. I lift with my legs and hobble back to the construction site and Tuck sledgehammers a stake into the hole. I feel the vibrations of each powerful strike through the rubber soles of my snow boots. Three more swings and the stake's set and out comes a tape measure. Tuck paces out exactly forty feet—regulation length. I wrap strips of red duct tape around the apex of each stake, and that about does it.

I ask Tuck, "Wanna give this thing a try?"

"Bring it on baby. Yeehoo!" he says, pounding his chest.

Tuck disappears into the storage tent and reappears a minute later with two red horseshoes and two blue horseshoes. "I brought these all the way from the States. They're the good ones," he says. "We had one snap in half last year and it almost ruined the entire expedition."

Dave and Melissa walk by so I peer-pressure them into playing.

Tuck's like, "Whoever wants to win can be on my team."

"Me and Leif'll kick your ass," says Dave, and that settles it.

Melissa throws first and it sails way past the pin and lands a foot away from the wall of the comms tent.

"Whoa. Heads up! Harness that cannon," I say.

"Shut up!" she says innocently. "It's my first throw."

"The women's tee box is up there," says Tuck, pointing to a line of red duct tape laid over the moraine.

"I don't need that," says Melissa, a little defensively.

"Yeah," I add, "didn't you see how far that went? If anything, she needs to step farther back."

"Okay. Okay," says Tuck, raising his hands like a soccer player who's just committed a foul. "I'm just saying. It's fine to use it. I would."

But Melissa's not the type to take shortcuts. Her second throw bangs loudly against the backboard and twirls off into the rocks.

Now it's Dave's turn. He swings his arm back and forth three times and releases a blue horseshoe at the apex. It arcs high into the air and, oh shit, it barely misses one of the seven strings of prayer flags attached to the tharshing. Then it dings into the backboard and ricochets violently and, somehow, beyond all reason, wraps around the stake. Dave raises his fists in the air like a quarterback who's just thrown a touchdown pass. "Ringer, ringer, chicken dinner," he says.

"Oh . . . my . . . God," says Tuck, mouth agape.

"Skills!" I shout.

"Are you kidding me? That was all luck," says Melissa.

"Straight talent," I reply.

Dave takes his next throw and it lands a good five feet short of the pin.

"Talent?" says Melissa.

"Maybe it was a little lucky," I concede. "But it's like Tuck always says: I'd rather be lucky than good."

Melissa's like, "I'd rather be both."

A gorak alights on the tharshing, watching the horseshoes fly like it's never seen such ugly birds.

The red team wins two of three matches and we're taking a break from horseshoes until later this afternoon, so Dave, Tuck, and I walk out to Icy Cyber. On the medial moraine of the Khumbu Glacier, about a ten-minute walk from camp, you can sit on a rock and surf the World Wide Web. From the comfort of our tents the wireless signal is too weak, but from here, on a mound of rock a few hundred yards from the start of the climbing route, the signal's powerful enough to load Facebook, send emails, and watch YouTube videos. Icy Cyber's biggest drawback in terms of user experience is glare. Being made mostly of ice, its walls and floor are highly reflective. Tuck's figured out a solution: he brings an extra jacket with him and drapes it over his head, shoulders, and laptop, creating a cocoon of darkness. Thanks to this cocoon, he's able to watch the Los Angeles Lakers game cast, read the online version of the *New York Times*, and scroll through photos of white sand beaches.

Inside my cocoon, Slate.com is all Treyvon Martin and Mitt Romney. I open Facebook. Eighty-seven notifications: about half strangers and half real friends. One random guy says he's "rooting for me." An older woman urges me to "stick with it." Thanks, ya'll. You'd be surprised how much a little friendly encouragement makes the mountain shrink.

On the other hand, why does anybody care? In a world full of real violence, real poverty, real disease, and real environmental catastrophe, how can climbing be considered anything but a wholly shallow and selfish endeavor? I've heard climbers use all sorts of justifications. "We're inspiring people." "We're providing an economic benefit to Nepal." "You can't help others find happiness unless you're happy yourself and the only thing that makes me happy is climbing." Gimme a break. Let's face it, I'm a cracker-white, right-handed, six-foot-five-inch male born in the "greatest country in the world," and how do I choose to spend my time? Putting one foot in front of the other over and over again on a giant heap of ice and stone.

It was different for Dad and his teammates. Besides being experienced climbers and professional guides, many of the team members were professors, researchers, and scientists. As James Ramsey Ullman wrote, "The educational level was positively frightening, with no less than three MDs, five PhDs, and five MAs or MSs (three of whom were working for PhDs)." That's not to mention the BAs and BSs. They studied glaciology, geology, high-altitude physiology, psychology, and many other disciplines during their time in the Himalaya. Additionally, though the team of American climbers did not have a premeditated goal to provide medical or educational assistance to the indigenous people of highland Nepal, they inevitably fell into that role when they encountered individuals who were in desperate need. Along the trail to Base Camp, the team doctors held a clinic each day for Americans, Sherpa, porters, and people from nearby villages. They passed out medications, extracted rotten teeth, cleaned infected cuts and even carried out a few simple surgeries. They also encountered a case of smallpox and could easily have been at the center of an epidemic were it not for a supply of vaccine that the World Health Organization sent from Kathmandu. Within the ranks of their own Sherpa and porters, there was a case of appendicitis and another of double pneumonia. Both patients survived. The expedition made a tangible, direct, and positive difference in people's lives.

I'm scrolling through my news feed and the Khumbu Icefall's right above me and, ugh, it feels like I'm breaking some sort of natural law, but here's a video of a kitten chasing a frog and it sure is cute.

Footsteps on the rocks.

I peek out from underneath my jacket. A tall woman looks for a seat on the moraine next to me. I recognize her. It's Hilaree O'Neill, the famed ski mountaineer. I've heard she's a member of the National Geographic/ The North Face team and that she's planning to climb the South Col this season, just like me. However, unlike me, she intends to *ski* from the summit if conditions are acceptable. She waves hello and takes a seat on a white granite boulder and unfolds her laptop and drapes an extra jacket over the screen. Her lithe, sinewy body hunches over the computer. She looks ridiculous. I must look ridiculous too.

"I'm done," I say, loud enough for Dave and Tuck to hear me.

"I'll walk with ya," says Tuck.

"I've got a bit more," says Dave. "I'll be a little behind you."

Tuck and I follow our footprints back to Base Camp. We slide between neck-high penitentes, cross a narrow stream, and drop into a runnel between mounds of ice. Water drips and rushes beneath me. I stroll through the bottom of the runnel and cross a bench of ice and, whoops, my right leg plunges through a thin veneer and into a foot-deep pool of water.

Tuck can't stop laughing. He offers his hand. I grab hold and pull myself up. "It got ya!" he says. "You all right?"

"Just wet feet," I say. "Surprised me, though. I guess I should pay more attention."

Back in camp Melissa notices my wet boot and asks what happened.

"Fishing accident," I say.

She smirks. "I'm ready for a game of horseshoes when you're dried off."

We're tied at five and it's Melissa's turn. She flings one hard and it slides through the gravel and leans up against the pin. Damn. I guess she's a quick learner. Another powerful swing and her second horseshoe's cartwheeling through the air and it looks like it's gonna be close and then, *BDOOOOOM*, Mount Everest erupts.

"Where is it?" I yell over the thunder, scanning the mountain for the telltale billow of frozen smoke.

"There," screams Melissa, pointing high above the Khumbu Icefall, high above the Western Cwm, to the whitecaps of ice near the summit of Nuptse.

She's right. There it is, a whitewash of powder falling six thousand feet, tumbling and breaking and crashing as it goes. The powder cloud explodes across the crest of the Icefall and slams against the West Shoulder and turns toward us like a wall of water rushing through a curving pipe. The cloud spills outward and crawls over seracs and plunges into crevasses, covering the entire upper half of the Icefall before finally dissipating near the elevation of the Football Field. The earth-shaking bellow fades away and a clear silence follows. Crystals hover in sunlight. Then the silence dies and pandemonium rises in its place.

We rush into the comms tent and Tuck cranks the volume on the radio and keys the mic and says, "Chhering. Chhering. This is RMI Base Camp. Please respond."

Chhering's supposed to be carrying a load to Camp 2 today with Kaji and Pasang. Were they beneath Nuptse when the avalanche hit?

No response.

Tuck tries again. "Chhering. Chhering. Chhering. This is Mark Tucker at RMI Base Camp."

I hold my breath. We're all holding our breath.

Nothing.

"Chhering. Kaji. Pasang. RMI team from Mark Tucker."

Dead airwaves.

Melissa puts her hand over her mouth and Tuck squeezes the edge of the table until his knuckles go white.

"Mark Tucker. Mark Tucker. Chhering here."

We exhale collectively.

"Hello, Chhering. Good to hear your voice. Are Kaji and Pasang with you? What is your location?"

"Yes-yes-yes. Kaji, Pasang. Big avalanche, going down now," says Chhering. He's speaking fast and breathing hard.

"Chhering. Calm down. Is everyone on our team okay?" asks Tuck.

"I think"—inhale, exhale, inhale—"many people . . ." and his transmission cuts out.

Chef Kumar barges into the comms tent and grabs a handheld radio and barks rapid Nepali into the mic. Then Chhering's firing a thousand words a minute and Kumar's interpreting the gist. Chhering, Kaji, and Pasang are all safe. They were close to Camp 2 when the avalanche struck. Chhering confirms that the avalanche came from high on Nuptse and he says the powder cloud crossed the entire width of the Western Cwm. The route between Camp 1 and Camp 2 is likely destroyed and Camp 1 may have been hit. There's no telling how many people are buried. Chhering's on his way to the scene to assist with the rescue effort.

Dave ducks through the door, completely out of breath, laptop case still in his hand. "Did it come from the Horseshoe Glacier?" he asks.

"Nuptse," I say.

The color drains from Dave's face.

I know how he's feeling because I'm also having trouble imagining an avalanche of such magnitude. I recall looking up at the hanging blocks a few days ago and being glad that I was wearing my helmet, but a helmet means nothing in the face of such power. An avalanche like this one—in this location, at this time of day—could easily bury hundreds of people. How many are dead?

Tuck tapes a list of teams and corresponding radio frequencies to the wall above the VHF. He presses the "Channel Up" button until the numbers match the first frequency on the list. "AAI Base Camp from Mark Tucker."

An American voice responds, "Hi, Tuck. This is Joe. All our guys are confirmed safe. How about you?"

"Good to hear, Joe. We're whole as well. I'm doing a roll call and I'll let you know who's missing."

"Copy," says Joe.

Tuck pencils a checkmark next to AAI and dials up the second frequency on the list. The rest of us are listening and waiting and I'm pretty certain we're all expecting tragic news. My heart falls to pieces with the thought of how many people might be dead, but each checkmark glues it back together bit by bit.

Twenty minutes later, Tuck checks off the last name. It's almost unfathomable, but there's only one person reported missing, a Nepali cook who was on the route between Camp 1 and Camp 2.

Willie Benegas, Argentine alpinist and owner of Benegas Brothers Expeditions, rushes inside, a handheld radio dangling from his neck. He's been at Base Camp recovering from a bad case of bronchitis for the past week, but his twin brother, Damian, is up on the mountain right now and he's running down from Camp 2 to search for the cook. Damian's voice crackles on Willie's radio, "Starting next to Nuptse, moving to West Shoulder. Route is completely gone." His Argentine accent is hard to understand, especially when he's talking so fast.

"DamianDamian, watch for second avalanche. More might come down," says Willie.

"Okayokayokay. Tendi will watch."

They'll be scanning for a sign of color in the white debris.

Tuck sits on the edge of his chair, one leg bouncing nervously.

"WillieWillieWillie. We found him. A hundred meters from route, ten meters down in a crevasse. I will go in. Tendi stays on top," says Damian.

"Okay, Damian. Is he alive?"

"I don't know."

Did the blast throw the cook a hundred meters across the ice? Could anyone survive that?

Rachel Anderson from the Himalayan Rescue Association (HRA) steps through the door and now the comms tent is at capacity. The HRA's involved with every serious rescue on Mount Everest, and I guess Rachel came to our tent because Willie and Tuck are helping to coordinate today's effort. Damian will be rappeling into the crevasse right about now and, meanwhile, guides, climbers, and Sherpa from dozens of different teams are contacting Tuck and offering their assistance. Conversations crisscross the mountain in Nepali, English, Spanish, Italian, French, and Hindi. If the cook's alive, he's going to need a lot of help.

"Okayokayokay. He's alive. Cold, hurting," says Damian.

"Good job, Damian. Rachel's here. She will walk you through the medical."

Rachel snags a radio and leads Damian through a proper evaluation. The cook has a head injury and he might have some broken ribs and he's complaining of back pain, but he's stable enough to haul out of the crevasse.

"Can we arrange a helicopter?" Rachel asks to nobody in particular.

An Italian accent comes onto the radio. It's Simone Moro, an Italian alpinist, sponsored athlete, and high-altitude helicopter pilot who has a great deal of experience in the Himalaya. Simone says, "Fishtail sends a helicopter from Lukla. It will be here within an hour."

I step outside and look up at the crest of the Khumbu Icefall. Wispy clouds are veiling the entrance to the Western Cwm. Most helicopter flights happen in the morning, when the weather's usually clear. Dave wonders out loud if it's possible for a helicopter to make it through the clouds. Tuck relays the question to Simone and he responds, "Oh yes. Oh yes. No problem."

Thuda-thuda-thuda echoes up the valley.

The timing couldn't be more perfect. Only minutes ago, Damian reported his rescue team had transported the injured cook to an icy roll on the glacier below Camp 1. It's the same landing zone that was used less than a week ago to extract the body of the fallen Sherpa.

I watch it wend into the wispy clouds above the crest of the Icefall and disappear.

A tense silence.

We're all outside now, waiting, watching, listening.

The sky's pink and gold.

Thuda-thuda-thuda.

The helicopter glides out of the clouds, descending rapidly across the slope of the Icefall with the cook in its belly. A collective cheer rises up as it cruises over our heads, less than a hundred feet from the deck, a beautiful bird on its way to Kathmandu.

Tuck says he'll make mountain mochas to celebrate. He rips open a package of instant cocoa and pours some into a plastic mug. He picks up a steaming French press and asks, "One shot of espresso or two?"

"That depends. Are we playing horseshoes?" I reply.

A mischievous gleam lights up Tuck's eyes. He rubs his hands together and says, "Fish on, baby. Fish . . . on."

27.
ROLL A DIME

"Rockfall everywhere up there. I don't like the route. I think there's a better way farther to the right," says Willie Benegas, munching a lox-and-cream-cheese hors d'oeuvre.

The Camp 2 dining dome is the same size as our comms tent at Base Camp, but it's much sparser. There are no twelve-volt batteries or solar panels or laptops or power strips or fabric flowers decorating the ceiling or laminated photos of surfers carving turquoise waves. None of that. It's a single folding table and four camp stools and a pyramid of oxygen tanks and a white sandbag filled with snacks. Even though the afternoon sun's burning the nylon walls, we're all wearing down suits and booties. On the table, there's a stainless-steel platter of torn-to-shreds salmon and a few remaining crumbs of multigrain crackers.

"We will go up there tomorrow and look for a better way," mumbles Willie.

It's our second acclimatization rotation and our first evening at Camp 2. This morning we climbed directly from Base Camp in seven hours and fifteen minutes, passing through Camp 1 without even opening the tents. It took half an hour to cross the avalanche debris. The glacier had been completely refurbished—crevasses filled in with refrigerator-sized chunks. I was relieved to discover that the wobbly ladder above Camp 1 had been buried, but it was impossible not to imagine what *could* have happened if the timing of the avalanche had been different. I counted fifty-three other people climbing through the debris next to us. I used to think it was a relatively safe part of the route. Now I realize how lucky we all were.

Our goal on this rotation is to touch Camp 3, located at twenty-four thousand feet in a jumble of bench-like seracs on the Lhotse Face, a four-thousand-foot wall of ice ranging from forty-five to fifty-five degrees steep. However, word on the Everest grapevine is that rockfall is showering the usual route up the Lhotse Face.

"That sure sounds like a lot of fun," says Dave, "but we'll let the *real* climbers figure that out before we head up there."

"Yeahyeahyeah. It's like a shooting gallery," says Willie.

"Some fresh snow'd be nice," interjects Melissa.

"Would it ever. Looking at the Lhotse Face makes you wonder if it snowed at *all* this winter," says Dave.

Melissa and Willie nod contemplatively.

"So if we're not going up to Camp 3, then what're we doing?" I ask.

"I was thinking we could go check out the beginning of the West Ridge route. I've never been up there, and it'd be a safer way to get higher while the Lhotse Face gets sorted," says Dave.

Above Advance Base Camp, the American Mount Everest Expedition split into two independent arms: the West Ridgers, spearheaded by Tom Hornbein and Willi Unsoeld, who aimed to explore the previously unclimbed terrain of Everest's West Ridge; and the South Colers, led by Dad, Gombu, Lute Jerstad, and Dick Pownall, who would follow a route—across the South Col and along the Southeast Ridge—that had yielded successful ascents for six previous climbers.

The idea of climbing the West Ridge had originated as a far-flung dream, but as Willi Unsoeld and Barry Bishop made the first journey into unknown terrain above ABC, they were overjoyed to find a feasible route. A snowy thirty-five- to forty-five-degree incline rose 2,400 feet to the crest of the West Shoulder. The West Ridgers made astounding progress on their first reconnaissance trips, establishing Camp 3W ("W" for West Ridge) at 23,800 feet. From there, the climbers could peer down into the glacier-filled basin of the Western Cwm and across the valley to where the other half of their team was climbing the Lhotse Face. For the next two days, thick clouds foiled the West Ridgers' reconnaissance above Camp 3W. The third and final day would determine whether the West Ridgers would continue their exploration of an unclimbed route, or scrap it and throw their energy into the South Col. Willi, Tom, and Barry climbed toward their previous highest point and continued to ascend diagonally over slopes of overlapping, plate-like rock. By 4:00 p.m. the team had made it to 25,100 feet. They traversed back to the crest of the West Shoulder and discovered a perfectly flat terrace. It was an ideal site for Camp 4W. Raising their eyes to the true West Ridge, they saw a formidable wall of rotten rock. It wasn't an appealing sight, but, looking closer, they could see a complex web of snowy couloirs laid over the black rock, leading up out of sight. Perhaps the West Ridge really *could* be climbed. At the very least, it was worth a shot.

To commemorate the fiftieth anniversary of the original climb, two teams are trying to repeat AMEE's route up the West Ridge this year. Eddie Bauer is sponsoring one of them. National Geographic and The North Face are cosponsoring the other. The National Geographic/The North Face team is a single pair of famed alpinists, Conrad Anker and Cory Richards. The Eddie Bauer team consists of Jake Norton, David Morton, Charley Mace, and Brent Bishop, the son of the late Barry Bishop. Their base camp neighbors ours. They sometimes visit for afternoon snacks and horseshoes, but we're usually on opposite schedules—they're climbing while we're resting and vice versa—so I haven't gotten to know them as much as I'd like.

A few weeks ago David Morton showed me some old photos he had found from the 1963 expedition and we talked about how tough climbers used to be. I asked him how many people had climbed the West Ridge since 1963. "It's so hard to tell," he said. "It depends on where you look and what you consider the West Ridge. Some teams have done it via the West Ridge Direct, which doesn't go out onto the face into the Hornbein Couloir. Others have tried the couloir from the north without the ridge, or from Base Camp without going into the Western Cwm, or from the Tibetan side. There are more than a few variations. Between three and twenty people have successfully climbed the route or the variations since 1963. But nobody's been up there in the past twenty years, so who knows what it's like now." I asked him how many people had died trying. "Again, I'm not sure," he said, "but somewhere around twenty." *Those aren't great odds* is what I wanted to say, but instead I told him I was rooting for him, which I am. I like the idea of their following Tom Hornbein and Willi Unsoeld's route while I'm following Dad and Gombu's, but so far neither of the West Ridge teams has been able to make it up to the crest of the West Shoulder. In fact, they haven't even come close. Conditions are reportedly dry and unstable. Rockfall and rotten ice are making for sketchy climbing and both teams are currently at Base Camp, recovering their strength and rethinking their strategies.

On a clear evening like this evening, the view from Camp 2's worth suffering a headache to see. The sun's dropping fast and a shadow's creeping up the Cwm toward me and in about fifteen minutes the temp will plummet to Pluto-like negatives, but right now it's the golden hour and a view like this is one of the main reasons people climb mountains in the first place. I'm standing on this little bump of moraine and off to the west there's the rolling belly of the Western Cwm and a pyramidal spire biting into twilight. To the south Nuptse's spikes of ice stab the sky like the spine of an iguana. To the north, there's the West Shoulder and West Ridge. The approach looks like a straightforward walk over moraine, across benched glaciers, and up a gradual slope of snow, but then the terrain steepens dramatically into a seamless face of ancient glacial ice, bare and uninviting, with a pale tint of baby blue. The face lacks any smidgen of fresh white snow. Winter's melted away. Easier climbing's melted away. It's a mirror reflecting the sunset.

The Lhotse Face is similar. The right side's all rounded seracs and humps of ice, but the left side's flawless, free of the tiniest scar or imperfection. I guess the normal route clings to the boundary between these two features, but according to Willie's reports, every loose rock on the Lhotse massif is funneling into there, and who knows when it'll calm down?

The line of shadow sweeps over me and I feel the tip of my nose go numb, so I dive into the tent and watch my foggy breath rise to the ceiling and think about how mountains are dipsticks that measure the health of the earth. The glaciers are low and it'll take more than a simple oil change to fix the problem.

The next morning I trace Dave's footprints over loose talus and onto a bench that's like the upper deck of a stadium. Ooh, there's a frozen pond up here and it looks ideal for figure skating. I can just imagine Michelle Kwan in a sparkly leotard performing a triple Salchow and carving graceful arcs with the West Shoulder towering in the background. ABC is a smattering of color on the dark moraine just a few hundred yards below us, but how many people have ever been to this place? Dave's climbed Everest almost a dozen times and *he's* never been here, so I think it's a bit of a secret, a beautiful one. It's amazing what you discover when you go off the beaten path, even a step or two.

Kent sets up a tripod and films Dave, Melissa, and me walking across the reflective surface, with crampons instead of skates. Then we're climbing again up a steeper slope of windblown snow that's patterned like a field of wheat bent over in a gust. It's uneven and sharp and hollow, but morning's already softening the sastrugi and they break away beneath our crampons.

Step. Breathe. Step. Step. Breathe.

The usual rhythm feels easier today so maybe the acclimatization rotations are working.

We reach a second bench where a boulder the size of an engine block rests, a strand of nylon webbing wrapped around it. Three ice tools, dozens of ice screws, and an almost-empty spool of white rope are clipped to the webbing. This must be where the two West Ridge teams are caching their gear. Is this the place that Tom Hornbein and Willi Unsoeld called the West Ridge dump? I take a seat in the snow next to the boulder and gaze at the seamless face above.

I don't see a weakness.

Two different paths of crampon prints mark the face. One path traverses diagonally toward the lowest point of the West Shoulder before dead-ending on a blank page of ice. The second path leads straight uphill toward a saddle in the West Shoulder between two prominent spires of crumbly-looking stone. That path's also a dead end. It peters out beneath a rotten section of glacier that's peppered with fist-sized rocks.

"I just don't see any obvious route," says Dave, shaking his head. "And if it's dry down here on the Shoulder, how's it going to be up higher in the Hornbein Couloir?"

"Who knows? But probably not very good," says Melissa.

"I don't think anyone thought it would be this difficult to just get to the Shoulder. And it certainly isn't going to get easier after that," says Dave.

"It's crazy to think how the glacier must've changed in the past forty-nine years," I say.

"I forget, how long did it take the 1963 team to reach the Shoulder?" asks Dave.

"A couple days. Certainly less than a week," I say.

"That's what I thought," says Dave.

"There must've been a lot more snow in '63. Climbing was a hell of a lot harder in almost every way back then, but I guess the conditions might've been a bit easier," I say.

"It makes you wonder if the West Ridge can ever be climbed again," says Dave.

"Yeah," I reply. "But isn't the unknown a big part of the appeal?"

"Maybe. This is a little different, though. It might not be worth the risk. Just look up there," says Dave. He holds out his hand and flicks his thumb like he's flipping a coin. "If you stood in the right place, you could probably roll a dime from the top and it wouldn't stop until it hit the bottom."

While the West Ridgers were exploring the uncharted topography above ABC, the South Colers were having their own adventures. On their first day of climbing past ABC, they reached a protected tier of snow at 22,900 feet beneath an overhanging wall of ice on the Lhotse Face. It was an excellent site for Camp 3. Dad and Gombu woke early on April 8 to pioneer a route to Camp 4. Dad broke trail in soft snow and the pair wove in and out of the seracs along the right side of the Lhotse Face, making it to twenty-four thousand feet before the day grew old. The descent back to Camp 3 gave no respite. Dad and Gombu ran out of marking wands and strayed off the route. They descended into the wrong basin and had to climb back up to return to Camp 3. That night, Dad wrote in his journal: "Down from 24000' on the Lhotse Face and the most beat I have been for a long time . . . Went to Indian route which wouldn't go and then put in new route which required 2 screw leads and they exhausted me. I no doubt worried Gombu below who thought I would peel off and pull us both down . . . Had no lunch—not even drink of water—came down slowly . . . "

Lute and Dick took the lead the following day while Dad and Gombu rested, but even with their fresh legs the Lhotse Face was no cakewalk. Dick took the first fall of his life when one of his crampons suddenly detached. Lute arrested the fall from above and Dick somehow caught the loose crampon before it slid out of reach. At the end of a long day, they finally attained Dad and Gombu's previous high point and pushed beyond it for a few hundred feet, but they failed to reach the planned altitude for Camp 4—twenty-five thousand feet. They returned all the way to ABC that same night, exhausted and unsatisfied.

One day after our visit to the beginning of the West Ridge route, Melissa grabs a handheld radio and jogs past me with a serious look on her face. Word is a Sherpa was carrying a load to Camp 3 when a falling rock hit him in the face. He isn't a member of our team, but that doesn't matter to Melissa or the others who are trying to help him. Broken jaw. Lost teeth. Disorientation. Concussion? Brain trauma? Here at 21,300 feet, a paper cut can take a month to heal and a runny nose can kill you. What's a concussion going to do? He needs to get down the mountain, and fast.

Melissa raises Tuck on the radio and asks, "Can we set up a helicopter evac?" One big-balled pilot with a stripped-down chopper can save the Sherpa's life.

Tuck says he'll call around and get back to her. Three, seven, ten minutes, and there's his voice: "It sounds like we have a problem with payment. No insurance." Dave rolls his eyes as if to say *of course*.

I can tell Melissa's pissed when she replies, "Get me a phone number for the guide service. I'll call them on the sat phone and explain the situation."

Many Everest guide services, including RMI, provide medical and rescue insurance for their employees, but I guess the injured Sherpa's working for a small, cut-rate company that didn't sign him up for anything, which means someone'll have to pay out of pocket. The going rate is about $5,000 for a flight from ABC to a hospital in Kathmandu. That could be more than the injured Sherpa makes in an entire year. I wouldn't be too surprised if Melissa or Dave put it on a credit card because that's just the type of people they are. But they aren't the ones who sent the Sherpa into the shooting gallery in their haste to stock higher camps.

Tuck comes back on and relays a number to Melissa.

Brinng... brinng... brinng. I have no idea what Company Owner looks like, but I imagine he's fifty pounds overweight with a half-untucked, grease-stained button-down and a patchy 'stache. Neck sweat, chewed stogie, and a knockoff gold watch, sitting in a stuffy Kathmandu office.

"*Namaste.*"

Melissa's voice is even-keeled and professional as she explains the Sherpa's injuries. Trauma to his brain could result in his injuries worsening overnight. He needs to get to a hospital immediately. Company Owner isn't buying it. I can't hear what he's saying to Melissa, but from the way her demeanor is changing—agreeable smoothness to angry squint—I can tell that Company Owner doesn't seem to realize how serious the situation is. That, or he just doesn't want to pay for the helicopter.

Can he even imagine the sight of the sheer Lhotse Face? Can he imagine rolling a dime from the top and watching it gain speed until it rockets across the climbing route and smashes into the Western Cwm? He can't see the mountain like we see the mountain.

I guess Melissa is done pussyfooting around because she's like, "Listen, how much is a man's life *worth* to you? How much is a man's life worth?" Her words cut into the Kathmandu office. Company Owner is silent. She goes for the close: "Right now you have a chance to save a man's life. All you have to do is get out your credit card and call Fishtail Air."

Fifty-eight minutes later, a red, white, and blue B3 helicopter glides through waning sunlight into the Western Cwm. The injured Sherpa's lying on a stretcher, his face and head bandaged. A crowd of us stands on a rib of moraine, watching the helicopter's flight. Up here in the thin air, the rotor blades don't provide as much lift as they do at sea level. Even though B3s are designed to operate above twenty-three thousand feet, there's only a tiny difference between how much power is available and how much power is needed. Changes in temperature, air pressure, payload, and weather can easily flip the margin, dragging the helicopter out of the sky, but it looks like this pilot is dialed in. The B3 glides over us, its blades dicing the sunset, and alights on the glacier like a feather landing on the surface of a lake. Melissa helps load the injured Sherpa into the fuselage. She slams the door shut, pats her palm against it twice, and runs away. *Thwucka-thwucka-thwucka.* The helicopter lifts off the glacier until its skids are less than ten feet above the ice. The sound grows louder but the helicopter doesn't rise any higher. It tilts forward and shoots down toward the Khumbu Icefall, rocketing over the undulating surface of the glacier like an albatross skimming the surface of the waves. It falls over the lip of the Khumbu Icefall and disappears from sight. Tense seconds tick by slowly. Hundreds of eyes stare down the valley, waiting for a sign. There it is, rising powerfully into the sky. It banks sharply left and disappears behind Nuptse.

Just another routine day above twenty-thousand feet.

"Gimme a bit of slack," says Dave, so I take a few steps forward and the rope between us drops to the snow. Dave launches himself over a black slot then lands on the opposite side with a thud. Dave keeps moving and the rope lifts up off the snow into a smile and our four-person team's a single entity again, our steps and breaths synchronized to Dave's pace.

In thirty feet I come to the edge of the hole and Kent gives me the same slack I gave to Dave. I plan the jump before I commit. I'll step in that little divot with my right foot and hurdle across and land with my left foot on that solid platform. One, two, three, and I'm flying and it's all wicked air beneath me and then my left crampon strikes and I'm walking again. Well, *that* was fun. I've been roped up like this on dozens of glaciers, but never on Mount Everest.

We're off the beaten path again, away from the fixed lines, over on the southern edge of the Western Cwm. This is where the alternate route goes, the route that Willie Benegas and a bunch of other guides are supposed to be working on today. It's still too dangerous to go up the standard route on the Lhotse Face, but we've got to get stronger somehow, so I guess the idea's to climb as high as we can without being exposed to the rockfall. Melissa, our anchor, executes a graceful jump and we're onto a rolling slope of glacier that tilts steeper and steeper the closer we get to the Lhotse Face.

I wouldn't mind being in front, in Dave's position, because he's taking the biggest risks and, consequently, having the most fun. He gets to pick the route and pick the pace and the glacier's not too complex here. It's not much different than the Emmons or the Easton or the Blue. I could lead us through here safely, but this is Dave's show, so I'll just hang back and try to be a good middleman. Not too much slack. Not too much tension either. If Dave punches into a hole, I'll be the one to catch him. Kent'll catch me and Melissa'll catch Kent and we'll all catch each other. It's exhilarating to be out here alone, just the four of us, exploring a corner of Everest that few people get to see. Out here, trusting our lives to each other, it's easier to imagine how the mountain *used* to be.

Step. Breathe. Step. Step. Breathe.

I'm stronger than yesterday. I can just feel it.

We climb between two tilted seracs that look like the prows of ship-wrecked tankers half buried in the glacier, and arrive at the base of a vertical wall. A group of guides is setting out on the route-fixing project. I recognize most of them because they've all visited our horseshoe pit at Base Camp or played cards in our dining tent. There's Justin Merle, Willie Benegas (or is it Damian?), Lakpa Rita, Max Bunce, and Ben Jones. Chad Kellogg's tied to the sharp end a hundred feet above. He hammers an ice tool into the glacier, pulls down, and kicks with his front points. Crystalline shards break off and swirl like dragonfly wings buzzing in sunlight. Chad twists two ice screws into the wall and waves down for the next climber to follow him up. A Benegas twin traces Chad's path and then climbs past him, wrapping around an overhanging serac and disappearing behind a glassy corner.

Dave peers at the new route with a suspect look. "Do you think clients'll be able to get up there?" he asks Justin Merle, nodding toward the vertical wall.

"I think the first pitch is the worst. It eases off after that," says Justin, his face gleaming with excitement.

Dave, Melissa, Kent, and I have no plans to climb the route today. It's the end of our second rotation and there's no need to go higher just yet. It's the smart decision, the decision that'll keep us healthy and alive, but I'd be lying if I said I don't feel a slight twinge of envy as I watch Justin sink his ice tools into the Lhotse Face. I wouldn't mind being tied into the sharp end of the rope, if only for the chance to see the mountain through Dad's eyes.

28.
WHITTAKER-SIZED BUMP

Day five of our second rotation and we're aiming for thicker air. It's my fourth trip through the Khumbu Icefall and I guess I know it pretty well by now because I'm hopping and sliding and running over the ice without thinking. My crampons bite and my shoulders twirl and I dance through an alleyway and tiptoe across a ladder, keeping Dave's backpack in sight. My brain can't memorize the patterns of the Icefall, but my feet and legs and hips have a memory too. Speed equals safety and our descent's just a controlled free fall. I jump off a kernel and pinball down a corridor and roll out onto a bench, sprinting beneath the A-Bomb serac. I feel like a badass, like I'm Daniel Craig in that parkour scene at the beginning of *Casino Royale*. No. Too angry. I'm smoother than that. I'm more like Sean Connery in his prime, around the time of *Goldfinger* and *Thunderball*, only faster, like Jackie Chan in *Rush Hour*. That's it. I'm the love child of Sean Connery and Jackie Chan. The Khumbu Icefall doesn't stand a chance.

Dave sidesteps to his left and disappears and I'm hustling after him when, oops, I catch a spike and trip. I thrust out my right foot and my knee bangs violently into a sharp corner of ice. *Ouch-ouch-ouch-ouch-ouch-ouch-ouch*. Pain shoots up my thigh and down my shin but at least I don't fall. I squeeze the muscles around my knee and it throbs dully, but everything seems to be working fine and running doesn't make it hurt *more*, so I start running again because there's no time to waste.

Down across the Popcorn and through the Little Bowling Alley and into the Up-Downs, where it's safe to stop for a minute and take off our harnesses.

"I banged my knee pretty good back there. I think it's kinda hurt."

"Really? How bad?" asks Dave.

"Pretty bad."

"Well, it's probably a good idea to take a look," says Dave in a nonchalant tone.

I roll up my pant leg and peel it back, revealing the knee, and, fuck fuck fuck fuck fuck, it's the size of a grapefruit. Literally.

"Aw jeez!" exclaims Dave. "I'd say that's worse than 'pretty bad.'"

"Yep."

"Can you walk all right?"

"Oh yeah. It hardly even hurts," I say. *Jackie Chan, my ass.*

We walk through the last of the Up-Downs and Dave tells me a story about breaking his patella during a past Everest expedition. He says he tripped while walking around Base Camp and smashed his knee on a rock. His entire leg was black and blue from his hip to his ankle. He sat around Base Camp for a month, letting it heal while the rest of the team did their acclimatization rotations. When the clear and warm weather of late May arrived, Dave went for the summit. "I felt great," he says. "Oh, to be young again."

Dave's story reminds me of my back surgery and how waking up after a five-hour operation that was supposed to be a two-hour operation isn't at all like they show on *Grey's Anatomy*. Nausea. Disorientation. Strips of skin ripped off your face from where the breathing tube was taped on. A deep aching pain in every joint of your body because you've been contorted into completely unnatural positions that'd be considered torture if you'd been conscious. Then there was Dr. Bennardo poking my legs and telling me to wiggle my toes and frowning disappointedly when the right leg wouldn't wiggle at all, even though it'd wiggled fine before they put me under. You *fucking did this, you bastard!* He handed me a photograph of the thing he'd removed from my spine, a clump of bloody tissue on a blue paper towel, more than an inch in diameter. *All this from diving for a loose basketball?*

"It was a Whittaker-sized disc," said Bennardo jovially. I would've liked to stab him with his own scalpel if I could've gotten out of bed. I stared at the clump in the photograph and imagined the fatheaded Bennardo leafing through my nerves with cooking tongs and a spatula. Then I puked off the side of the bed. The nurse came around and told me if I didn't pee within the next two hours, she'd have to insert a catheter. I tried to hobble to the bathroom, but my right foot was just a dead stump on the end of my leg. No matter how hard I tried to keep it straight, the ankle would roll sideways into the polished linoleum floor. Empty. Lifeless. Detached. I leaned against the wall, sobbing, absolutely certain that I'd never walk normally again.

People told me to stay positive. They told me to look on the bright side, that it could be a blessing in disguise, but I knew that was all bullshit. I was twenty-three and I'd been an athlete for most of my life and now I was debilitated. There wasn't a bright side.

For the first few months of recovery, I'd wake up in the middle of the night with intense cramps in my hamstring and calf. I had to crawl out of bed and prop my leg against the wall to stretch it out. Physical therapy three times a week and hours of exercises every day strengthened the ankle enough for me to walk again, albeit with a noticeable hitch in my giddyup. I've worked it pretty hard in the past four years, but my right leg is still way smaller and weaker than my left. My toes fold over with the tiniest pressure. My calf twitches and cramps after exertion. No big deal. I try to tell myself, *It doesn't slow you down too much.* But I doubt the nerves will ever be normal again.

Back at Base Camp, I drop my backpack next to the dining tent and walk directly to the HRA. I don't recognize the doctor on duty. He takes one look at the bump on my knee and lets out a long whistle. A poke here, a squeeze there, and he puts his hand on his chin and frowns. "Nothing's broken," he says, "but you have an enormous hematoma here."

"What's a hematoma?" I ask.

"Basically a big pocket of blood."

"So you're telling me that entire bump is filled with blood?" I ask.

"Yep."

The doctor says I have two options: I can let the hematoma dissipate on its own or I can have it drained. The former option might take a while and will manifest into an impressive bruise, but the knee will heal eventually. The latter option will accelerate the healing process but carries an increased risk of infection.

"What would *you* do?" I ask the doctor.

"Drain it. I don't think it'll get infected. And you'll be climbing again before you know it."

The doctor cleans the area around my knee, repeating the process twice for good measure. Then he gets a syringe sealed in plastic. It's the size of a beer bottle and the needle on the end looks thick enough for household plumbing.

"Aren't you going to numb me up?" I ask as he removes the plastic seal.

"No need," he says, aiming the needle.

I recall a story Dad often tells.

In 1978, a few weeks before he was supposed to leave for his second attempt on K2, Dad cut himself while stripping bark from logs at a construction project on the remote Washington coast. He was using a drawknife when it slipped and cut the top of his hand, severing three tendons.

Hours later, he sat in an operating room at Swedish Hospital in Seattle while an anesthesiologist prodded around Dad's collarbone, searching for the best place to inject the anesthetic. Dad, aware that his seven-liter lungs were a full liter above average, warned the anesthesiologist that he was going to puncture his lung, but the anesthesiologist just chuckled and said not to worry.

Dad's arm went numb. A surgeon repaired the tendons and Dad fell asleep in the hospital. Later that night, he woke up with a start, unable to catch his breath. Of course, he had a collapsed lung.

He was the leader of an expedition that was about to leave for the world's second-highest mountain, and he had only one healthy lung and seven working fingers. He decided to have an operation that allowed his lung to expand again. Then, when he was sitting in the hospital bed with a rubber tube sticking out from between his ribs, the anesthesiologist came in. He said something like, "So this is the famous mountaineer who's going to climb K2." Dad wanted to kill him, and he probably could have, but he wasn't going to let a little injury stop him.

A few months later, the 1978 American K2 Expedition put four climbers on the summit.

The doctor sits on a stool in front of me and shoves the needle into the side of the hematoma. He pulls gently on the plunger, but nothing comes out. He drives the needle deeper. Still no blood.

"I'll have to come at it from a different angle," he says, extracting the needle.

On his second try viscous red blood spills into the barrel. The doctor pulls the plunger slowly and the bump starts to shrink until the barrel's nearly full. Then he yanks out the needle, slaps a bandage over my knee, and says, "Ice it. Twenty minutes on. Twenty minutes off. Keep an eye for signs of infection. Come back to see me in a few days and we'll take a look."

I find Dave and Tuck playing rummy in the dining tent.

"What'd they say?" asks Dave, hardly looking up from the cards.

"No big deal. They drained the blood. I'm supposed to ice it. I should be good to go for our next rotation," I say. *Will I really heal in five days?*

"Okay," says Dave, drawing a card.

I actually appreciate Dave's and Tuck's lack of concern. It makes the bump on my knee feel smaller.

"Hey, Tuck. How can I ice this thing?" I ask.

Tuck pauses for a moment, inspecting me with raised eyebrows. "Look around, man. This whole place is made of ice," he says, and then all three of us break into a fit of laughter.

I take a ziplock bag and my ice axe to the edge of camp. I scrape off a layer of rock and sink my axe into underlying ice, unseating brittle shards. After crawling inside my tent, I plop the ziplock full of ice on my knee. I think about Dave's fractured patella, Dad's punctured lung, and my surgically repaired spine. Compared to those injuries, my hematoma's nothing more than a scratch. I've been through worse and I've come out fine. I can get through this.

I pull off my sweaty socks and shove my bare feet into my sleeping bag. Goose feathers wrap around my cold ankles. I take a deep breath and wiggle my toes.

29.
PERSONAL BEST

On April 12, 1963, Dad wrote in his journal, "Tomorrow, if the weather's all right, we're going to put in 4 or else."

The next morning was dark and bitter cold, but as Dad and Gombu set off, the sun rose to greet them, ushering them onward, buoying their spirits. The first two hours were relatively easy. Then the face steepened to fifty degrees and turned from malleable snow into unyielding ice. Dad bent over at the waist and hammered his three-foot axe into the Lhotse Face, chopping hundreds of steps as he painstakingly ascended toward a large serac that, weeks earlier, had been observed from afar as a likely location for Camp 4. Along the way, Dad and Gombu passed the remnants of two old tents that must have been left by the successful 1956 Swiss expedition. But Dad chose not to stop there because they were still far below the large serac. On they went, chopping and kicking, their arms and legs burning. At 24,900 feet, they came to a protected shelf, and Dad was finally willing to halt. Whittling the shelf with their adzes, they built a level platform and anchored a tent.

The view must've been breathtaking, but they took little time to soak it in. After an hour they began their descent, perfecting the stairway and adding fixed ropes along the route. When they finally returned to Camp 3 in the evening, Dad wrote in his journal, "Consider this last real problem of climbing. Hooray."

Three days later, Lute Jerstad, Dick Pownall, Nima Tenzing, and Chotari began the reconnaissance of the route above Camp 4. Turning sharply left, they set out on a prolonged traverse across a giant funnel-shaped wall of the Lhotse massif. Soon they came to the Yellow Band, a layer of bronze schist that ran horizontally across the entire Everest formation, all smooth slabs and shelf-like steps sloping dangerously toward three thousand feet of exposure. To make matters worse, a sheet of bulletproof ice covered the rock. They made slow progress, unable to hammer in pickets or even fasten a coat hanger. It took two hours to ascend the Yellow Band, and by that time the sun was already falling in the sky.

The agreed-upon goal for the day was to forge a route over the Yellow Band. Norman Dyhrenfurth had given specific orders to turn around there. Sinister clouds swarmed the western horizon, but the four men were feeling strong. The two Americans had been breathing bottled oxygen since climbing above Camp 3 and they had plenty left in their tanks. The two Sherpa were climbing without supplementary oxygen, but they were easily keeping up with Lute and Dick. Though there were many reasons to go down, the men looked at the Geneva Spur looming above and decided to continue.

The Geneva Spur, a steep and rugged buttress of dark stone, guarded the ridgeline between Lhotse and Mount Everest. Most previous expeditions had chosen to climb above the elevation of the South Col and over a crown of snow at the very apex of the Geneva Spur, which meant they had to descend about two hundred feet to the site of Camp 5. Lute and Dick decided to follow this route, but Chotari and Nima Tenzing did not. The two Sherpa angled sharply left toward the middle of the Geneva Spur, aiming directly for the South Col. When the Americans crested the crown of snow and looked down on the South Col, they saw their Sherpa teammates already waiting there, grinning cheerfully.

It was April 16 and AMEE had reached the South Col weeks ahead of previous expeditions. They had pulled off an impressive feat and the entire team would benefit.

The highest I've ever been before is 22,841 feet, the altitude of Aconcagua, but that's 6,194 feet lower than the summit of Mount Everest. We're part way up the Lhotse Face and I just stepped across an invisible boundary, breaking my personal record—22,842 feet.

Breathe.

Step.

22,843.

It's our third and final acclimatization rotation and it's a beautiful day—muted cobalt sky, a gust of freezing wind brushing against my bare cheeks, and a wall of naked ice glinting above. I haven't seen any rockfall, at least not yet, maybe because we're using the alternate route. It feels like *real* climbing, especially that one vertical wall at the base. I'll admit it: I was glad I wasn't on the sharp end. I had sewing-machine legs and boiled-lobster shoulders even *with* my ascender gnawing on the fixed line, but it was fun too. It felt like a true challenge.

Step.

Breathe.

Breathe.

Breathe.

Step.

22,845.

A trail of black ropes traces a rudimentary stairway that's been carved into the ice by hundreds of kicking crampons. The stairway climbs over a convex roll, traverses beneath a serac with the texture of a steel drum, and angles toward a camp of red and yellow tents picketed to snowy shelves. Pale sunlight reflects off every facet of the Lhotse Face. The sun's burning the inside of my nostrils and the roof of my open mouth. I can't put sunscreen up my nose because it makes me sneeze. Trust me, I've already tried. I can't put sunscreen on the roof of my mouth either because a warning on the bottle says you shouldn't swallow it. And I can't close my mouth because I'm breathing too hard.

Breathe.

Breathe.

Breathe.

Step.

22,846.

My knee's feeling fine even though the stairway's disappearing now and the ice is harder than my crampons. I try to flex my downhill ankle to allow all twelve points to engage, but it's too steep for that here, so I've got to balance on my toes, my calves burning.

Breathe.

Breathe.

Breathe.

Step.

22,883.

The stairway reappears and I lean forward, bending my uphill leg and resting my forearm on my knee, my head pointed at the fifty-degree slope. I probably look like I'm about to vomit, but I don't feel like I'm about to vomit. I feel like every breath's coming from a sandwich bag. My feet are concrete pier blocks. Camp 3's at about twenty-four thousand feet and our goal's to touch it. It's a final piece of training, like the last few reps in the weight room. It's supposed to be hard, and maybe because it's so hard it produces the largest gains. Suffering today equals strength tomorrow. Climbing mountains is less about strength and more about perseverance.

Breathe.

Breathe.

Breathe.

Breathe.

Step.

22,953.

My thoughts wander to Dad. I recall him trudging up an arbitrary hill outside Lobuche just a few weeks ago. I'll never forget that look he gave me when I tried to stop him. He wouldn't let me stop him until he got to the top of the hill, even though the hill was just a tiny hill in a sea of mountains. Did I inherit his determination? Do genes contain a history?

Breathe.

Breathe.

Breathe.

Breathe.

Step.

23,121.

The Lhotse Face goes on for-fucking-*ever*. It'd be *so* easy to turn around. I could just tell Dave I'm too tired to continue and we'd spin around and the pain'd be gone in an instant. Who am I kidding? I'm not strong enough to do this. I'm no Reinhold Messner or Edmund Hillary or Big Jim Whittaker. I'm a half-crippled, full-of-doubts, searching-for-himself twentysomething in a better-than-you, fame-driven, compassionless world. It'd be *so* much easier to give up.

Breathe.

Breathe.

Breathe.

Breathe.

Step.

23,330.

I think about Dad and Uncle Lou and how they'll look at me if I turn around. I think about Thanksgiving, about cousins asking me if I'd climbed Rainier, and about what they'll say if I fail on Everest. I think about the salmon-breathed guy in the shimmering suit and the gray-haired woman on the Mount Townsend trail and how I'll have to say, "Actually, I *tried* to follow in his footsteps, but it was too hard." Maybe it's easier to keep going up.

Breathe.

Breathe.

Breathe.

Breathe.

Breathe.

Breathe.

Step.

23,577.

Dad loves to tell a story about Ed Viesturs, the first American to climb all fourteen of the world's eight-thousand-meter peaks without using bottled oxygen. Viesturs sometimes uses the number of breaths per step to judge whether or not he's moving fast enough. Five breaths per step is too fast. Thirty breaths per step is too slow. The perfect pace is somewhere in between.

Breathe.

Breathe.

Breathe.

Breathe.

Breathe.

Breathe.

Breathe.

Breathe.

Step.

23,781.

Breathe.

Breathe.

Breathe.

Breathe.

Breathe.

Breathe.

Breathe.

Step.

23,966.

Dave unclips from the fixed line and traverses to an uneven ledge where Chhering, Kaji, and Pasang are digging out a level platform for our tents. I stomp over, set my backpack in the snow, and sit down on it. We still have 5,069 feet of mountain to be climbed, but this place feels like a summit in itself. I'm 1,125 feet higher than I've ever been before. A sense of euphoria washes over me as I peer down at the sun-bleached trough of the Western Cwm.

"Nice work," says Dave. We shake hands.

"Thanks. You too. That was *hard*. I hope I didn't slow you down too much," I say.

Dave glances at his watch. "We did it in six hours. Not bad. Next time I bet we do it in five."

"If you say so," I reply, but my inner voice is like, *yeah right.* We won't be back here until our summit bid at least a week from now, maybe two depending on the weather and the crowds.

"Have a sip of water and something to eat. We'll get the tents up soon," says Dave.

He grabs a shovel and starts digging next to Chhering.

Digging's probably the most exhausting thing I can imagine right now, but when Neil Fiske told me I'd be climbing with guides, I promised myself I'd show the guides I could contribute to the team. I wanted to prove that I could be a partner instead of a helpless client. This is one small chance to earn their respect, so I snatch a shovel.

Chhering greets me when I walk onto the platform. "Hello, Leif-bai! Very tired?" he asks, smiling brightly.

"Yes. Very, very tired," I reply. "Now, how can I help?"

30.
CARNAGE

We've been at Base Camp for a week, watching the weather reports, waiting for the first good window of the summit season, and today's shower day. Jetta collects pails of frigid water from a nearby glacial tarn, carries them up to the shower tent, and pours the water into a thirty-gallon drum. It's sunny today so I'm sure the solar panels are producing enough electricity to power the little pump that pushes the water through an on-demand propane heater. Melissa walks up to my tent, wet hair gleaming, and says, "All yours. It's nice and hot."

"All right. How was it?" I ask.

She smirks and lets out a sigh. "Better than sex."

I step into the first compartment of the shower tent—the changing room. Stripping off my clothes, I glance into a mirror that's propped in the corner and, yikes, what happened to me? It's been more than a month since I've seen myself naked. Every centimeter of fat's gone. My arms and torso are emaciated, except for a band of muscle beneath my rib cage. Is that my diaphragm? Are those the muscles that control my breath? My legs, in contrast to my upper body, are thick and defined. My thighs are so large they seem oddly disproportionate compared to the rest of me. Weird. I look kind of like a grasshopper.

I step into the second compartment and flip a switch on the wall. Water pours out of a showerhead that's tied to a metal stanchion. It's numbingly cold on my hand at first, but a second later it's almost scalding. I slide beneath the stream and, *ahhh*, I see what Melissa was talking about. Hot water's the simplest of things when it's available all the time, but spend a month without it and it becomes a gift from heaven. I stand there and let the water run down my bony back. Warmth seeps into my core. I rub shampoo into my hair and massage my scalp and, yep, Melissa was absolutely right.

All I can think about are the luxuries of normal life. I wish I could sleep in a real bed in a real house with Freya cuddled next to me. I wish I could run barefoot across a field of freshly cut grass and dive for a perfectly thrown Frisbee. I wish I could plop into Dad's recliner with an enormous bowl of mint chip and watch Felix Hernandez spin changeups at bewildered hitters. I cover my body in soap, close my eyes, and dip my head beneath the water again, relishing every lavish drop, lost in my imaginings.

Then a gust of wind blows against the tent and, all of a sudden, the stream of water turns ice cold.

They can probably hear my shriek all the way up at the South Col. Certainly, everyone at Base Camp must wonder where the noise came from—a high-pitched scream of which only Mother Nature could be the creator.

I jump away from the water and nearly fall through the wall of the tent, naked, half covered in soap.

What the hell happened? Maybe the wind blew out the pilot light on the water heater. I flip the switch on the wall, turning the shower on and off, but the water remains as cold as the glacier.

What can I do? I can try to call for Jetta to come and light the pilot. I can wipe the soap off my body with my towel, climb back into my dirty clothes, and light the pilot myself. Or I can shower like a polar bear.

Maybe it's a blessing in disguise. Maybe I was getting too comfortable. Maybe I needed to be reminded that I'm still on Mount Everest, that the luxuries of normal life aren't close at all. Not yet.

I jump beneath the frigid stream. It floods through my hair and down my spine, so cold it takes my breath away.

After years of preparation and months of exertion, there came a moment when Dad and his teammates had to choose to either go up and attempt to reach the summit, or go down to rest and recover at Base Camp. On the morning of April 27, the sky dawned clear and full of promise. It was an easy decision. Dad lashed an American flag to a four-foot aluminum stake. He strapped the stake to his fifty-pound backpack and trudged out of ABC.

Dad, Gombu, Norman Dyhrenfurth, and thirteen Sherpa were the first team, while Lute Jerstad, Dick Pownall, Barry Bishop, Girmi Dorje, and four other Sherpa were a second assault team, following a day behind. Barry had earlier departed the West Ridge effort for a better chance to reach the summit. On the afternoon of April 29, in windless conditions, the first team reached what was known as the most desolate place on earth—the South Col. Four of the Sherpa dropped their loads and descended to ABC, leaving twelve men to spend the night at the South Col jammed into three billowing tents. The men soon found out they had only eleven sleeping bags. Ang Dawa, Norman's Sherpa climbing partner, squeezed in between Big Jim's meaty shoulders and Gombu's heaving chest.

The Triangular Face and the Southeast Ridge waited above. A plume of snow boiled in eddies of black.

Meanwhile, Tom Hornbein and Willi Unsoeld descended through the Khumbu Icefall, returning to Base Camp, where they had started their endeavor six weeks earlier. They felt both envy and admiration for the men headed up. Tom and Willi had declined offers to be included on the South Col team, instead remaining focused on the new route. They hoped that their teammates would make it to the top. If Big Jim and Gombu made it up, it would free Tom and Willi to pursue their ultimate dream.

Dark-as-oil coffee, pancakes, maple syrup, rice porridge with dried blueberries, and Spam: the breakfast of Everest champions. Dave, Melissa, Kent, Tuck, and I are sitting in plastic lawn chairs in the little courtyard in front of the dining tent. The handheld radio hanging from Tuck's neck is set to SCAN. Clear skies. Calm winds. Warm temps. It's a perfect summit window. I scarf my fourth Spam patty and gaze toward Everest and ask, "So how many people are up there today?"

"About two hundred," says Dave.

"And all of them are going for the summit?"

"Pretty much. Sounds like Garrett and Lakpa Rita are waiting at the Col till tomorrow to avoid the crowds, but it's supposed to get cold and windy tonight."

"How many climbers does that leave at Base Camp?"

Dave glances at Tuck. Tuck screws up his face and says, "About two hundred. Give or take."

Tuck's radio picks up wind sweeping across a mic. Between Camp 4 and the South Summit, the mountain tends to block radio signals, so maybe that transmission of scratchy wind was coming from somewhere higher up. The Hillary Step? The Cornice Traverse? From Base Camp, it's impossible to tell what's going on up there. Reality is filtered through hypoxia, fogged-up goggles, clunky oxygen masks, and 11,500 feet of mountain.

It's eight o'clock on the button, which means it's been more than twelve hours since the first team of summit hopefuls departed the South Col. They should be getting close to the top by now. Should be.

Tuck's radio crackles to life again and this time it's a Nepali voice. A garbled message of unfamiliar words rings out from the speaker. I don't know his language, but I don't need to. His tone swells with pride and triumph. He must be at the summit.

A moment of silence and then a celebratory response—*bing-bong, ting-ting, bang-bang-bang*. Cooks and support staff drum metal utensils against pots and pans, cheering into the mic. It's a harsh and dissonant song, but it's joyous nevertheless. It echoes across the airwaves and across the still air at Base Camp.

I take the last pancake and drown it in syrup and there's another voice. Male. Australian accent. "Base Camp, Base Camp, Base Camp. We're on the top!" More pots and pans and *yeehooos!* and a loud "Good on ya, mates!" comes over the radio. Simultaneously, I hear the banging and cheering start up from a camp to the east of us.

I'm guessing the whole day's going to sound like this.

I'll admit it: I'm jealous. I'm jealous that they've put their challenge behind them. I'm jealous that they chose the first good window and it worked out and now they're heading back to ice cream and fresh-cut grass and real beds. Why are we sitting here twiddling our thumbs while

Hedge Fund and the guy who doesn't know how to attach his crampons are probably standing on the special patch of snow where *I* should be standing? I know Dave wants to avoid the crowds and all, but it's May 19 already and the monsoon will be here in T minus eleven days, and will there even *be* another feasible window before then? They call Dave the "Everest guru" because he's reached the summit every year for like the last decade, which means he's good at reading tea leaves. Still, streaks are made to be broken. Is this the year the tea leaves lie?

2:45 p.m. and I think everyone's still okay. Mostly. Justin Merle just checked in from the South Summit, and I guess there was a traffic jam on the Hillary Step that forced him and his clients to wait there for an hour. But Justin sounded crisp and aware and professional on the radio, like he usually does.

We're in the dining tent playing rummy and following the progress as much as we can. Tuck's handheld is blowing up with English, Sherpa, Nepali, Spanish, Italian, Tibetan, Hindi, and Chinese. There are still a few pots and pans being beaten at Base Camp, but the cacophonous revelry's mostly died down now. Some of the voices on the radio are taking on a hint of desperation.

One guy with a gravelly baritone mentions there's an exhausted and combative man on the route between the South Summit and the Hillary Step. Combativeness is a telltale symptom of high-altitude cerebral edema (HACE). Who is the man? Is anyone caring for him? There's no way to know from down here and there's no way to help. The baritone's gone and it doesn't reappear. To us, it's a single anxious sentence lost in the confusion.

There's a report of a woman running out of oxygen because she'd set her regulator to a six-liter-per-minute flow rate, far higher than normal. Our regulators max out at four liters per minute. Is the woman still climbing? Is there an extra oxygen tank available? Our oxygen tanks are at the South Col, far below her, along with the oxygen tanks for the two hundred other climbers who are listening and waiting at Base Camp, impotent like we are.

A British accent asks if anybody can see three Sherpa helping a worn-out client descend the Triangular Face. Apparently, they were at the Balcony when they last checked in and nobody's heard from them for hours. "Can anybody see them?" asks the British accent. There's no response.

A Nepali accent asks about a Nepali man and his sixteen-year-old daughter. When the father-daughter team last checked in, they'd reached the summit and were on their way down. Now they're unaccounted for. "Has anybody seen them?" Again, no response.

A pit of anxiety forms in my gut. Is being able to say you've climbed Mount Everest really worth dying for?

Seven o'clock sharp and Ang Jangbu's voice comes onto the radio, asking for a status report from Justin Merle. Over the course of the day, Justin has become IMG's sweep man, which means he's at the back of the procession, responsible for ushering the last and slowest of IMG's clients to safety. "Well, we're all still alive," says Justin, and leaves it at that. He's been climbing and descending for more than twenty-four hours, but his voice doesn't waver, not in the slightest.

Of course, Justin is strictly responsible for IMG's clients and Sherpa. Many other climbers are still unaccounted for. It's impossible to know exactly how many people remain on the mountain, but it's clear by now that some of them won't make it down alive. It's not the result of a storm or avalanche either. Simple exhaustion is enough to kill you. People assume Everest is a tame adventure and maybe that's their biggest mistake. How many will be missing when morning comes? Six? Eight? A dozen? It could be one of the worst losses of life in Mount Everest history, worse than the 1996 tragedy made famous by Jon Krakauer's *Into Thin Air*. Or it could be a day of miraculous survival. We just don't know.

It's 8:45 p.m. when Garrett Madison, senior guide for Alpine Ascents International, and Lakpa Rita, AAI's head climbing Sherpa, lead their team away from the South Col and toward the Triangular Face. Tuck brings a radio into his sleeping tent and monitors AAI's frequency. Temps will be plummeting and the wind will pick up, carrying pellets of ice that'll stick to the team's jackets and beards, covering everything with a layer of rime. Garrett and Lakpa Rita will be setting a fast pace to keep their clients warm. At least there isn't a crowd anymore. Soon Garrett and Lakpa Rita climb out of radio contact, the mountain blocking their signal.

The atmosphere is somber this morning. Garrett checked in a few minutes ago and one of the words he used is stuck in my head: carnage. He didn't give too many details over the radio, but at least four people are dead, maybe more. It sounds like one body's clipped to the fixed ropes three-quarters of the way up the Triangular Face and another's just below the Balcony. A third was blocking the route between the South Summit and the Hillary Step. It sounds like Lakpa Rita had to cut this body loose and tip it out of the way in order to get past safely.

Dave and Tuck look into each other's eyes and shake their heads solemnly. Dave's voice is heavy with sympathy when he says, "It's too bad they had to go through that."

The one shred of good news is that the Nepali father and daughter are completely fine. Apparently, they'd climbed fast and descended smoothly and they were resting safely in a tent at the South Col yesterday afternoon when the Nepali voice was asking if anyone had seen them. They'd been warm and healthy all along.

Still, too many climbers will not descend at all. Others will lose fingers and toes to frostbite.

Carnage.

And for what? To say they've climbed the highest peak on planet Earth? To check it off their bucket list? To prove they can do it? To make their parents proud?

It's so selfish and shallow and tragic and, even though my inner voice says *you're different*, I'm pretty sure that's a lie. Today we'll let our hearts ache for those who were lost and we'll do what little we can for those who still need help, but tomorrow we'll bury the awkward truths deep in the soil of our pampered self-importance and start packing our things for our own summit push.

31.
NOSES TO ASSHOLES

I crawl out of the vestibule into harsh sunshine and look past IMG's Eureka! tents, and my heart takes a seventy-five-foot whipper onto a questionable screw and goes *splat*. A single-file line of climbers is trudging up the Lhotse Face and there's got to be at least two hundred of them, but it's impossible to count because I can't tell where one climber ends and another begins. Chests and necks and shoulders blend together. Legs bend and straighten in unison. It's a red, yellow, and orange centipede that's undulating over the baby-blue ice toward the Geneva Spur. Dad and Gombu could never have imagined such a sight.

"Noses to assholes the whole way up," says Dave. "Don't let anybody get in between us."

It's May 24 and half of the Everest population is back at Base Camp, nursing their wounds, celebrating their triumphs, mourning their losses, and packing for the journey home, but the other half of us aren't finished yet. It's our turn now. This is the final weather window of spring and we're dashing madly for the summit.

Dave stomps across our hand-carved platform and slices into the centipede without asking permission. He straddles the fixed line and sticks his butt into the next climber like he's blocking out for a rebound. Dave gives me a let's-go-let's-go wave, so I jostle in behind him. Melissa and Kent make their own incision and then we're cruising along together, a four-person link in the chain.

The valve on my oxygen mask clunks with every breath. Step. Step. Step. Clunk. Step. Step. Step.

There are about fifteen people in front of us, but I think we're moving faster than most of them. We're pulling away from the people behind and gaining on the people in front. The stairway's even and firm. Step. Step. Clunk. Step. Step. Clunk. Cold air rushes into my throat. Every breath stings. Dave unclips from the fixed line and motors past a group of three Sherpa without breaking rhythm. I slide a few feet off the stairway and follow him. It's steeper without the stairway and my calf muscles strain to hold me up. Climbing's so much harder when you forge your own path. Thirty feet and my legs are twitching. At least I'm in front of the three Sherpa now and it looks like open water ahead. Dave reduces the pace a notch or two. I hear steps and clunks behind me. It's not just Melissa and Kent either. The rest of the centipede's slithering after us. *Let's go, let's go, let's go!*

The stairway bends sharply left and turns into a sidewalk—a two-foot-wide shelf traversing the Lhotse Face. It's not much different than a trail cut into a steep hillside in the Cascades or Olympics, except it's all ice and a fall here would mean a 2,500-foot slide into the Western Cwm. Step. Step. Step. Clunk. Step. Step. Step.

The slabs of the Yellow Band are the color of rotten straw. Thin scratches pattern the rock like the engravings of a thousand fingernails on a chalkboard. Are any of the scratches from Dad and his teammates? My spikes leave their own impression as I scramble over the slabs after Dave. Up ahead, Mount Everest pokes into the blue. It's not far now. Off to my right, the Lhotse Couloir's a bumpy line of white like the contrail of a jet.

At the foot of the rocky Geneva Spur, I look up and see a dozen climbers with cumbersome packs coming down. They must be carrying loads of equipment back to ABC, so maybe there will be fewer people at the South Col. Since there's no way to get past them, we wait, leaning into our harnesses, ascenders biting the black fixed line.

Twenty minutes and we're moving again, crossing the Geneva Spur where Chotari and Nima Tenzing discovered a shortcut forty-nine years ago. The rock of the Geneva Spur forms interlocking sheets, some as thin as cardboard and others as thick as the spine of a dictionary. The entire Spur looks like a sculpture of a library tilted on its side, books falling out of the shelves here and there. We crest the Spur and the wind immediately picks up. Lhotse's no longer protecting us. The South Col, a saddle in the ridgeline that connects Mount Everest to Lhotse, is directly ahead. A layer of stale, wrinkled ice covers the saddle like old skin hanging loosely from a bony spine. Dozens of bright tents cling to the ice, their walls flapping and their poles flexing beneath gusts. My watch says 26,013. Welcome to the death zone.

The death zone isn't too stormy today, so I guess our window's holding. Lhotse and Mount Everest funnel the weather through here, but right now it's just wispy clouds in an indigo sky. A horizon like a blank page torn in half. A wall of snow-etched stone. It wouldn't be a bad day to be standing on the summit, although the plume's churning like those photos I've seen of Saint Helens erupting.

Dave, Melissa, Kent, and I scurry into the South Col. Chhering, Pasang, and Kaji are already here, constructing tents. They don't have to ask for our help. Dave and I wordlessly take over the construction and anchoring of one tent. Pole tips into grommets. Plastic hooks over aluminum. I hold it in place while he guys it out. The tent goes together without a wasted motion. I like when we work as a team.

I unclip my crampons and toss them in a corner of the vestibule and dive inside. Dave dives in after me.

"You can take your mask off," he says. "We'll use the cannula in the tent. Set your regulator at a half-liter flow. Try not to use it all the time, but definitely when you're sleeping."

Off comes the rubber Darth Vader mask that's been sealed against my cheeks all day and in goes the two-pronged plastic tube. It's exactly what you'd see on an emphysema patient. The prongs go in your nostrils and the tube wraps over your ears. I twist the knob on my regulator until the tiny arrow lines up with "0.5." Cold gas stings my nose and it hurts worse than it should so I pull out the prongs and, uh oh, they're red with blood. I'm twenty-seven years old and I'm dying like I'm ninety-fucking-three. The blood's not dripping, though. Maybe it's too thick and dry to drip. Thirty seconds off the O's and a headache swells behind my temples. My toes are going numb and my heart's racing at 114, 115, 117, 120 beats per minute. I jam the prongs back in. Every breath stings, but it's better than the alternative. The swelling in my temples recedes. Still, it's not gone completely. It'll probably be there for the next two days, two weeks, two years, or however long it takes me to recover from this little vacation.

Dave's cracked thumb flicks the flint of a red Bic. Onto the flame goes an aluminum pot and into the pot go chipped-off shards of the South Col. *Ksshh.* The stove's a miniature rocket shooting from the floor of the tent between Dave and me.

"So we're going for the summit at midnight?" I ask.

"Ideally. But we'll see what the weather and crowds are doing," says Dave cagily.

"The weather's supposed to be good. Right?"

Dave shrugs. "Sup*posed* to be. But Everest makes its own weather."

"How long can we stay here before we run out of fuel and O's?" I ask.

"Tonight and tomorrow night. If we haven't made it up by then, we'll be too dead to go up there anyway."

Living in the death zone is a gradual deterioration like a battery running out. There's no way to recharge, and the longer we spend here the weaker we get. Climbing tonight is the best option, but if the crowds and weather don't cooperate, we'll be forced to spend a day interned in the tent, muscles melting and lungs shriveling up. Fuck that. I've been patient long enough. The summit's only three thousand feet away. Just try to stop me.

Twelve men awoke at the South Col on April 30. Dad and Gombu led the pack across a gradual plateau and then into a steep couloir rising to the Southeast Ridge. Norman Dyhrenfurth and Ang Dawa trailed behind, snapping photos and recording video as they went. The wind picked up to a gale. Sheets of windblown powder cloaked the couloir ahead. Norman caught flashes of Big Jim and Gombu belaying over loose rock, traversing blue ice, and inching their way up the couloir.

Dad and Gombu crested the Southeast Ridge and curved left toward the South Summit, where they discovered remnants from past expeditions. Here was a tattered tent with rusty poles. There was a pile of discarded oxygen bottles. At 27,450 feet, just past the remnants of a Swiss camp, the men dropped their loads and began digging out a flat platform big enough for two tents. They dug for two hours without breathing bottled oxygen. When the tents were secure, one to rock and one to snow, eight of the Sherpa departed. They wished Dad and Gombu good luck, waved good-bye, and disappeared into the windblown snow.

Norman and Ang Dawa soon arrived and crawled wearily into the second tent next to Dad and Gombu's nylon domicile. At forty-four, Norman was one of the oldest members of the expedition and he had now climbed higher, by many thousands of feet, than he had ever been before.

Sunset waned and the wind accelerated to deafening gusts. A blizzard streaked the darkness. The tents thrashed in the storm.

Inside, the men began the arduous process of melting ice. At that altitude, even the mildest exertion caused a feeling of suffocation. Cooking was no small task. Water at a boil was cool enough that Dad put it directly to his cracked lips and drank it down in a single gulp. Sleep was nearly impossible. They floated in and out of consciousness as the storm raged, straddling the ridge between reality and imagination.

With the storm blossoming into its most sinister stage, Dad must've had doubts. Would the wind ever stop? Would Mount Everest allow them to reach the top?

Six o'clock and the weather's gone to shit. It's like someone accidentally hit the button labeled BLIZZARD. Big ol' cumulonimbus sweep across the South Col and, in seconds, the evening sky goes from an inviting golden hue to a choking mess of white. A humming sound comes from outside like a soft breath pushed through a harmonica. What *is* that? It's making my skin crawl. I peer outside. I can't see Melissa and Kent's tent even though it's only a few yards away. I can't see Mount Everest even though it towers thousands of feet above. Night swoops down and the landscape is a pixel pattern of TV static.

Inside, Dave turns on his headlamp. A tube of lifeless blue light shoots out from his forehead. His face is all shadowy and it makes his skin look like a threadbare rug. I send him a this-fucking-sucks look and he pinches his lips together in fatalistic agreement. He picks up the radio. "Melissa. Melissa. This is Dave. How's it going over there?"

"Hi, Dave. Not too bad, except for the weather," Melissa responds.

"Yeah. I don't think tonight's our night. So let's rest up for tomorrow."

"Copy that."

My heart and stomach trade places. Is the weather really going to get better tomorrow night? What if it gets worse? We'll have less strength and energy to cope with a storm. Dave doesn't seem too concerned, which is annoying. Sure, he's been to the summit eleven times already, but *I* haven't been up there once. Maybe it means more to me than it does to him.

He peeks under the pot lid and says, "Might as well have another hot drink. Then we should sleep. Or close our eyes, at least."

32.
DOT

On a night like tonight, when frozen clouds obscure the stars, when bursts of wind punch the tent walls into my face, the South Col's a humbling place. The landscape and the storm don't care that I'm the youngest son of the first American to summit the highest peak on planet Earth. They don't care how much I've trained or how strong I am or how long I've dreamed about Mount Everest. They don't care about the Saint Christopher medal and the red string. On a night like tonight, the flame of our stove is what matters. The warmth of my sleeping bag is what matters. The strength of the pickets driven into the ice around our tent is what matters. A night like tonight whittles away emotion and imagination. It breaks things down to their simplest form. I have to pee.

But on a night like tonight, peeing's a dangerous proposition. The water bottle marked "Leif's Pee" is already full. I've been guzzling grape Tang like it's pouring from the Fountain of Youth and I think I've peed half a dozen times since we got here. The good thing is my pee's the color of lemonade, which is a lot better than the color of 10W-30, but the bad thing is I have to crawl out of my warm cocoon and go outside. It's all swirly and white out there. I still can't see Melissa and Kent's tent. But I can't think of a way to avoid it.

My boots are frozen stiff, so I yank out the liners and slide my socked feet into the shells. I strap a pair of clear-lensed goggles over my face, touch the button on my headlamp, pull the cannula out of my nose, and crawl through the vestibule into black and white. The wind's picking snow up off the ice and flinging it all over the place. Crystals coat my goggles in a split second and I can't see a thing. I can't even see the moraine beneath my feet, so I slide the goggles down around my neck and squint into the storm. I don't need to go far. Just a few steps.

The wind jukes and darts like a fish evading a predator. Half of the contents of my bladder end up in the snow and I think the other half's divided between my boots and down suit. At least it's out. I crouch low to the moraine and empty my pee bottle in a crevice. Thank God I won't have to leave the tent again until morning.

Where *is* the tent? I thought it was right behind me but, oh fuck, it's gone. In fact, Camp 4's gone entirely, engulfed in the blizzard. A rush of fear and adrenaline runs through me like I used to get, when I was a kid and terrified of the dark, stepping outside our house at night. I could die here, just a few steps from the tent, and nobody'd be the wiser. FAMOUS CLIMBER'S SON DISAPPEARS WHILE URINATING or JIM WHITTAKER'S SON FEARED DEAD ON WORLD'S HIGHEST PEAK. The news stories will identify me as the son of Jim Whittaker, but they'll fail to mention me by name. No more than a paragraph will be devoted to explaining the circumstances of my death, but the story will go on for another five pages with quotes from Dad and a description of his legendary ascent. A cloud of frozen dust stings my eyes. The beam of light coming from my headlamp runs into the storm's white flecks of static. I don't know which way to go.

Another cloud of frozen dust swirls at me and I instinctively close my eyes. When I open them again, I see something in a patch of snow. Relief floods me. I see a footprint.

The wind's filling it in quickly, but there it is, clear as day—an arrow home. I step into the footprint. I guess the wind's changed it because the outline's a bit bigger than my boot.

Three more steps in a straight line and I glimpse a tab of reflective fabric glowing back at me like a wolf's eye. It's the vestibule of my tent. My crampons are lying in the corner, right where I left them. I unzip the door and dive inside. Dave's lying on his shoulder, facing away.

"How was it out there?" he asks without rolling over. His voice sounds like it's being transmitted from deep underwater.

"Not bad. I almost died emptying my pee bottle, but otherwise not bad," I reply.

"I'm glad *that* didn't happen," he says.

"Me too."

"You should try to get some sleep," he says, emptily because he knows it's impossible.

I shove the cannula in my aching nose and turn off my headlamp and listen to the wind—a raspy hum coming from the east. I try to let my neck and shoulders relax. Breathe deep. Let the breath go like it's sand slipping through spread fingers. Imagine climbing to the summit. *I will climb Mount Everest. I will come down alive.*

Dawn. The sky's clear enough for me to glimpse a distant line of climbers inching up the Southeast Ridge toward the South Summit, like the dots in vanilla-bean ice cream. There must be over a hundred of them. Dave twists the knob on his handheld radio and eavesdrops. There's a report of frostbite and a potential HACE victim, but his Sherpa guides are ushering the man to safety. More than anything, there are pots and pans and crackly *yeehoos!*

I give Dave a questioning look and he brings his open hand up under his armpit as if to say, *Don't blame me.* But he's the one who made us wait until the very last good window of the season, and he's the one who decided *not* to go for the summit last night. Now we're committed to tomorrow. Our bodies can't afford to wait any longer than that, no matter what the weather does. If it's too stormy to leave the tent at midnight tonight, we'll be going home without even having a chance to touch the summit. I'm probably stronger than most of the tiny black dots, but that doesn't really matter now. Strategy's what matters. Luck's what matters. Maybe Dave's got the wrong strategy and maybe his luck's finally run out.

A door zips open and a head sticks into our tent.

"Hi, Dave. You guys wanna join me for a walk?" It's Conrad Anker. He's not wearing a cannula or oxygen mask.

Weeks ago, Conrad and Cory Richards abandoned their attempt on the West Ridge, as did the four-person Eddie Bauer team. Conditions were ultimately too dry and dangerous on that part of the mountain. Some new aerial photos of the Hornbein Couloir showed a veritable death-gulley of choss and rotten ice. I heard that Conrad had switched his permit to the Southeast Ridge and would attempt to climb without bottled oxygen. Like us, Conrad arrived at the South Col yesterday, hoping to make a summit attempt last night.

"I wasn't feeling very good, so I bailed," says Conrad. "But I've got to collect some rock samples for Montana State University and I need a partner or two."

It sounds like an exhausting way to break the monotony, but I guess there's nothing better to do and I probably won't need my energy reserves tomorrow anyway.

"Maybe we can find an oxygen bottle or something from '63," says Dave.

I like that idea but I just nod curtly, sending him a whatever-you-say look.

Our crampons cut a scar into blue ice. Scattered cobbles pool in divots and trenches. There are remnants of past expeditions everywhere—tent poles poking through faded nylon like broken bones through skin, empty fuel canisters, packages of ramen noodles, torn sleeping bags with synthetic fill spilling out, toilet paper folded into clumps of desiccated shit, twisted pickets, a single boot with a missing sole, a pair of navy fleece pants partially buried in the rocks, a threadbare lime-green backpack, a plastic water bottle without a lid, chemical hand warmers, furry climbing rope, corroded carabiners, and dozens of yellow and orange oxygen bottles.

Dave and I follow Conrad easterly, toward a pillowy outcrop the color of a cast-iron skillet. Even without O's, Conrad's faster than us. There's no rush, though, because there are lots of old oxygen bottles to inspect.

"Let's split up," says Dave. Fine with me. I turn my back on him while Conrad jogs off in search of his samples. The glacier is bare ice here, not a hint of snow, and the old oxygen bottles stick out like pills strewn across a glass tabletop. Each one's different, but the older ones are long and skinny—bazooka shaped—rather than short and tubby like the newer ones. Numbers and letters—some of them Russian—are stamped on the bottles, and there's usually a date. I'm looking for anything before the seventies.

I peer across the ice, trying to imagine, to sense, where Dad and his teammates might've put their camp. It feels like I'm in the right place, off to the east of the fixed ropes, beneath an icy couloir hanging from the Southeast Ridge. There's a nice flat dell in the glacier where a tent might've gone, so I trace the dell from east to west, hopping from old bottle to old bottle. I find an ancient-looking one with yellow casing that's partially unwound. It looks like a stretched-out Slinky, which is pretty cool because it's different than the others. There's a date stamped into its neck: 1976. That's the oldest one I've seen, so I hoist it off the ice. It's ten pounds easy, maybe fifteen. I don't think it's worth carrying down, but maybe Dave has found a bottle from '63 and we can trade.

Dave and Conrad are both wearing red down suits, but I can tell them apart from Dave's loping stroll and Conrad's bouncy hover.

"What'd you find?" asks Dave. He's not carrying anything.

"This one's from 1976," I say. My throat stings when I talk.

Dave and Conrad debate whether the bottle came from a British and Nepalese Army expedition or from an American expedition. There's no way of telling, but it's an artifact either way.

"Are you going to keep it?" asks Conrad.

"I don't think so. Too heavy," I say.

"Do you mind if I take it?" he asks.

Conrad climbed all the way up here without a full bottle of oxygen on his back and now he wants to carry an empty one down. Is a piece of history really worth the extra suffering? Maybe I *should* want to keep it. "Go right ahead," I reply.

Conrad slings the bottle over his shoulder like a bindle and jogs off toward the tents. I turn to Dave and shoot him an are-we-done-here look. "So nothing from '63, huh?"

"Nothing. I guess it's all been taken already," he replies. "Sorry."

"No worries," I say brightly, trying to veil my disappointment.

Maybe there's really nothing left of the mountain Dad and Gombu climbed. Maybe the pundits and message-board commenters and armchair climbers and desk-bound journalists are right. Maybe Everest is not worth climbing anymore. Then why do I still want to stand on the summit so badly?

Climbers are coming down from the summit now, filtering into Camp 4 one at a time, or in groups of two and three. A man sways back and forth with every step like he's hanging from a noose. People walk on each side of him, holding him up by his shoulders like cops escorting a convict. A lone woman stumbles toward the tents a few steps at a time. Between stumbles she bends over at the waist, puts her hands on her knees, and points her head at her feet. I don't think I'd ever be that fatigued, but you never know.

The mountain disappears and we're inside a cumulonimbus again. People keep coming down out of the white, one after another. More banging of pots and pans on the radio. More *woot-woots!* Everyone's alive. It's been a good day on Mount Everest, and instead of celebrating we're melting glaciers into water again and chugging fruit punch Kool-Aid. Dave peers out of the tent into the white. He furrows his brow like he's stuck on a Sunday crossword clue and his chest falls with a sigh.

The volume of the wind ticks up a notch or two. The clouds thicken into a heavy alfredo. Sunset's an hour-long fade to black. There's an odor in the tent like burnt popcorn mixed with turpentine. How has it come to this?

We've done everything right, but we're going to fail. We're subject to the whims of the mountain now. The mountain's simply happening, and for a brief moment we're watching it, feeling it. Tonight I feel like a dot of graphite on a clean sheet of paper—insignificant and erasable. In all my life, I've never felt this small.

33.
ONE CHANCE

The wind gusted to seventy miles per hour on the morning of May 1, 1963. Sir Edmund Hillary, who was camped at the base of a nearby peak, saw a wild plume rolling off Mount Everest's summit. He called the weather impossible. Nobody would dare make an attempt that day. Dad and Gombu had a more intimate view. Ice crystals peppered their tent—the sound of a hundred snare drums. The wind punched the walls of the tent into Dad's head and shoulders. Dad boiled snow and prepared a breakfast of freeze-dried crabmeat, tea, and red Jell-O.

When Dad peered outside the tent, he had probably already made his decision to go for the top. Based on his and Gombu's climbing experience, and the confidence they had in their strength and will, the weather didn't matter much. According to James Ramsey Ullman, Dad would later say, "We had climbed in worse, and we decided to go on up and make our try." He turned to Gombu, pointed his forefinger in the air, and said, "We go up." Gombu simply nodded.

When Dad crawled outside, he was enveloped in a chest-high blizzard. Above, the sky was clear. Below, it was a whiteout. Gombu's goggled head appeared to be floating on a layer of blowing snow, eerie and bodiless. I can imagine Dad thinking, "Dammit, we've come this far. I'll crawl the rest of the way if I have to."

On his feet he wore three pairs of wool socks, his Lowa Eiger double boots, knee-high nylon overboots, and a pair of twelve-point Grivel crampons. On his legs he wore cotton-wool underwear, down underwear, wool pants, and a pair of down-filled outer pants. On his top half he had a cotton turtleneck T-shirt, a down sweater, a wool shirt, a waterproof jacket, and a down parka. On his hands he had lightweight nylon gloves and wool mittens with leather and canvas shells, and he would later switch to down mittens. On his face went ski goggles with dark lenses and his Maytag oxygen mask. He covered the top of his head with a wool beanie, the hood from the waterproof jacket, and the wolverine fur–lined hood of the down parka. His backpack contained two full oxygen bottles, a length of three-eighths-inch nylon climbing rope, a Nikon F camera, two water bottles, a radio, a first-aid kit, extra clothing, food, a minus-thirty-degree sleeping bag, and a four-foot aluminum stake with the American flag lashed to it. All together, it weighed about forty-five pounds. At 6:15 a.m. he took his first deliberate steps toward the summit, Gombu close behind. There was no turning back.

Storms seemed to follow Dad. The weather was equally dismal for him almost thirty years later, when he returned to Everest for the 1990 International Peace Climb. Bud Krogh and Warren Thompson had approached Dad more than three years before the fall of the Berlin Wall with the idea to send climbers from the world's three superpowers—China, the Soviet Union, and the United States—to the summit of Mount Everest together in order to demonstrate what could be accomplished through teamwork and cooperation. Amid Cold War tensions, the expedition would represent the desire of common citizens for a safer, saner, more peaceful world. They also wanted to climb the mountain leaving as little trace as possible and even remove decades' worth of garbage from Mount Everest. Dad would be the overall leader of the expedition. He and Mom worked tirelessly for more than four years to organize the complex international effort. Mom would have likely been a member of the climbing team if she hadn't had to take care of my brother and me. If she and Dad had gone to Tibet together, they would've had to leave us for three months, not to mention risk both their lives. So Mom remained in Port Townsend, working as the executive director of the expedition. "That decision turned out to be fortunate," Dad wrote, "for without her help from home at a critical point in the expedition, we might not have climbed the mountain at all."

By May 1, 1990, the team of American, Soviet, and Chinese climbers had established camps high on Mount Everest's North Ridge. Everything was in place for their summit bid, but the weather wasn't cooperating. Gale-force winds hammered the mountain throughout the day and night. A blizzard deposited one inch of new snow per hour. Dad called Mom on the satellite phone and updated her on the situation. "It's so windy people are flying like kites on the fixed ropes. If this wind doesn't stop, we're going to have a hard time making the summit," Dad said.

Mom called her friend, Susanne Page, who had spent years amongst New Mexico's Navajo and Hopi tribes. In an effort to change the weather on Mount Everest, Susanne contacted her Navajo friend, Mare Sultclah, a highly respected medicine woman. According to the medicine woman, it was sheer arrogance to think of stopping the wind. However, she said, she might be able to move it.

At dawn on the morning of May 6, the wind on Mount Everest suddenly vanished. Dad called Mom on the satellite phone.

"It's amazing," he said. "It's perfectly calm here. It's a great summit day. I guess Susanne's Navajo friend must have moved the wind."

"She sure did," said Mom. "It's blowing about eighty-five knots here, four trees are down in the yard, and a couple of boats were capsized in Puget Sound—that's pretty unusual for this time of year."

Even though I was only five, I remember when the storm hit Port Townsend that May. From the kitchen windows I watched the cedar trees in our backyard sway and groan in the wind. From the living room I watched whitecaps crash together in the Strait of Juan de Fuca. Menacing clouds swept the sky like spilled ink. It was a furious storm and it terrified me, the way it pressed everything closer. I wanted Dad to be there. I wanted his booming voice to drown out the storm and his huge presence to fill our house again. I was upset with him for being gone. I didn't understand why he had left.

That morning, six climbers—two from each country—reached the summit together. Over the next three days, in perfect weather, fourteen others reached the top, making the 1990 International Peace Climb the most successful expedition in Mount Everest history. One of these climbers, Ekaterina Ivanova, became the first Soviet woman to stand on the summit. Her radio message to Base Camp brought tears to everyone's eyes. She said:

"I stand on top of the highest mountain on planet Earth, for all the women in the world. Let there be no more borders, no more war; let us make a safe and clean world for our children and our children's children."

It's nine o'clock at night and failure appears more likely than success. The clouds are thick and the wind's humming a frequency I feel in my teeth. Nobody would dare climb into this storm, but I'd rather give it a shot than run home with my tail between my legs. How much am I willing to sacrifice? A pinkie toe? Probably. A big toe? Maybe. My life? Certainly not. But hell, if I'm losing big toes, my life can't be far behind. Dad and Mom'll be devastated. My friends'll cry at the funeral. The world'll wonder why I climbed into the storm, why I accepted the risk. Jon Krakauer will write a best-seller about my demise.

Failing to even make an attempt to reach the summit might be worse than dying. Dad and Mom'll console me. Everyone in Port Townsend will be so disappointed. My sponsor will never fund me again. People will ask why five hundred others could make it up, but I couldn't. I'll try to explain the situation—the weather, the dwindling oxygen supplies, the debilitating death zone—but people won't understand. Worst of all, I'll never have another chance to summit Mount Everest.

My watch says 10:03 p.m. and the storm's still here. Dave melts pot after pot of ice. I don't really want to ask him what he's thinking because I'm afraid of what he might say. I'm afraid he'll tell me, in his casual guide tone, that we've got to go down. I'd rather not hear those words uttered out loud.

10:33 p.m. and the clouds are as thick as the ocean in the middle of the Pacific. We're probably done now, but there's still a shred of hope in me. I can think of nothing else to do but ask for help.

But what or who is going to help me? I can think of nothing more powerful than the very mountain I hope to climb. *Please, Mount Everest. Please, Chomolungma. Give me one decent shot to climb. That's all I ask for. One chance. Please give me one chance.*

I repeat the request over and over in my mind. The tent walls snap in the wind like the leech of a drum-tight sail. I bring my hand to my neck and grasp the Saint Christopher medal tangled with the red string and repeat the request again until, by some small miracle, I fall fast asleep.

A strange sound wakes me. It's a sound I haven't heard for days: silence.

I jolt upright. The tent walls are as still as a pair of trousers hanging slack on a clothesline. It's 10:57 p.m., which means I've been asleep for only about twenty minutes, but it's the longest sleep I've had in the last thirty-six hours. I stick my head out the vestibule and, wow, the sky's alight with stars. A dotted line of headlamps shimmers on the Triangular Face. There's not a whisper of wind. The glacier reflects the ghostly light of a half-full moon. Mount Everest grins like it's mildly amused and beckons me upward.

On a night like this, when footsteps and deep breaths are the only sounds to break the vast silence, Mount Everest is a friendly place. Dad and Gombu weren't so lucky. Nor were Sir Edmund Hillary and Tenzing Norgay in 1953. After eleven summits, how many times has Dave Hahn seen the mountain so calm and clear?

Thank you, Chomolungma. Thank you for this chance.

"Dave, are you seeing this?" I ask, turning back into the tent.

He gives me a do-you-realize-who-I-am look and lights our stove.

"Did you know this was coming?" I ask incredulously.

"I had an idea," he says, and his bent smile curls all the way up into his eyes. I could hug him.

11:15 p.m. and I crawl out of the tent, crouch down, and tighten the laces on my boots. Dave squeezes out behind me and steps into his crampons. To my right, Melissa adjusts her oxygen mask and Kent presses a button on his GoPro, red light flashing on the ever-watchful eye. To my left, Chhering, Kaji, and Pasang are already clipped to the fixed rope, shuffling their feet eagerly. In tranquil moonlight, we double check each other's harnesses and oxygen regulators.

"Everything good?" Dave asks. "You ready?"

"I was born ready," I reply.

"Okay." He points a finger to the heavens and says, "Up we go."

34.
GRAVEYARD

In the tube of blue-white light streaming from my headlamp, Dave's crampons claw the rock. Tattered ribbons of blue and orange rope hang over snow-coated gullies and cracks. A strand of new yellow rope trails past Dave's hip, through his ascender, and into the blackness beyond the reach of my headlamp. Regulators clunk between frantic breaths. Nylon pant legs swipe together and a caress of wind tries to pry beneath my goggles, which are fogging up around the bridge of my nose. From somewhere high above, a penny-sized stone tumbles through the night and hits me in the bicep, tearing a penny-sized hole in the arm of my down suit. Feathers spill out into the darkness and dance in the wind like dragonflies. Good thing it wasn't a bigger stone.

Put your head down and keep climbing, one foot in front of the other. Don't think about how far you have to go.

We come to a nearly vertical, eight-foot wall of crumbly rock. The rock's a pattern of loose squares and rectangles like it's made of Legos. I watch Dave scramble up it and then try to imitate his moves, but the climbing's awkward. There's no easy balance. I'm completely on my toes and it leaves me gasping for air. Spit drips out of the exit valve on my oxygen mask and freezes instantly to the chest of my down suit. An icicle's forming, a milky horn protruding from my chin. I inhale, but the rim of my oxygen mask draws tighter against my cheeks. Something's wrong. The mask's suffocating me. Maybe my ambient air valve is clogged. I blow out hard—*hoooh*—like the Big Bad Wolf, but it's still clogged, so I might as well rip it out. I wrap my gloved hand around the knobby protrusion and yank. The rim of my mask loosens instantly as frigid air rushes in through a quarter-sized hole. I can breathe again. Oxygen from the tank in my backpack mixes with the air that's coming through the hole. I inhale the concoction. My lungs fill up to my belly button and I hustle to keep up with Dave.

Step.

Breathe.

Breathe.

Breathe.

Step.

What's that mound of red-and-white fabric off to my left? A body? Yes. Prostrate on a ledge. Legs twisted together unnaturally. Arms splayed overhead. There's no skin showing, but even with the puffy down suit protecting it, I can tell the body's limp and crumpled. It's within an arm's reach of the climbing route. Wrinkles of fabric flutter in a gust, shiny and reflective and brand new. The body can't have been here more than a few weeks or else the wind would've torn the fabric to shreds. It's probably one of the four people who died on May 19. Maybe it's Shriya Shah-Klorfine, the thirty-three-year-old Nepali-Canadian woman who ran out of oxygen as she was descending. Were the colors of her down suit made to match the colors of the Canadian flag? I've seen a dead body before, when Dad and Mom took Joss and me to the back room in the mortuary so we could say good-bye to Grammy, but this is different. This woman wasn't much older than I am and she was only an hour away from the safety of the tents. It's hard to imagine how exhausted she must've been— how heavy her boots felt and how starved her lungs. I've never been so exhausted that I can't take another step and I probably never will be. Probably.

Then again, didn't Shriya Shah-Klorfine believe the same thing?

Step.

Breathe.

Breathe.

Breathe.

Step.

Am I doing something wrong by climbing past a body? It feels like it, but there's not enough time and energy to dwell on morals and ethics.

There's only the rhythm. The moment I stop is the same moment I start to die too. I don't want to die here, crumpled inside my down suit like a shriveled peanut inside its shell. No. We've got to keep moving.

Step.

Breathe.

Breathe.

Breathe.

Step.

But here's a second body—head downhill, perhaps how it landed after a fall—and, Jesus! a third—chalk-white skin visible around the wrists where gauntlets and sleeves are pulled apart. Maybe it's Song Won-Bin, a forty-four-year-old Korean man, and Ha Wenyi, a fifty-five-year-old Chinese man. They died a week ago too, in much the same way as Shriya Shah-Klorfine—starved of oxygen, frozen, and too exhausted to continue.

What can we do? Nothing. There's not enough life up here for a funeral. There's nowhere to dig. Just putting one foot in front of the other is like sprinting for the finish line of a marathon with a plastic bag wrapped around your head. I step over Won-Bin and around Wenyi without breaking rhythm.

Step.

Breathe.

Breathe.

Breathe.

Step.

We climb over another Lego wall and along a shoulder-width gulley and up to a platform of snow that's not much larger than an elevator compartment. Condensation's creeping up the clear lens of my goggles from my nose to my forehead. I can't see my feet anymore, so I rip off the goggles and try to wipe out the inside, but the condensation's frozen. It's a spiky pattern like you'd see on a car windshield after a frosty night and I don't have a scraper. I stow the goggles in my chest pocket. It's still too dark for sunglasses, so I'll have to climb with bare eyes until the sun comes up. Dave's not wearing goggles either. The wind sweeps across us from right to left and I drape my hood around my face to block it. The toes on my right foot have gone numb, but they're not stinging yet. Not yet. I flex them against my insole with every step like I'm trying to pick up a sock off my bedroom floor.

Step.

Breathe.

Breathe.

Breathe.

Step.

We reach the Balcony and it's time for our first break. Swallow a packet of mocha GU. Chug half a liter of burnt water. Switch our regulators to fresh oxygen tanks. Take ten, expect five, get two. Thirty seconds and I can already feel the cold creeping in.

There are remnants here—shreds of fabric, snippets of unbraided rope, discarded oxygen bottles. Is this where Dad, Gombu, Norman Dyhrenfurth, and Ang Dawa made their highest camp? With the blue-white light of my headlamp, I sweep the platform for signs of the past.

Dad and Gombu needed daylight to see the route ahead. Without a trail of fixed ropes or an obvious bootpack, climbing at night would've been dangerously inefficient. As it was, the raging storm veiled the Southeast Ridge in a torrent of swirling snow. It penetrated their goggles and brushed across their eyes. The gusts threatened to push them down the southwest face into the Western Cwm, more than one vertical mile below. Dad and Gombu took turns kicking steps in deep snow. When they encountered sections of hard ice, they chopped steps with their axes, but the surface was soft for the most part and they made consistent progress. Through rare breaks in the sweeping clouds they glimpsed the enormous masses of Lhotse and Makalu puncturing the sky at their backs. And it was not long before they were higher than these great summits, but they hardly noticed because they could see almost nothing except the curving slope of the Southeast Ridge.

At 8:00 a.m., they reached a point where the route steepened. Here, about a thousand vertical feet below the summit, they cached their partly used oxygen bottles in a noticeable place. Then they hooked their regulators into their last full bottles and continued climbing.

Norman Dyhrenfurth and Ang Dawa left the tent at 7:15 a.m. and began inching toward the South Summit, trying to follow Dad's and Gombu's steps, which the windblown snow had already begun to fill in. Their fifty-pound packs full of camera equipment were cumbersome and the weather was far from ideal for filming, but they trudged on nonetheless. About five hundred feet below the South Summit, Norman realized he had reached his limit. He knew he couldn't make it to the summit and back alive. Cinematography was pointless in the whiteout, so Norman and Ang Dawa descended to Camp 6, where they waited anxiously for the return of the two men who were still going up.

"All right, Leif. We're off and running again," says Dave, his voice muffled behind the oxygen mask.

"I'm with ya," I reply.

There's no time to dwell on the past.

We're stepping and breathing again before our sweat's had a chance to freeze.

Step.

Breathe.

Breathe.

Breathe.

Step.

Above the Triangular Face and onto the Southeast Ridge we climb. It's a cresting wave of snow with a waist-high trench eaten into it. Hundreds of crampons have left imprints, but there are no corpses here and no other climbers in sight. I'm matching Dave's rhythm and listening to Melissa's steady breaths behind me and watching Kent frame the mountain in his viewfinder. I like how Chhering, Kaji, and Pasang move—fluid and efficient, without a wasted step or breath. Dad and Gombu are here too, climbing alongside us. I can't imagine a better team.

Sunrise. Morning brightens the sky, so I stop and turn around and take in the contours of the world below. Bony glaciers cut through brown earth like the spines of alligators stalking prey in a muddy pool. River valleys scoop into misty shadow. Frail clouds crawl westward like dinghies adrift in an ocean. Pumori's a snowcapped canine tooth. Nuptse's a crenellated battlement protecting the vast courtyard of the Western Cwm. Lhotse's the nib of a fountain pen, with a pure-white couloir slitting its tines in two. I've seen sunrises from high mountains before, but this one's different. This is more like watching a sunrise from the window of a jetliner that's cruising at thirty thousand feet. As rose light accentuates the black and blue, it feels, for a few seconds, like I'm floating in midair. I can see so far that the horizon droops down at the corners of my field of vision. I'm looking at the curvature of planet Earth. Then a fiery orb crosses the serrated border between land and sky. This could be the most beautiful sight I've ever seen. No. It *is* the most beautiful sight I've ever seen. Period.

Warmth hits my cheeks and euphoria comes with it.

We *will* make it to the summit.

Just stick to the rhythm.

Nothing'll stop us now.

I'll stand in Dad's footprints today.

There's not a doubt in my mind.

Step.

Breathe.

Breathe.

Breathe.

Step.

We're a smidge higher than any other mountain and it's one of those days you dream about. The cross breeze is a tickle. I'm wearing my darkest sunglasses now, but I still have to squint a little because the snow's too bright even for the category-four lenses. My toes have come back from the dead thanks to the rhythm and the sun. Valves clunk. Pant legs swish. Crampons click into plasticky snow. Aluminum carabiners jangle on harnesses. Otherwise it's as silent as space. Looking up, I see a final, fifty-foot slope that leads to the top of a snowy pinnacle: the South Summit.

From there, we should be able to glimpse the Cornice Traverse and the Hillary Step, the final obstacles before we arrive at the top of the world.

Step.

Breathe.

Breathe.

Breathe.

Step.

Lock your downhill leg. Thrust your hips into the slope and rest your weight on your skeleton. Purse your lips and push the air from your belly like you're trying to blow out a candle five feet away.

This is really happening.

We're going to make it.

Three more steps and another loud breath and I finally crest the South Summit and . . . no, no, no, no, no. Euphoria changes to dread as more than a hundred climbers shuffle down the ridgeline toward me. They must've left the South Col earlier than we did last night and now we're crossing paths and there's no safe way to get past them.

Dave sighs into the valve of his oxygen mask and says, "Just like usual on Everest. Hurry up and wait."

35.
GRATITUDE

Curl and uncurl fingers. Think about Fijian beaches, bikini-clad blondes, and mai tais. Think about Oreo cookie ice cream. Think about how fun it was to get lost on Mount Olympus, not to care where you're going or where you've come from, to take pleasure in the act of exploration. Drift off into the thumping of a racing heart.

Thirty minutes.

Wiggle toes. Think about Dad sitting in a Royal Nepalese Airlines DC-3 and seeing Mount Everest for the first time. Think about stainless-steel bands, broken drums, and a nondescript hill above Lobuche. Think about rum and Cokes. Drift off into the continuous hiss of oxygen rushing through a tube.

Sixty minutes.

Gaze out at the Tibetan Plateau—a rolling sheet the color of coir. Think about waking up in a hospital bed with a paralyzed leg and how the ankle rolled over and over against the polished linoleum floor. Think about the butterfly kisses Mom gave me when I was a kid and couldn't fall asleep. Think about sinking into my memory-foam mattress topper, the scent of freshly cut grass. Drift off into the swishing of nylon.

Ninety minutes.

This is getting ridiculous, and dangerous. If I'm not careful, I might drift off forever.

Finally, there's the caboose of the crowd—someone in a cherry-red down suit. The oxygen mask and goggles and balaclava hide the person's origins and gender. They could be richer than 99 percent of people on the globe or they could be supporting a family of twenty all on the $4,000 they'll earn if they make it down alive. Or they could be somewhere in between. There's no way to tell and it doesn't really matter either, not up here. All that matters is how much juice they've got left in their legs, how much oxygen their lungs can capture, and whether or not they'll keep putting one foot in front of the other regardless of how tired and hypoxic and hypothermic they might be.

Whoever they are, they're not moving fast enough for my taste. I'd like to scream, *Get the hell out of the way!* but it's not really their fault. They're stuck in the crowd and clipped to the fixed line just like we are, and it'd be nearly suicidal to attempt the alternative.

Dave's been a statue for the past half hour. I can't see his eyes behind his mirrory sunglasses and I'm too far away to hear if he's breathing. He could be dead for all I know, but then he notices the caboose and stirs to life. He shakes his gloved hands like he's trying to get rid of pins and needles and says, "Okay. It's our time. Everyone ready?"

A grunt, a tired sigh, and a gentle nod. We've succumbed to hibernation and it's brutal shaking it loose. My muscles are as stiff as a straight shot of bourbon and I might as well've left my toes in the tent, but I'm ready. The Hillary Step's vacant. Kent cranks open my regulator and I suck a breath all the way to my thighs. Dave unpauses the rhythm.

Step.

Breathe.

Breathe.

Breathe.

Step.

It feels incredible to be moving again after a protracted stillness. My joints creak comfortingly. A familiar ache sets up shop in my lungs. I don't mind the pain. It's a reminder of a worthwhile effort, a recommitment. We're free on the mountain. This is how I like to climb.

Chhering's climbed the Hillary Step before and it shows. He's precise with his crampons and quiet with his upper body. I catalog his moves— left leg splayed out wide, right arm extending his ascender on the fixed rope, a sharp tug, and he's up. That looked easy. Dave goes next and it looks goofier. His crampons skitter and he dangles momentarily from the rope like one of those metal tubes on a wind chime. He grunts and yanks and he's over it, out of sight. It's my turn.

I don't care how it looks. I'm just anxious to get up. I know I shouldn't hurry, but I do, which is why I get into an awkward position. My left leg's splayed out like Chhering, but I can't find a hold for my right foot. It flops around impotently. I've got my fingers latched through the handle of my ascender and I'm swaying on the fixed rope. Thank God for the fixed rope. It's suspending me over eight thousand feet of pure Himalayan air. Dad was fucking *crazy*. Gombu was fucking crazy. I'll never be as crazy as they were.

My forearms burn. The pull of gravity pools around me like quicksand. Yank and grunt and drive upward off the left leg while simultaneously advancing the ascender. Once more. It's not pretty, but it's working and it's fast. I step away from rock and back to snow where Dave and Chhering wait.

"I'm not sure if I did that right," I say, gasping.

"There's no *right* way, Leif," says Dave. "You're doing just fine."

Once Melissa, Kent, Kaji, and Pasang are queued up behind me, we continue as a team.

Step.

Breathe.

Breathe.

Breathe.

Breathe.

Breathe.

Step.

The glaciers and mountains below are miniature models. We crawl onto the final ridge. Time accelerates. It's probably been an hour since we left our perch below the South Summit, but it feels like minutes. We straddle an ancient boundary between solid ground and cornice. The angle eases off and there's a series of drifts and dips like sand dunes. From crest to trough to crest again, we climb. And each crest is a little higher than the last, each trough not quite so deep.

It didn't look much different for Dad and Gombu. Add a storm and erase the fixed ropes. Otherwise it's the same mountain. It's easy to see it through their eyes. All that's left to climb is a wavy ridgeline. Keep moving. Keep the rhythm. One of these crests is bound to be the ultimate crest. It's achingly close. Dad believes he can make it. I do too.

Step.

Breathe.

Breathe.

Breathe.

Breathe.

Breathe.

Step.

I feel the apex getting closer. Dad and Gombu are here. Leif Patterson and Jake Breitenbach are here. We're climbing these last few feet together—up one crest, down a trough, and up again. We're falling and rising and falling and rising, but the key is to keep moving forward.

There it is, fifty feet away. The white dome curves against a cobalt sky, pristine and empty, and a place where thousands of climbers have been, where a nest of faded prayer flags luffs in the breeze.

Dad coils the rope, bringing Gombu to his side. "You first, Gombu!" says Dad.

"No, you first, Big Jim!" Gombu shouts back.

They sling their arms around each other's shoulders and walk side by side to the highest point on planet Earth.

Dave stops and turns to face me. "Hell of a job, Leif," he says. "It's all yours."

"Thank you, Dave. Thank you so much. But you go first. You've led us the entire way," I reply.

"No. This is your moment. When your dad and mom left us, just before the helicopter took off in Lobuche, your dad told me something. He said you have a gift. I didn't really know what he meant at the time. But I see it now. You have a gift, Leif."

My vision blurs with tears. "I couldn't have done it without you."

"It's been a pleasure," he says. "Now go get it."

Fifty more steps and three hundred more breaths and I'm standing above *everything*. The mountaintop punctures a flawless sky. I remove my oxygen mask and stare out at the world beneath me, taking it all in. The landscape begins at the corniced summits of the greatest Himalayan peaks—Makalu, Lhotse, Nuptse, Cho Oyu, Pumori, Ama Dablam, and countless others I cannot name. Walls of ice gleam in stark sunlight and dive to glacier-flooded valleys. Lower down, the ribbed tongues of the glaciers peel back from speckled moraines. Lower still, emerald forests bunch in misty strips. The layers are so well defined it's like they're painted on a map. To the west, the terraces of rural Nepal are like contour lines. To the north, there's the vast umber of the Tibetan Plateau stretching out endlessly like a dry ocean. To the east, the striking curvature of a torn-paper horizon. To the south, fingers and spines and teeth and fins jut from the surface of the planet. Waiting was a blessing in disguise because all the other climbers are gone and we've got the summit to ourselves. On a day like today, Mount Everest is a friendly place.

Chhering embraces me and says, "Congratulations, Leif! You're at the top of the world!"

"Thank you, my friend," I say, fighting back tears. "The top of the world." I can hardly believe I'm here. It doesn't seem quite real, but we've made it. Here we are.

I take a seat on a bump of snow next to the heap of prayer flags and let memories wash over me. I think about the first hike I ever went on with Spencer and Chris and Danny up to Boulder Shelter. I think about Joss yelling, *It's not too bad. Only one scary part,* and about Sam spiking a Ping-Pong ball. I think about Dad saying, *He was a prince of a man,* and Chhering rubbing tsampa on my cheeks, and Melissa saying, *It makes sense to me if we stay here for the night.* I think about the look in Mom's eyes when she saw the musk deer and about the sunrise this morning. I think about the knife stabbing into my throat when I first saw the Khumbu Icefall and about a streak of blood on the wall of a crevasse and about the glassy funnel that's the Lhotse Face. I think about a bloody clump of tissue resting on a blue paper towel and Dad's face when he said, *Let me get to the top of this hill. Then we'll see.* I think about the question, *What are you doing with your life?*

I admit it: part of me feels like I could accomplish anything I set my mind to, but the overwhelming emotion isn't pride or a sense of power. No. It's gratitude. Maybe it's the lack of oxygen, but I feel the overwhelming urge to say thank-you to everyone and hug them and tell them I love them, including the mountain itself. *Thank you, Mount Everest. Thank you, Chomolungma, for allowing me to be here.*

The mountaintop punctures the blizzard and the sky's the type of dark blue only astronauts, pilots, jetliner passengers, and high-altitude climbers ever get a chance to see. A boiling plume obscures the view into Tibet.

Dad peers across the Himalaya and the world's greatest peaks look up at him. He unstraps a four-foot aluminum stake from his backpack, places its point at the very apex of the dome, and pounds it in with the wooden shaft of his ice axe. The gale unfurls the Stars and Stripes. It whips and cracks. Dad stands in front of the flag and raises his ice axe in the air. Gombu rotates the camera vertically in order to fit Dad, his ice axe, and the American flag into the frame. The shutter clicks.

Starved of oxygen, half blind, toes and fingers nearly frozen, Dad doesn't feel expansive or sublime. He doesn't feel like he's conquered the mountain or accomplished an historic feat. No. There's none of that. Instead, he feels only like a frail human being.

Gombu deposits a khata on the summit. His uncle, Tenzing Norgay, gave him the khata for this specific reason. Gombu holds his ice axe aloft. He's tied a Nepalese flag, with its white sun and crescent moon, and a flag from the Himalayan Mountaineering Institute to his ice axe. Dad snaps the picture, accidentally capturing a bit of his fur-lined hood in the frame. At this moment, Gombu doesn't feel a sense of power or victory. Nothing of the sort. His first and only thought is *how . . . to . . . get . . . down.*

Kent says it's time for photos. We've already discussed how I'm going to pose. I bend my uphill leg, lock my downhill knee, and raise my ice axe into the air, trying to look as heroic as possible. The Eddie Bauer flag tied to my ice axe flaps lightly in the breeze. It's weird. I used to resent the image of Dad on the summit but, hell, I guess he *did* have a pretty badass pose.

Peering down at Kent's camera through a lingering haze of tears, I notice a lone figure in a red down suit coming up the ridgeline toward us. It's a solo climber and as he gets closer I notice he's carrying only a small day pack and his face is bare. He's not using bottled oxygen, but he's climbing steadily nevertheless. He's breathing so loudly I can hear him from fifty yards away.

"Conrad?" asks Dave with a no-fucking-way tone of voice.

"Howdy, Dave," says Conrad Anker as he joins us. "Do you mind taking my picture?" Conrad unzips a chest pocket, pulls out a point-and-shoot camera the size of a cell phone, and hands it to Dave. He poses for a second or two while Dave snaps away.

"Hey, Kent, will you get a picture of Dave and me?" Conrad asks.

Dave and Conrad sling their arms over each other's shoulders and grin for the lens. It's not the first time they've been here together. They're so casual about it, like buddies who've run into each other on their favorite hiking trail. What a nice little coinkydink.

Five minutes on top and Conrad's trudging away. "Will you keep an eye on me on the way down?" Conrad asks Dave over his shoulder. "I'm pretty beat and I think you're the last people up here. I'm sure you'll catch up to me."

"No problem," says Dave. "We'll be along soon."

Watching his red figure disappear behind a snowdrift reminds me that we're only at the halfway point. There's an entire mountain beneath us and, from here, it looks steeper than it did from below. A slope of brittle ice arcs toward emptiness. A vertical step of chunky rock tumbles into space. Did we really *climb* that stuff?

The euphoria and pride and gratitude ebb away as the rhythm approaches, but the haze of tears remains. Why? I shouldn't be crying anymore. Wait, I'm not crying. Something's wrong. I blink and blink and blink. I wipe at my eyes with my gloved hand. The haze remains. There's no pain, but the mountain's sharp angles are softer than they should be. The ice and rock are foggy patches of burning light and impenetrable dark. This is *not* good. It's time to get down.

36.
GET THE HELL OUT OF THERE

The right eye's worse than the left, but they're both as steamy as a shower door after a hot rinse. There's a pinhole of clarity that I can look through when I really need to see details—feeding a rope into my belay device, or adjusting my regulator. Otherwise, the mountain's painted in broader strokes. Dave's an out-of-focus silhouette against an overexposed backdrop. He's close enough to reach out and touch. I watch his feet—red-and-gray splashes on a fresh canvas—and sink my own feet exactly in his footprints. It's no problem keeping up. I just wish I could enjoy the view.

It isn't snow blindness because it doesn't hurt. Dave says my corneas are probably frosted. I should've been more careful when I removed my foggy goggles at the Balcony. It must've been the sideways breeze that did it in the hour or two before sunrise when my eyes were bare. It's scary how Everest magnifies the tiniest mistakes.

Rappeling the Hillary Step's a bit unnerving because I can't tell how close the bottom is until I'm practically sitting on the snow. I've always been comfortable rappeling though, ever since Joss showed me how at the bunkers in Port Townsend. Just lean back until you're perpendicular to the wall and walk your feet down as you let the rope slide through your fingers. Maybe it's less intimidating with frosted corneas because I can't judge the exposure. It could be eight thousand feet of air or ten feet. It's all a chaotic pattern of black and white.

We march past the cleft where we waited for ninety minutes and up the pinnacle of the South Summit. It truly is all downhill from here, but the downhill isn't necessarily easier, or safer, than the up. Very few people have died while ascending Mount Everest. Accidents always happen on the *de*scent, when you're tired and you've already reached your goal and you've relaxed your focus. All the bodies I've seen so far are people who touched the summit, but I'm not going to add to the carnage. No way.

We catch up to Conrad midway down the Southeast Ridge. He lets us pass and then clips into the fixed line behind Kaji. Dave eases off the gas pedal so Conrad can keep up, which is fine with me because it gives me a chance to think about Dad and Gombu. My mind's eye isn't frosted. I can see them clearly. They're on the Cornice Traverse, and Dad has just realized he's sucking on an empty oxygen tank. Gombu is empty too. Their half-full tanks are waiting below the South Summit, still so far away.

A crooked fracture suddenly cut along the ridge like a bolt of lightning and a huge section of cornice calved off, disappearing down the Kangshung Face. A gaping void remained, the edge of which was only a few inches to the left of the trail of footprints. Dad looked up and saw Gombu standing on the opposite side of the void. The rope between them arced into space, vibrating in the wind. Oxygen-starved and exhausted, Dad simply took a few steps to his right and continued descending. The half-full oxygen bottles waiting below were their salvation.

Below the Hillary Step, not far from a narrow cleft, Dad felt the undeniable urge to take a crap. It was without a doubt the highest and most uncomfortable pit stop a mountaineer had ever made. Dad later wrote, "It was a humbling—not to mention numbing—experience. I felt very mortal."

Meanwhile, Gombu, unaware of what was happening behind him and unable to hear Dad's repeated shouts, continued down. Soon the rope grew taut and Gombu, thinking it must be caught on a rock, tugged hard. Dad had dressed quickly and was hustling to catch up when the tug came. It spun him sideways and he toppled over backward, a mess of rope, loose clothing, and who knows what else.

Dad untangled himself and struggled to the crest of the South Summit. He rested for a brief moment and then the pair continued down to their cache of oxygen. They'd been climbing for more than two hours without oxygen, and since Dad's two water bottles had frozen solid almost immediately after leaving camp, they hadn't taken a sip of water the entire day. They hooked up their regulators, set them to a two-liter flow, and took a few life-giving breaths. Then it was, as James Ramsey Ullman put it, "down, down, down."

At 5:45 p.m., just as darkness crushed in on them, Dad and Gombu trudged into Camp 6, where Ang Dawa and Norman Dyhrenfurth were waiting with cups of hot Jell-O.

Dad awoke at midnight. His oxygen bottle had run empty. The three other men had emptied their bottles too and, since they couldn't sleep, they lay there feeling the cold creep inward from their frozen toes and fingers toward their hearts. When morning finally arrived, their faces were swollen and tinted blue from hypoxia, but they forced themselves out of the tents and down toward the South Col. Norman and Ang Dawa decided to lag behind, snapping photos and filming as they descended. Dad and Gombu were wasting no time. They were going down, down, down as fast as they could.

Lute Jerstad, Dick Pownall, Barry Bishop, and Girmi Dorje met them and, for the first time, heard the news that Big Jim and Gombu had reached the summit. They all shared in the joy of victory because each man had contributed to the effort. But celebration would come later. The six teammates returned together to Camp 5, where Dad and Gombu sipped oxygen and chugged hot liquids. An hour and a half later, Norman and Ang Dawa came into view and, with the help of the other men, stumbled into camp. Then they were all descending together—across the Geneva Spur, over the Yellow Band, and down the Lhotse Face, aiming for thicker air.

Over the course of the next few days, AMEE departed the frozen heights and returned to Base Camp. Dad had spent thirty days at 21,300 feet or above. He was bruised and battered from the ordeal, at least on the surface. His toes were black with frostbite and he soaked them in a tub until feeling gradually returned. Portions of his face that the oxygen mask and goggles had not covered were frostbitten. He had a bracelet of frostbite blisters on his left wrist where there had been a tiny gap between his glove and parka. All these signs of struggle—the story written into his skin—would heal after a few weeks. They were only minor nuisances, forgotten amid the pleasures of life at 17,500 feet.

Dad stripped naked and lay on a boulder in the clear heat of spring. Norman shaved his stubble and some of the men gave each other haircuts. They ate fresh eggs and mutton, which tasted spectacular compared to the instant meals they'd consumed higher up. The mundane concerns of normal life—the details they'd taken for granted before the expedition— were now reasons for utter delight.

I can practically taste the mint chip, but right now it's down, down, down over knobby crags, through trenches in the snow, past faded refuse, and onto the Balcony, where we stop to swallow our last drop of water.

"Do you want to call your parents?" asks Dave, rummaging through his backpack.

"Seriously?" I reply.

"Yeah, of course. Why not?" he says with a what's-the-big-deal tone. "Aha. Here it is." He pulls out a satellite phone and extends the antenna. "What's the number?"

I tell him Mom's cell number. He dials it in, listens for a ringtone, and then passes me the phone. She answers on the third ring.

"Hello?" she says.

"Hey, Mom. It's Leif. We just got to the summit and we're on our way down."

"Oh my God! Hold on a second. Dad is with me. I'll put you on speakerphone." I hear rustling and frantic talking in the background. Then the speakerphone engages and I hear Dad's voice.

"Son? Can you hear me?"

"Yeah, Dad. Loud and clear. I'm at the Balcony on my way down. We just made it to the summit!"

"Oh-ho! Good for you! That's incredible!" says Dad.

"Yep. Pretty amazing," I say, but it comes out sounding like I'm talking about a particularly good slice of pizza. "Where are you guys?"

"We're in a hotel room in Bellevue," says Mom. "I'm glad I answered the phone because it was an unknown number and I wasn't going to answer."

"I'm on Dave's sat phone. We're all here and we're all safe. My eyes are a little messed up but I'm fine."

"Messed up how? Snow blindness?" asks Dad.

"No. Just kinda frosted my eyeballs. My vision's a little blurry, but no big deal."

"The same thing happened to me," says Dad. "It was the wind getting in underneath my goggles. It passed in a few hours once I got back to camp."

"Exactly. My goggles got iced over on the way up and I had to take them off to see. That's when it happened, I think. But Dave lent me an extra pair of goggles so I'm okay now. We're almost at the South Col. I hope they clear up quickly."

"Good. Will you stay the night there?" asks Dad.

"I'm not sure. I think our plan was to try to get down to Camp 2, but if my eyes don't get better, we might spend another night."

"Be careful, Leif," says Mom. It dawns on me that my parents must be very worried. If they've been following the news, which I know they have, they're aware that it's been one of the most deadly seasons in Mount Everest history.

I try to sound reassuring when I say, "We'll get down. Don't worry."

A short pause and Dad says, "This is amazing. Here we are in a crappy Bellevue hotel room and you're all the way over there on Everest. I can hardly believe it."

"I know. A crappy hotel room sounds pretty good right now. We still have a long way to go. I should probably say good-bye."

"Yep. Okay," says Dad. "Go. Go. Go. Get the hell out of there."

"I love you, Mom and Dad."

"We love you too," they say in unison. I press the red button and pass the phone back to Dave.

"How was that?" he asks.

"My dad said we should get the hell out of here," I say.

Dave's chuckle is a roll of thunder. "I tend to agree with him."

Partway down the Triangular Face, there's another body. Even with blurry vision I can see the crumpled outline. I can tell it's a man from the broadness of his shoulders. He's lying facedown and the back of his ragged suit's torn open between his shoulder blades, revealing the skin beneath. It's ivory white and it looks as hard as leather. There's no decomposition visible.

"Scott Fischer," mumbles Dave as we trudge past. Any magazine will tell you that climbing mountains is all about strength and skill and perseverance, but you've got to be lucky too, and respectful. Even the strongest climbers in the world can't control the mountains. Nobody can.

Apparently, the Sherpa working for the National Geographic team have already struck Conrad's tent and carried it down to ABC because it's no longer at the South Col. Dave and I have extra space in our three-person capsule, so Conrad crawls into our tent with us and falls asleep on my Therm-a-Rest. Conrad's snoring and Dave's melting ice for hot drinks and I'm inspecting my toes. The right one's thawing out, I think, and there's none of the telltale whiteness of frostbite. I swallow a boiling mug of cocoa in a single gulp and then a boiling mug of Kool-Aid. Hot fructose tastes so damn good.

Conrad awakes with a start and says, "I gotta go," so we shake hands and he slides out through the vestibule and then he's gone, a tall red blur running for ABC across the shingles of the Geneva Spur.

Dave says, "How're your eyes?"

"Still foggy," I say. I'm wearing the goggles Dave lent me, but the haze hasn't dissipated.

"They'll clear," he says, "but I don't know how long it'll take and it's probably safer if we avoid the Lhotse Face until they do."

I just nod.

The South Col's emptying out like a sinking ship. Everyone's rushing to pack up tents and equipment. In less than a week, every camp on the mountain will be gone. The Icefall Doctors will remove the ladders.

The monsoon snows will arrive as they do every June, erasing any sign we were here, returning the mountain to an ancient cycle of rebirth. But before that happens, Dave and I will spend one more night in the death zone.

I stretch out on my pad and listen to the pain throbbing in every corner of my body. My head's pounding. My throat's aching. My legs are cramping and twitching. I feel my energy retreating inward, toward a glowing core. And when I fall asleep, it's as if I'm dying. The calm and silence and depth are absolute. I do not move a muscle. I do not dream.

Most expeditions would have returned home after Dad and Gombu's summit, but AMEE was a team of highly driven individuals, only two of whom had reached the top. Tom Hornbein and Willi Unsoeld returned their gazes to the vast and unexplored West Ridge. If everything went according to plan, the West Ridgers hoped to rendezvous on the summit with Lute Jerstad and Barry Bishop, who would be climbing from the South Col. However, the men knew that a meeting at the world's highest point would be very difficult to pull off.

On May 14, the West Ridgers completed a carry to Camp 4W, an ideal terrace at 25,100 feet. At 3:30 p.m. on May 16, they reached a bench of limestone at 26,250 feet. Peering up a gulley, which they named Hornbein's Couloir, they glimpsed five hundred vertical feet of smooth snow before the couloir doglegged out of sight. It looked like an excellent way forward. They returned to Camp 4W full of enthusiasm, but an inescapable adversary would soon wash away their spirits: the Himalayan wind.

Barry Corbet, Al Auten, and four Sherpa had come up from Camp 3W the same day and now the eight men hunkered in three tents to pass the night. A storm descended. The gusts broke the one-hundred-mile-an-hour mark, lifting two of the three tents and tossing them toward Tibet. Unable to escape from the nylon prisons, the men couldn't arrest their blind and chaotic ride. Mercifully, the tents slammed into a shallow depression a hundred feet down the slope. It caught them and held them fast. The reeling occupants tried frantically to secure what little shelter they had left. Al Auten ascended through deafening blackness to Tom and Willi's tent, the only one that remained anchored to the snow. Then all the men worked to save as much equipment as they could, using their axes and climbing rope to tie it all together, struggling for their own survival in the vicious currents.

Sunrise was no respite. A wicked blast tore the last tent free. Tom Hornbein lunged for the door. He later wrote, "A metal rappel picket was lying on the snow. I rammed it in, spreading my legs in the vestibule, and held tight. The tent stopped." The others escaped and tossed anything they could find on top of it. Miraculously, everyone was alive, but in the shattered forms of their tents, they saw a portent of their own impending failure. Their dreams had been literally demolished.

They retreated to Camp 3W and could have abandoned the West Ridge then and there, but their resolve was absolute. They still had time to make an attempt before the monsoon arrived. It would be much smaller, faster, and more dangerous than planned, but there was a chance at the summit nevertheless. They continued to believe.

On May 20 the West Ridgers returned to the ruins of their old camp, adding two four-person tents to the windblasted plateau. Ten men were on the team: Willi Unsoeld, Tom Hornbein, Barry Corbet, Al Auten, Dick Emerson, Ang Dorje, Ila Tsering, Tenzing Nindra, Passang Tendi, and Tenzing Gyalsto. With warm drinks spreading outward from their stomachs, they passed a fairly cozy night. The next day was a carry to what would be the last and highest camp on the West Ridge, Camp 5W. For the first three hours the men climbed over known terrain—up the Diagonal Ditch to the base of Hornbein's Couloir. Above that, the route was unknown and, with Al and Barry chopping steps in the lead, they made excellent progress toward the bulging golden rock of the Yellow Band. Even with enormous loads on their backs, the men achieved an altitude of 27,250 feet by 2:00 p.m. Here they found a tiny ledge of snow to which they secured a single two-man tent. Then there were rushed good-byes between the two men who would risk it all and their eight faithful companions who had, through their selfless work, given Tom Hornbein and Willi Unsoeld the chance to make history.

37.
SECRET

A nail hammers into my third eye and I jerk awake with a gasp. My heart's going ballistic and my skin's a soggy dishrag and the blackness reeks like leftover stir fry that's been ignored in the fridge for a month. Where's my headlamp? I rummage blindly through folds of nylon and find an empty wax casing from a mini cheese and my last Jolly Rancher and two packets of instant oats and a mucus-saturated Buff and my Maui Jims and my insulated mug and, finally, my headlamp. Press the button and a beam slashes into the darkness and I trace the clear tube coming from my nostrils through the folds of my negative-twenty-Celsius bag to where it connects to the regulator. The black needle's in the red shed, so I guess this bottle's empty and, judging from the galvanized steel inserted in my frontal lobe, it has been for quite some time. I unzip the tent door and reach into the vestibule and, thank God, there's one more full bottle and it's got my name on it.

Dave's raspy, half-choked voice emanates from the black. "How're your eyes?"

I hardly realized it, but my vision's perfectly clear. The chaos inside the tent is splayed out in fine detail. I can read the nutrition facts on a torn Snickers wrapper and the washing instructions on the tag of my sour-milk-smelling base layer. "Perfect," I reply.

"Good. We have some long days ahead," says Dave like we're in the center of the Sahara and our only camel just died of thirst.

I spin the tank onto my regulator and adjust the knob to "0.5." Cold gas bites my nostrils, but at least it's prying out the nail breath by breath. Sleep's impossible again and my iPod's been dead for hours, days, weeks, so I'll just lie here and stare into the blackness and think about how the mountain has changed and how the mountain has changed *me*. I'm stinkier and skinnier and weaker, that's for sure. What else?

Utter darkness lightens to a dim gray sky. The only reason to eat breakfast is so we can carry the raisins and spice down in our bellies instead of in our packs. Outside, we peel off the waterproof fly and collapse the poles and unhook the inner walls of our temporary home. I jam the fabric in around empty oxygen bottles, empty fuel canisters, and my compressed sleeping bag. Lift with your spine, not with your legs. A precalibrated scale would tell you my pack's sixty-five pounds, but the truth is it's closer to five hundred. No biggie. It's not like I have back problems.

A nod, a deep breath, a final look back at the tilted witch's hat of snow-etched stone, and we're going down, down, and down again across the shredded-paper slabs of the Geneva Spur, beneath the thin-as-a-doorway Lhotse Couloir and through the straw veneer of the Yellow Band. Sometimes we rappel and sometimes we spiral the rope around our arms like it's a cephalic vein, controlling our free fall with the squeeze of a gloved hand. The rope singes my leather palm and paints a meandering line of grease onto the right forearm of my down suit. I lean forward so my torso's perpendicular to the fifty-degree ice. Gravity does most of the work and our job's to resist it only enough that we don't land with a crunch at the pitiless foundation of the Lhotse Face. It's a fast way to go. Look at that, we're already at the edge of Camp 3 and Dave sits down, his tether clipped to an anchor, so I guess it's time for a quick break. I glimpse through swirling murk a few scraps of partially buried orange fabric and a broken aluminum pole—more fragments, more trash leftover from a nameless expedition and an unknown decade. What imprint, what legacy will our team leave behind?

I sweep my eyes in all directions, looking for signs of other climbers, but we're completely alone. Solitude's rare on Mount Everest these days, and for a few scant seconds as Dave arranges his next rappel, I allow the vast emptiness to wash over me. Is Everest really that much different than it was in 1963? Certainly, climbing the mountain has changed, and must continue to evolve. The ugly side—injustice, ego, and tragedy—is undeniably present, and I am complicit in these wrongs. But if I had to guess, I'd say there's a mystery hidden in this landscape that's always been here and will always be here. I can't prevent the mountain from entering my memory and imagination and dreams. To me, it remains an incredible challenge. It remains beautiful beyond description. It will always deserve our love, fear, and respect. But enough of that. If we move fast and everything goes just perfectly, the warm grass at Chetzemoka Park in Port Townsend is only a week away and that sounds like nirvana right about now. Down, down, down.

At 4:30 a.m. on May 22, Tom Hornbein, Willi Unsoeld, Lute Jerstad, and Barry Bishop awoke on their respective sides of the mountain and prepared to go up. Willi and Tom were huddled in a two-man tent secured to a tiny platform on the unexplored West Ridge. Lute and Barry were at Camp 6 on the Southeast Ridge. Could the two climbing parties rendezvous at the apex of the Himalaya?

Tom and Willi's preparations went smoothly, but Lute and Barry had an accident that could've easily ended their efforts, and their lives, that very moment. As Lute attached a fresh cartridge to a stove, there was a sudden explosion. Flame and smoke shot into the tent. Lute dove through a door and nearly tumbled down the ridge. Barry followed, grabbing the burning stove and drowning it in the snow. Due to the accident, they did not set off until 8:00 a.m.

On the other side of the mountain, Tom and Willi were making slow progress. At 11:00 a.m., after four hours of climbing, the pair had ascended only four hundred vertical feet. A sixty-foot cliff of rotten yellow rock guarded the way forward, sloping downward in a collection of loose plates. Tom climbed around a corner, sending showers of rock down on Willi's belay position. Tom continued to work up and left until he reached a final, vertical eight-foot step. He removed his mittens and, in the few seconds before his fingers went numb, tried with all his might to clamber over, but could not. Willi would have to make an attempt. Tom lowered to the belay position and Willi took the lead. He moved up to Tom's previous high point, removed his mittens, and let his arms extend, his frozen hands clinging to what he hoped were solid holds. Their dreams hinged on this moment. If Willi didn't succeed, it would all be over. He let go of his connection to the world below and focused entirely on the one move that would get him and his teammate higher. It was perhaps the most incredible and daring piece of climbing the expedition would see, and still one of the most legendary feats in American mountaineering history. Willi pulled hard. His body pivoted on an edge. His crampons broke loose a tremendous gush of stone. And then he was up.

Tom soon followed, and when the pair were standing on more level terrain at 27,900 feet, they pulled out their walkie-talkie and tried Base Camp. It was Dad's voice that echoed up to Tom and Willi.

"This is Base here, Willi. How are you? How are things going? What's the word up there? Over."

"Man, this is a real bearcat!" Willie replied. "We are nearing the top of the Yellow Band and it's mighty tough. It's too damned tough to try to go back. It would be too dangerous."

"Don't work yourself up into a bottleneck, Willi. How about rappeling? Is that possible? Over."

Willi knew that Tom's willingness matched his own and he spoke for both of them when he said, "There are no rappel points, Jim, absolutely no rappel points. There's nothing to secure a rope to. So it's up and over for us today"—Dad must've heard these words and wondered if he would ever see his friends again, but Willi didn't allow much time for contemplation—"and we'll probably be getting in pretty late, maybe as late as seven or eight o'clock tonight."

It was already afternoon, but the summit, they knew, was not far off—only eight hundred feet, now seven hundred, now six hundred. The climbing here was, for the two men, the most enjoyable of the expedition. They balanced on solid holds, gliding upward with all the grace of ballet dancers.

At 6:15 p.m., just before sunset, Willi stopped in his tracks and coiled the rope as Tom came up next to him. There, forty feet above, was the tattered American flag that Big Jim had planted three weeks earlier. Tears streamed out and froze to their cheeks as the two frail men stood together on top of the mountain.

Like Dad and Gombu, Tom and Willi had little time for philosophy. They too spent only twenty minutes on the summit and their overriding thought was to get down as quickly as possible. They began searching for a sign of Lute and Barry—some remnant, something to lead them home. Footprints. "Thank God for the footprints," Tom Hornbein would later write.

About three hours earlier, Lute and Barry had, against all odds, reached the summit themselves. May 22 was a brilliant day and Barry and Lute sacrificed what life was left in their fingers when they pulled off their mittens to operate the metal camera equipment. Photography complete, they waited and watched for any sign of Tom and Willi coming up the West Ridge. At 4:15 p.m. they could wait no longer and they started down, the flapping Stars and Stripes soon disappearing from sight behind the snowdrifts.

But Lute and Barry were almost completely exhausted. It took them three and a half hours to descend past the Hillary Step and over the South Summit, a vertical drop of only six hundred feet. It was 8:00 p.m. and the last gleam of light was long gone from the horizon. Could they make it back to Camp 6 alive? As if in response to this question, a voice suddenly echoed through the darkness.

"Helloooo."

It was Tom and Willi hollering from above. The four climbers united and it was soon clear that Tom and Willi were in far better shape than the other two. Tom took the front rope position with Lute and Barry in the middle and Willi last in line. In this fashion, the four men crawled and fell and slid and shuffled down for three more hours until the steepness of the Southeast Ridge eased off. Partially frozen, half lost, and completely exhausted, they could no longer continue. They had gone only four hundred vertical feet in three hours, a distance that, by Tom Hornbein's estimate, would have taken fifteen minutes in daylight. Their only option was to wait for sunrise. Without sleeping bags, tents, stoves, or bottled oxygen, the four men settled in for what would be the coldest and longest night of their lives.

At over twenty-eight thousand feet, it was the highest bivouac in history. Incredibly, it was the type of night that happens perhaps once a year on Mount Everest—utterly silent and still. The temperature remained at eighteen degrees below zero. Tom was the only man with enough energy and wherewithal to take off his steel crampons. When he complained of pain in his toes, Willi offered to put Tom's feet on his warm belly. Tom accepted and offered to return the favor, but Willi declined, saying his feet didn't hurt. Neither man was lucid enough to recognize that Willi's feet were not paining him because they were completely numb and frozen white. Lute wiggled his toes, banged his boots together, shoved his fingers in his armpits, and repeated these thrashings throughout the night in an effort to stave off the death that he thought would come with sleep. Barry tried to do the same before he realized it was a useless effort. They all drifted off into their wandering thoughts and dreams. In the far distance, lightning crashed against the Indian plains, but the flashes were as silent as the darkness.

When the wave of morning finally struck their crag, it revealed four beating hearts and eight open eyes. Dave Dingman and Girmi Dorje rounded a corner with the sun and helped the injured men down to safety.

Lute, Barry, and Willi had suffered severe frostbite, although Lute's was the least worrisome of the three cases. Tom Hornbein was the only one of the four to avoid frozen appendages. Barry would eventually lose all his toes as well as the tips of his pinkies. Willi would have every toe except one amputated. All four of them walked through the Khumbu Icefall for the last time under their own power, hesitating momentarily to remember their fallen friend, Jake Breitenbach. As they walked over his icy grave, they had no feelings of conquest or of a great battle being won. There was not a hint of nobility or self-satisfaction in their posture. It was a procession of starving and hobbled men whose dream was finally, mercifully done. They had completed the first American ascent of Mount Everest, the first ascent of the West Ridge, and the first traverse of an eight-thousand-meter peak. And now the whole team was dropping into thicker air, down, down, down, to what Tom Hornbein called the "world of living things."

After a final night at ABC, we rise before the sun and half walk, half run toward the Khumbu Icefall. It's a clear day and the air betrays the mystery of spring, wafting over the surface of the ice like the warm breath of a lover. The glacier talks—creaking, popping, and snapping. The crevasse with the bloodstained wall has grown enormous. Five sections of lashed-together aluminum ladders span the gap. It must be fifty feet across. I step out into the middle and the ladders bow under my weight, the ends lifting off the edges of the crevasse. Don't think about it. Six steps and six breaths deliver me to the opposite side.

Down, down, down beneath the Horseshoe Glacier through the Damn Deep Ditch along Sugar Hill and under the H-Bomb serac. It's not worth stopping for a break at the Football Field because the fatigue's too deep. A sip of melted glacier and a carrot cake Clif Bar aren't going to heal me. No. I'll need weeks, months, years to get over an expedition like this, so we continue down, jumping and sliding and shuffling between kernels of frozen popcorn, rolling through the Little Bowling Alley, and finally, doggedly emerging into the safety of the Up-Downs, where each successive rise is slightly crueler than the last. I glimpse the colorful Base Camp tents and I feel the cares falling away. Each step and breath sheds a worry. We're one hundred yards from the dining tent now and pure joy courses through me. Mark Tucker spots us from his perch next to the comms tent and raises his fists in the air like a starting pitcher who's just thrown the last strike of a perfect game. Every member of our climbing team has reached the top and come down alive. Here we are. We've done it.

A peek through the door of the Benegas Brothers Expeditions tent exposes a revelry steeped in relief. Green and red Christmas lights dangle from the rim of the ceiling, blinking in synchronicity with the bass-heavy pop that's rumbling from a set of battery-powered speakers. A platter of sushi, salty meats, smelly cheeses, and crackers rests on a folding table. Bottles of Coke, Fanta, and Sprite are piled in a corner next to a case of San Miguel beer. There's also a box of red wine and a few bottles of liquor—rum, whiskey, and vodka. The tent's stuffed tight with a mix of Sherpa, Argentine, British, and American climbers, most of whom have stood, over the course of the last few days, on the summit of Mount Everest. They dance wildly, spinning and stomping in flashes of light. Melissa bounces through the crowd, graceful and giddy, laughing the whole time. Chhering sways with the rhythm, a huge smile squeezing his cheeks. In the sunburned and chapped faces of the partygoers, there's a powerful release of pent-up energy. For some, this moment signals the safe completion of a season of dangerous, backbreaking work. It means a wad of cash in the pocket and easier living to come. For others, it signals the accomplishment of a long-sought-after goal. It means bragging rights, prestige, and an avoidance of further climbing, at least for a while. For everyone, it's a time to forget inhibitions and carouse the night away, but something's missing.

I'm three rum and Cokes deep and I'm still not feeling it. I can't let myself go. Maybe it's because Dad and Mom and Joss aren't here. Maybe I simply want to be home after so long away. Maybe I want to walk beside the ocean and glimpse the shrouded sea stacks and let the damp air press into my skin. Or maybe I don't want this journey to be over. The part of me that was, for so long, focused on climbing Mount Everest is empty now and I don't know how to fill the void.

I step out of the tent and take a seat on a nearby boulder and open my journal and scratch words onto blank pages. It's mostly nonsense, but as I read it over and add more sentences to the end, I begin to feel a flow. Then the words pour out in a flood. They dive and splash and erupt onto the page, unwilling to slow even as my fingers cramp. I never noticed how the rhythm of writing is a lot like the rhythm of climbing—one word in front of the other. The pencil burns a blister between my fingers until the flow gradually slows and finally ends in a single graphite dot.

Dave walks out of the tent and strolls over to me. Noticing my journal, he says, "What? Are you writing a fucking book?" Dave's smirk is bent like a tilde.

We both laugh from our hearts and I say, "I think maybe I am."

38.
GREEN

Dad likes to tell a story about coming down after months in a world of rock and ice. Spring was blooming in Nepal as the men of AMEE departed Base Camp. They hiked the same trail on which they had approached the mountain, but it was strange and unfamiliar. It was alive. A cozy mélange of yak and juniper hovered in the moist air. Women and children peered shyly at the weary, pale men, smiling and giggling from windowsills, doorways, and the corners of sun-soaked homes. Chickens pecked and cackled on the edges of the muddy trail. The pungent ground softened beneath the blistered balls of their feet as they left the infertile glaciers behind and burst into the world below.

Out of the corner of his eye, one man noticed a lick of bright green shooting from the earth. It was a blade of fresh grass. He hollered for the other men to come take a look. It was the first living plant they had seen in nearly three months. Some of them fell to their knees and wept. Dad knelt there and thought about Jake Breitenbach buried in the Icefall. A friendly dog ran over to him. Dad hugged it tightly, feeling its warmth and softness as it licked the tears from his face.

Base Camp hums with the sounds of departure—yak bells dinging, tent poles clicking together, zippers zipping, and dozens of helicopters gliding onto the cobbled landing pad at the south end of camp. It's a three-day hike to Lukla, past head-high emerald potato plants, through blooming plains, and over rivers coursing with turbid spring runoff. I'm looking forward to a casual walk so I can think about what's next. Climbing a mountain's such a simple thing. The risks are known and the route's visible. If only life were so straightforward.

"What do you think about a little helicopter ride?" asks Dave in an it-could-be-pretty-fun tone.

"Aren't they expensive?" I ask. I think I'd rather make a slow readjustment to normal life, but Dave's hiked this trail dozens of times and he leaves for Denali in about three weeks, so he probably wants as much time to recuperate as he can possibly get.

"Not too bad right now. Simone says he'll give us a deal. And Tucky got word that no plane flights have gone out of Lukla to Kathmandu in like a week because of bad weather. So there's a big lineup to get out of there. We could be stuck for a while if we don't go now," he says.

"Can they take us all the way to Kathmandu?" I ask, thinking how heavenly it'd be to step into a hot shower at the Yak and Yeti.

"They'll take us to Lukla first and then if the weather holds, we can go onto Kat in a separate heli," Dave replies.

"So helis have been flying, but planes haven't?"

"Yes. They do a better job of maneuvering through cloudy valleys."

"Okay. I guess I'd go if that's what everyone else wants to do," I say.

Tuck calls Simone Moro, who says, "Be at landing pad in twenty minutes. Don't be late."

So that's that. One phone call and the journey's over. We each sling one sixty-pound duffel over our shoulders and carry another in our arms and jog along the moraine. *Thwucka-thwucka-thwucka.* A red, white, and blue B3 sets down. There's only enough room for half of us on the first flight, so Kent and I volunteer to wait for the second revolution.

"See you in Lukla," says Dave, and jumps on board. Kent and I step back as the rotors spin faster and faster. The noise rises and the helicopter shudders and lifts a few feet off the ground. Then it sets back down. The pilot waves frantically at a Nepali man who's standing nearby. The Nepali man runs up to the helicopter, opens the rear door, pulls out a single sixty-pound duffel, and drags it away from the landing pad. The noise rises again. The skids lift off the rock a few feet higher than before. This time the helicopter lurches dramatically forward, gaining momentum and at last ascending into the warm sky.

Kent and I lounge on top of our duffels as yak drivers saunter past, shepherding their heavily laden animals toward Lobuche, Pheriche, and Namche Bazaar. We drink cans of San Miguel and talk about what we're going to eat when the helicopter delivers us to Kathmandu. Ice cream's a priority, we agree.

There are moments of silence between our conversations, and in those short seconds I find a way to say good-bye to the mountain and the Icefall. A piece of me doesn't want to leave. A piece of me's going to miss it—the intensity, simplicity, camaraderie. Will I ever find in normal life the sort of closeness I have with my teammates? Are there other mountains that will touch my heart, memory, and imagination in the same way? I'm not sure. Maybe I'll be back one day with less self-centered goals in mind. Maybe Dad, Mom, Joss and I will come together and build a shrine for Gombu in the secret place amongst the blooming rhododendrons. Who knows?

Thwucka-thwucka-thwucka.

Another B3 glides up valley. I crouch behind a boulder and shield my eyes as it lands. What follows is a frantic rush to load our bags and climb inside before any fuel's wasted. Simone's at the controls. He shoots me a get-ready look and gives me a thumbs-up. A Nepali man closes the doors from the outside, trapping Kent and me in the fuselage. Simone grips the controls and the noise rises, drowning all other sound. The skids lift off the ground. Through the cockpit windows I see jagged mounds of moraine less than twenty feet beneath us. The machine slams forward and for a split second it looks like we might plummet to our deaths, but the blades gain purchase and then we're flying through the glacier-carved valley, tracing the river less than a hundred feet off the deck.

The landscape rushes beneath me in a blur of changing color. The umber hillsides and speckled, lichen-sheathed rocks of Gorak Shep transform into the olive, drab hummocks and bister, yak-beaten earth of Lobuche. Always, pure-white snow and blue glaciers cap the layers of this place, a mighty contrast to the increasing lushness of lower elevation. Simone lands on a grassy field in Pheriche and motions for us to get out.

I glance confusedly at Kent before I realize what's happening. Simone wants to fill the fuselage completely, but he can't take off in the thin air at Base Camp with a heavier load, so he's shuttling Kent and me to thicker air at fourteen thousand feet.

The grassy basin's vivacious, the warm air a shock to my stinging throat. Tiny purple flowers with yellow stigmas grow in the meadows that cling to the dendritic fingers of the creek. Dogs bark behind mossy rock walls, their excited yelps mixing harmoniously with chirping birds. Kent runs to a nearby guesthouse to purchase more beer. I get down on my hands and knees and stare at the magnificent intricacy of the purple petals and the blades of grass.

Before long, the helicopter's back. The flight to Lukla takes twenty minutes. Down, down, down past the rhododendron forest near Rivendell, over Tengboche Monastery, and around the corner to Namche Bazaar, where terraces are sprouting with big-leafed plants. These places have taken on a different meaning since I visited them last.

Tenzing-Hillary Airport in Lukla is bursting at the seams with climbers and trekkers waiting for plane rides home. Kent and I find the rest of our crew at a ramshackle building to the west of the downhill landing strip.

"We should be pretty used to this drill by now," says Dave, rolling his eyes. "Hurry up and wait."

We drain thermos after thermos of lemon tea. Every few hours a helicopter lands on a graveled terrace in front of the building, but they're all reserved for different teams. Now that we're so close to the comforts of the Yak and Yeti, I've forgotten about my desire for contemplative walking and solitude. I just want to be home as quickly as possible, but as afternoon flushes toward evening, our departure becomes more and more unlikely. There's no telling how long we might be stuck here.

At 6:00 p.m., about an hour before sunset, a gray-and-red B2 helicopter glides between the clouds and lands on the terrace. The pilot hops out gingerly. He's a five-foot-three-inch pot-bellied Indian man in rumpled khakis and a short-sleeved navy-blue polo shirt. The top three buttons are undone to reveal a neck of folded chub and a sweaty chest. He flaps his hand at Tuck. It's the signal to load our gear.

While Tuck jams duffels into a storage compartment, two men walk to the rear of the fuselage, open the fuel cap, and shove a five-foot length of clear plastic tubing into the hole. One of the men puts his mouth around the open end of the tube and sucks. A stream of bluish fluid runs through the tube and into the man's mouth. He spits it out and feeds the tube into a waiting jerry can, spilling a few ounces into the grass. As I'm watching, the pilot saunters up next to me and lights a cigarette.

"We *verrry* heavy," he says, pointing toward the siphoning operation with a camouflage Zippo. The pilot orders the siphoning to stop when seven jerry cans have been filled. According to the pilot's calculations, we're now light enough to take off.

Because there isn't enough room in the storage compartment, we each sit with an enormous duffel on our knees. The passenger cabin's stuffed so full of gear and bodies there's no need for a seat belt. One of the attendants closes the door from the outside. At least I can see through the front windows and, if I strain my head to the left, I can glimpse through a square of clear plastic the skids touching the ground. The pilot starts the engines. The world vibrates violently as he gradually increases power. A gauge in the cockpit indicates we're at 102 percent lift when the skids finally rise from the grass. The aircraft darts forward with surprising fluidity and, thank God, we're flying. The only problem is, we're flying directly into a mountain of inky black clouds.

The rain falls in opaque sheets like tinfoil pulled from a roll. It hammers the windshield—*rata-tat-tat*. I'm peering through the front windows and I can hardly see a thing when, all of a sudden, the windshield wipers creep to a halt. Oh shit. Visibility goes to nil. Without warning or conference, the pilot pushes against the controls and dives the helicopter steeply into what looks like a river valley. Dave glances my way with an expression that says he's thinking the same thing I am. After surviving Mount Everest we're going to die in a freak helicopter crash at the hands of a pack-a-day smoker. The pilot leans closer to the flooded windshield like a myopic grandparent trying to read the newspaper. He scans for a place to land and selects a diamond-shaped island of pebbles on the edge of a half-flooded river. The rotor wash startles a herd of black dzopkyo and they gallop off into the jungle. The sides of the valley are densely vegetated—vines, towering trees, and stocky bushes the color of kryptonite. There are no houses, roads, or other manmade structures in sight. Once the helicopter's safely on the ground, the pilot pulls out a map from an overhead hatch and peruses it intently. Tuck looks at Dave and shakes his head in disbelief. His eyes say, *This has* got *to be a joke.* We're lost somewhere in the wild valleys of northeastern Nepal and our windshield wipers are broken.

We squeeze out of the passenger cabin. I'm soaked to my core in seconds. The rain's so hard that it stings the top of my head where my hair parts. Dave and I crouch beneath the helicopter's tail boom while Tuck and the pilot attempt to fix the windshield wipers. Lacking any sort of real tools, they can't reasonably hope to make it work, but we've got to try.

Just then a teenage boy in an oversized orange T-shirt appears. Maybe he's in charge of the dzopkyo herd because he's carrying a thin bamboo switch. I can tell from his expression that he's never seen a helicopter before. His eyes are all wonder and fear and distrust and curiosity. He inches closer, but he's shy and he remains partially hidden behind the trees and sparse shrubs. A funny thought pops into my head. Maybe someday this boy will learn to fly.

The pilot crouches next to Dave and me and asks, "You have tents and sleeping bags? Extra for me?"

Dave chuckles fatalistically because our tents and sleeping bags are still at Base Camp, waiting there to be carried down to Lukla and flown to Kathmandu over the course of the next week. I check my backpack. I've got three Clif Bars. At least it's enough to keep us alive until the storm abates, unless this storm's the beginning of the four-month monsoon.

The sky continues to darken. Night's approaching. If we don't take off within half an hour, we'll be stuck here until morning. Will the boy in the orange T-shirt welcome us into his home? Or will we have to spend the night huddled beneath the tail boom?

We get back inside so we can leave at a moment's notice if the rain stops. We need one break in the clouds, one decent chance, one last blessing from the Himalaya.

A beam of rich orange light busts through the clouds at the head of the valley. The rain lessens, although it still pounds against the windows—*rata-tat-tat.* The pilot leans forward and peers at the high ridges, which are visible for the first time since our emergency landing. This is our chance. We've got to take it.

The pilot turns around to look at us and, without a hint of sarcasm, he says, "I step outside. Have one little smoke. Then we try."

One little smoke? Is he trying to calm his nerves? Or is he like a prisoner asking for a final cigarette before stepping in front of the firing squad?

He finishes his cigarette, climbs inside, and yells in Nepali through the window at the boy in the orange T-shirt. The boy runs behind a tree trunk and peeks out, watching suspiciously as the rotors spin up. The pilot turns around again and gives us a thumbs-up. Then he pushes the engine to its absolute maximum. At 105 percent lift, the skids rise less than five feet above the pebbles. In one terrifying, earsplitting instant, the helicopter slams forward violently. The force throws my head backward and it slams into the metal wall of the cabin. We bank sharply to the left, smashing me against the door as we trace the meandering course of the river. The rain hammers the aircraft like gunfire.

Suddenly the rain stops and the helicopter arcs into clear air. Sunset paints the red-and-green contours of rural Nepal in golden light. We fly low above terraced hillsides, tumbling rivers, and precipitous footpaths. It's incredibly beautiful. It's like I've never seen it before. I inhale the warm atmosphere, gazing out at the distant white mountains, and I know exactly how wonderful it is to be alive.

ACKNOWLEDGMENTS

Writing a book, no less than climbing a mountain, is a collaborative effort, and I would not have succeeded at either without the insight, generosity, and partnership of many wonderful people.

I am profoundly indebted to everyone involved in my 2010 and 2012 expeditions to Mount Everest. Specifically, I owe my thanks to Dave Hahn, Melissa Arnot, Mark Tucker, Kent Harvey, Michael Brown, Ken Sauls, Seth Waterfall, Casey Grom, Chad Peele, Jeff Martin, Lambabu Sherpa, Chhering Dorjee Sherpa, Tendi Sherpa, Kaji Sherpa, Pasang Sherpa, Kumar, Yubaraj, Raju, Jetta, Lhakpa, Kami, Cancha, Jiban Ghimire, and Sagar Poudyal, truly the world's best teammates, whose courage, strength, and intellect carried me to the summit. Many thanks are owed to Neil Fiske, Kristen Elliot, Kirsten Kinkead, Andrew Turner, and the rest of the staff at Eddie Bauer who have been incredibly generous in their support of my far-flung dreams. Thanks to Jake Norton, David Morton, Brent Bishop, Charley Mace, Grayson Schaffer, Conrad Anker, Rachel Anderson, Luanne Freer, Scott Jones, Rob Suero, Wendy Booker, Ben Jones, Garrett Madison, Lakpa Rita Sherpa, Ang Jangbu Sherpa, Lama Geshe, Chad Kellogg, Willie and Damian Benegas, Joe Kluberton, Simone Moro, Justin Merle, Michael Horst, Sam Isherwood, and countless other friends from the horseshoe pit, card table, and guesthouses along the trail. I was lucky to share the mountain with all of you.

This book wouldn't exist without the fantastic work of the staff at Mountaineers Books, including Kate Rogers, Helen Cherullo, Mary Metz, Margaret Sullivan, Doug Canfield, Emily White, and Jen Grable, as well as Mountaineers Books' freelance designer Heidi Smets. Thanks to Shannon O'Neill for many insightful suggestions and contributions, without which this story wouldn't be nearly as good. Thanks to Kirsten

Colton for her precision and care, lessons that I will surely carry to my next piece of writing. Thanks to Dave Costello for sending me a message at the perfect time, spurring this project forward, and pursuing it with honesty and excitement. Lee Ann Chearneyi supported this book in its infancy and provided valuable advice as I developed the idea. Sam Nowak, Robert Rich, Kaity Teer, Brenda Miller, and Lee Gulyas offered productive suggestions along the way.

Of course, I am grateful for all the members and participants of the 1963 American Mount Everest Expedition. That expedition and the people involved have influenced me in such profound ways that I had to write a book to make sense of it. Specifically, the writing of James Ramsey Ullman, Tom Hornbein, and Barry C. Bishop has been a priceless source of information and inspiration. The leadership of Norman G. Dyhrenfurth is something I aspire to replicate in my own adventures, and the joyous, selfless spirit of Nawang Gombu is an example we can all hope to live by. Thanks also to the families and descendants of AMEE, many of whom have reinforced my belief that each member of the team had extraordinary qualities.

Everyone who appeared in this book was important to the creation of it, including Jake Beren, Spencer Edwards, Chris Brady, Danny Milholland, Peter Whittaker, Lou Whittaker, Steve and Kerry Sutorius, Tyler Lappetito, and Leif Patterson.

For guidance, advice, and friendship during numerous adventures, outdoors and otherwise, special thanks to Bobby Whittaker, Henry and Karen Nichols, Namgya Sherpa, John and Lynn Nowak, Janet and Kenny Barron, Motup and Yangdu Goba, Daniel James Brown, Barb Richey, Freida Fenn, Hank Fly, and John Lockwood.

To my family and friends who have provided their unwavering support over the years, I will express my gratitude the next time I see you. As you've hopefully figured out by now, I love you all very much.

Deepest thanks to my parents, Jim and Dianne, always my most ardent proponents, and to my brother Joss, a constant inspiration, who I blame for teaching me how to tie into a rope.

Finally, thanks to my radiant partner, Freya Fennwood, who reassured me when I was in doubt, nudged me when I was procrastinating, and will drop everything for the sake of playing outside; you bring unimaginable joy to my life. I couldn't have done it without you.

BIBLIOGRAPHY

The following books, articles, and film were helpful in supplying details and context for descriptions of events of the 1963 American Mount Everest Expedition (AMEE), as well as general background on the Himalayan region.

Arnette, Alan. "Everest 2012: Season Recap: A Study in Risk Management." The Blog on alanarnette.com. May 30, 2012. www.alanarnette.com/blog/2012/05/30/everest-2012-season-recap-a-study-in-risk-management/.

Band, George. *Everest: The Official History.* London: HarperCollins Publishers Ltd, 2003.

Bishop, Barry C. "Mount Rainier: Testing Ground for Everest." *National Geographic, 123* (5), (1963): 688-711.

———. "How We Climbed Everest." *National Geographic, 124* (4), (1963): 477-507.

Caple, Jim. "Fifty Years Since the Climb of a Lifetime." *ESPN* (blog). May 1, 2013. espn.go.com/blog/playbook/fandom/post/_/id/21489/fifty-years-since-the-climb-of-a-lifetime.

Costello, Dave. *Flying off Everest: A Journey from the Summit to the Sea.* Guilford, CT: Lyons Press, 2014.

Douglas, Ed. "Babu Chhiri Sherpa." *The Guardian.* May 2, 2001. www.theguardian.com/news/2001/may/03/guardianobituaries1.

———. "Nawang Gombu Obituary." *The Guardian.* May 24, 2011. www.theguardian.com/world/2011/may/24/nawang-gombu-obituary.

Dyhrenfurth, Norman G. "Six to the Summit." *National Geographic, 124* (4), (1963): 460-473.

Hahn, Dave. "Aces High." *Outside* (blog). January 25, 2008. www.outsideonline.com/1909271/aces-high.

Hawley, Elizabeth and Richard Salisbury. "Season Lists." *The Himalayan Database.* 2015. www.himalayandatabase.com/seasonlists.html.

Heil, Nick. "The Man Who Matched Our Mountains." *Outside* (blog). December 1, 1999. www.outsideonline.com/1889526/man-who-matched-our-mountains.

Hornbein, Thomas. *Everest: The West Ridge.* Seattle: Mountaineers Books, 2013.

Hornbein, Thomas and Willi Unsoeld. "The First Traverse." *National Geographic, 124* (4), (1963): 509-513.

Ives, Katie. "The End of the Everest Myth." *Alpinist* (blog). April 28, 2014. alpinist.com/doc/web14s/wfeature-everest-myth.

Jenkins, Mark. "The Sherpas" *National Geographic* (blog). May 9, 2012. ngm.nationalgeographic.com/everest/blog/2012-05-09/the-sherpas.

Leonard, Brendan. "Jim Whittaker Looks Back on 50 Years Since Everest." *Adventure Journal* (blog). February 27, 2013. adventure-journal.com/2013/02/jim-whittaker-looks-back-on-50-years-since-everest/.

Morton, David, Jake Norton, and Jim Aikman. 2013. *High and Hallowed: Everest 1963* (motion picture). highandhallowed.com/.

Norgay, Jamling T. and Broughton Coburn. *Touching My Father's Soul: A Sherpa's Journey to the Top of Everest.* New York: HarperCollins, 2001.

Payne, M. M. "American and Geographic Flags Top Everest." *National Geographic, 124* (2), (1963): 157-157C.

Poston, Pete. "Chomolungma Nirvana—The Routes of Mount Everest." *Mounteverest.net.* May 29, 2004. www.mounteverest.net/story/stories/ChomolungmaNirvana-theRoutesofMountEverestMay292004.shtml.

Potterfield, Peter. "Conrad Anker Recounts Avalanche Tragedy on Shishapangma." *Mountainzone.com.* 1999. www.mountainzone.com/climbing/99/interviews/anker/#ankervideo1.

Schaffer, Grayson. "Second Death on Everest Raises Safety Concerns." *Outside* (blog). April 24, 2012. www.outsideonline.com/1929211/second-death-everest-raises-safety-concerns.

———. "Take a Number." *Outside* (blog). September 12, 2012. www.outsideonline.com/1929136/take-number.

———. "Lost on Everest." *Outside* (blog). May 2013. www.outsideonline.com/o/outdoor-adventure/climbing/mountaineering/lost-on-everest.

———. "The Disposable Man: A Western History of Sherpas on Everest." *Outside* (blog). June 10, 2013. www.outsideonline.com/1928326/disposable-man-western-history-sherpas-everest.

Strickland, Ashley. "Everest Men: On Top of the World in 1963." *CNN* (blog). May 26, 2013. www.cnn.com/2013/05/24/us/everest-1963-expedition-whittaker/.

Ward, Alex. "In Rarefied Air, Rarefied Company." *The New York Times.* May 25, 2003. www.nytimes.com/2003/05/25/travel/in-rarefied-air-rarefied-company.html.

Whittaker, Jim. *A Life on the Edge: Memoirs of Everest and Beyond.* Seattle: Mountaineers Books, 2002.

Whittaker, Lou and Andrea Gabbard. *Lou Whittaker: Memoirs of a Mountain Guide.* Seattle: Mountaineers Books, 1994.

Wickwire, Jim and Dorothy Bullitt. *Addicted to Danger.* New York: Pocket Books, 1999.

Ullman, James Ramsey. "At the Top—And Out of Oxygen." *Life, 55* (12), (September 20, 1963): 68-92.

———. *Americans on Everest: The Official Account of the Ascent Led by Norman G. Dyhrenfurth.* Philadelphia and New York: J.B. Lippincott Company, 1964.

Unsworth, Walt. *Everest: A History,* (2nd ed.). Seattle: Cloudcap, 1989.

ABOUT THE AUTHOR

Freya Fennwood

Leif Whittaker is a writer, speaker, and adventurer from the Pacific Northwest. He discovered a passion for writing at age eleven while trapped on his parent's sailboat in the middle of the Pacific Ocean with nothing better to do. He currently resides in Bellingham, Washington. This is his first book.

MOUNTAINEERS BOOKS is a leading publisher of mountaineering literature and guides—including our flagship title, *Mountaineering: The Freedom of the Hills*—as well as adventure narratives, natural history, and general outdoor recreation. Through our two imprints, Skipstone and Braided River, we also publish titles on sustainability and conservation. We are committed to supporting the environmental and educational goals of our organization by providing expert information on human-powered adventure, sustainable practices at home and on the trail, and preservation of wilderness.

The Mountaineers, founded in 1906, is a 501(c)(3) nonprofit outdoor recreation and conservation organization whose mission is to enrich lives and communities by helping people "explore, conserve, learn about, and enjoy the lands and waters of the Pacific Northwest and beyond." One of the largest such organizations in the United States, it sponsors classes and year-round outdoor activities throughout the Pacific Northwest, including climbing, hiking, backcountry skiing, snowshoeing, camping, kayaking, sailing, and more. The Mountaineers also supports its mission through its publishing division, Mountaineers Books, and promotes environmental education and citizen engagement. For more information, visit The Mountaineers Program Center, 7700 Sand Point Way NE, Seattle, WA 98115-3996; phone 206-521-6001; www.mountaineers.org; or email info@mountaineers.org.

Our publications are made possible through the generosity of donors and through sales of more than 800 titles on outdoor recreation, sustainable lifestyle, and conservation. To donate, purchase books, or learn more, visit us online:

MOUNTAINEERS BOOKS
1001 SW Klickitat Way, Suite 201 • Seattle, WA 98134
800-553-4453 • mbooks@mountaineersbooks.org • www.mountaineersbooks.org

An independent nonprofit publisher since 1960

OTHER TITLES YOU MIGHT ENJOY FROM MOUNTAINEERS BOOKS

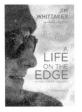

A Life on the Edge: Memoirs of Everest and Beyond
Jim Whittaker
"Jim Whitttaker is an American adventure hero of the highest order—on the highest peaks and deepest oceans. His story is a timeless tale of inspiration and living life to the fullest—on the edge and at home. He's a model for us all."
—Tom Brokaw

Everest: The West Ridge
Thomas Hornbein
The fiftieth anniversary edition of Thomas Hornbein and Willi Unsoeld's first glory-or-death ascent of Everest's West Ridge, with never-before-published expedition photographs and a new foreword by Jon Krakauer.

Sherpa: The Memoir of Ang Tharkay
Ang Tharkay with Basil P. Norton
Never before published in English, *Sherpa* is a curious blend of innocence and insight, of adventure and hardship, offering a priceless glimpse into the lives of the local guides and porters of the Himalaya and Karakoram.

Sixty Meters to Anywhere
Brendan Leonard
Kinetic, funny, and heartfelt—a painfully honest story of a life changed by climbing. "A transformative personal journey, showing the power of climbing and the courage that lies within."
—Kelly Cordes

Psychovertical
Andy Kirkpatrick
Winner of the Boardman Tasker Award for mountaineering literature, *Psychovertical* is written with dark humor and a sense of the absurd—a book to appeal to the conflicted adventurer in all of us.

Climbing the Seven Summits: A Comprehensive Guide to the Continents' Highest Peaks
Mike Hamill
"Mike Hamill's consummate coverage of the Seven Summits is far more studied and detailed than anything I could have ever written."
—Dick Bass

www.mountaineersbooks.org